Scribus 1.3.5

Beginner's Guide

Create optimum page layouts for your documents using
productive tools of Scribus

Cedric Gemy

[PACKT] open source
PUBLISHING   community experience distilled

BIRMINGHAM - MUMBAI

Scribus 1.3.5
Beginner's Guide

First published: December 2010

Production Reference: 1021210

Published by Packt Publishing Ltd.
32 Lincoln Road
Olton
Birmingham, B27 6PA, UK.

ISBN 978-1-849513-00-5

www.packtpub.com

Cover Image by Fillipo Sarti (filosarti@tiscali.it)

Credits

Author

Cedric Gemy

Reviewers

Robert Charles

Alessandro Rimoldi

Acquisition Editor

Dilip Venkatesh

Development Editor

Meeta Rajani

Technical Editor

Hithesh Uchil

Indexer

Tejal Daruwale

Editorial Team Leader

Aanchal Kumar

Project Team Leader

Priya Mukherji

Project Coordinator

Jovita Pinto

Proofreader

Aaron Nash

Graphics

Nilesh R Mohite

Production Coordinator

Adline Swetha Jesuthas

Cover Work

Adline Swetha Jesuthas

About the Author

Cedric Gemy is a French freelance graphic designer and training advisor who lives in Rennes but travels a lot to teach Scribus, GIMP, and Inkscape. He has been working with these software since around 2003.

Besides his freelance activities, he also teaches communication design in some French universities and private schools.

He is an active member of the Scribus and Inskcape team, involved in the user interface refactoring project of Scribus and in the documentation of Inkscape. He is a creator of the French Free Graphic Designer Association (AFGRAL) and FLOSSMANUALS Francophon.

This is his fifth book; he has already written two books about GIMP, one published under GPL licence, one about Inskcape, and one in French about Scribus.

He can be reached through his websites `http://www.cgemy.com` and `http://www.creationlibre.org`, where he provides information about free graphic software news and usage.

I would like to thank all the people who have supported me during the writing of this book, especially my wife, and the reviewers who made this book better than I could have made alone.

About the Reviewers

Robert Charles first dabbled in computer programming in 1984 when his family purchased a Radio Shack TRS-80 (AKA)- CoCo, Tandy Color Computer, and the Trash Eighty. Financial limitations kept Robert from pursuing a career in the technology fields until 1998, when he attempted to capitalize on the dot-com boom through web design.

After the dot-com crash, Robert joined the IT department of a financial company and was introduced to the Open Source community through a work colleague.

Robert started his own company in 2006, employing and touting many open source solutions, such as OpenOffice, GIMP, Scribus, SME, and Paint.Net in his business and personal use.

Alessandro Rimoldi lives in Zurich, where he promotes free software, especially through the workshops created for the Grafiklabor. He has been part of the Scribus community since it began, and since 2009, he has been an active member in the board of the Libre Graphics Meeting.

www.PacktPub.com

Support files, eBooks, discount offers, and more

You might want to visit www.PacktPub.com for support files and downloads related to your book.

Did you know that Packt offers eBook versions of every book published, with PDF and ePub files available? You can upgrade to the eBook version at www.PacktPub.com and as a print book customer, you are entitled to a discount on the eBook copy. Get in touch with us at service@packtpub.com for more details.

At www.PacktPub.com, you can also read a collection of free technical articles, sign up for a range of free newsletters and receive exclusive discounts and offers on Packt books and eBooks.

http://PacktLib.PacktPub.com

Do you need instant solutions to your IT questions? PacktLib is Packt's online digital book library. Here, you can access, read, and search across Packt's entire library of books.

Why Subscribe?

- ◆ Fully searchable across every book published by Packt
- ◆ Copy & paste, print, and bookmark content
- ◆ On demand and accessible via web browser

Free Access for Packt account holders

If you have an account with Packt at www.PacktPub.com, you can use this to access PacktLib today and view nine entirely free books. Simply use your login credentials for immediate access.

Table of Contents

Preface

Scribus is a relatively new software that is becoming famous thanks to the nice features it provides and the good printed results that it creates. As a layout program, it helps in creating business cards, brochures, newsletters, magazines, catalogs, and many other documents that need to be exported in high-level PDF, be it for high resolution printing or web interactive purposes. Scribus is free and is an open source application that provides all the features that one might need to create appealing designs productively. It is so easy to use that it can be used by beginners as well as more advanced users.

In this book, we will explain the most important features, those that you will really need, and many others, with the purpose of giving you the best of the software. As Scribus is intended to make printed documents, we will explain, when necessary, some specifics of the print workflow with the purpose of helping you to understand why the software is made like this.

What this book covers

Chapter 1, *Getting Started with Scribus*, will show the place that Scribus can have in a graphic workflow, what type of documents it can create, and how a layout program is different from other kinds of software. Then we will look at the main Scribus window to help identify the main tasks that will be done.

Chapter 2, *Creating a First Layout*, is a huge step-by-step tutorial to introduce you to the main Scribus functionalities and logic. We will create a simple business card using simple shapes, a vector logo, and of course some text.

Chapter 3, *Mastering Pages*, is where we deal with one of the most important concept of a layout program, namely, the page. As laying out mainly consists of placing objects and content on a page as nicely as possible and arranging those pages more consistently, we will see how to create or delete a page and how to get help to make it as structured as it needs to be and easily understandable to the reader.

Chapter 4, Using Text in Scribus, will of course be very important for many kinds of documents and will mainly contain text that can be written within Scribus or that can be imported. In this chapter, too, we will see how to look for text, make replacements, and link frames to help you work with long documents.

Chapter 5, Formatting Your Text, will show you the Scribus options to give it the aspect you like, as text needs to be set nicely and can sometimes be very long, and use a paragraph or the character style to use those properties as efficiently as possible. Beyond this chapter, we will talk about methodology as well as typographic preciseness.

Chapter 6, Special Frames for Complex Content Management, will mainly explain how to create tables in Scribus. They can be empty or can be imported from another application like OpenOffice.org Calc. After that, we will have few tests with render frames, which is a nice and very original way of including the result of any other applications in Scribus dynamically.

Chapter 7, Drawing Advanced Frames and Shapes, will show what possibilities Scribus has in the customization of the standard rectangular frame. You will then convert frame types, use several kinds of shapes, and mix or distort them with some advanced Bezier drawing and modification tools.

Chapter 8, Importing Images, is one of the more complex and theoretical chapters because even if pictures are used to make nicer and lighter documents, it's something else to have them printed well. Here, file formats and their specifics will be at the center, and resolutions, clipping path, or layers that they contain will be used to set the page according to the graphical and readability needs.

Chapter 9, Applying and Managing Color, will, in some ways, follows the previous chapter. It shows how Scribus can use flat colors as well as gradients or patterns, with or without transparency. More importantly, we will see how to create a custom swatch to work more efficiently with them, as well as creating spot colors, which are very specific in the print process. Color management will be part of this to help us get the most accurate results.

Chapter 10, Print Your Layout, is mainly dealing with PDF options to help produce the best document before sending it to a print-shop as a print-ready file. We will see that Scribus provides a verifier to help you evaluate your layout, which can have some kind of PDF format. A basic knowledge of the PDF versions will be necessary and we will see them as well as the very nice and complete Print Preview window and print options.

Chapter 11, Customizing the Creation or Viewing Process, will be a different chapter in which we will see form and interaction options of Scribus and how to make simple calculations into the file or modify the rendering on the reader's screen. Finally, it will be time to see how to extend Scribus with Python script to add some new custom functionality or perform a repetitive action.

What you need for this book

To read this book, you just need to be comfortable with using your computer. You need to understand how the directories can be organized and used. Except for that, just manipulating the mouse, being patient, and being creative will be the most desirable qualities you'll need. Of course, having some knowledge in other software can be helpful, especially on photo retouching, for example with GIMP, vector drawing like Inkscape, or Office suite. This book doesn't explain all this. However, any document you'll import into Scribus will need to be prepared beforehand and will have to be well managed from the beginning to the end.

Who this book is for

This book will help you if you have never used Scribus and if you are interested in creating documents that need to be printed by a print professional. This book will be for every person who works as a graphic designer or those who play a similar role in a company. It can sometimes offer you advice on how to create a layout, but this is not the main subject. And if you already know another layout program, it will help you understand how to migrate to this new and promising software.

Conventions

In this book, you will find several headings appearing frequently.

To give clear instructions of how to complete a procedure or task, we use:

Time for action – heading

1. Action 1
2. Action 2
3. Action 3

Instructions often need some extra explanation so that they make sense, so they are followed with:

What just happened?

This heading explains the working of tasks or instructions that you have just completed.

You will also find some other learning aids in the book, including:

Pop quiz – heading

These are short multiple choice questions intended to help you test your own understanding.

Have a go hero – heading

These set practical challenges and give you ideas for experimenting with what you have learned.

You will also find a number of styles of text that distinguish between different kinds of information. Here are some examples of these styles, and an explanation of their meaning.

Code words in text are shown as follows: "In any case, you'll need to import Scribus module for your Python script to access the Scribus-specific functions using import scribus."

A block of code is set as follows:

```
scribus.setText(row[2]+' '+row[1], txtName)
scribus.selectText(0, len(row[1])+len(row[2])+1, txtName)
scribus.setStyle("name", txtName)
```

New terms and **important words** are shown in bold. Words that you see on the screen, in menus or dialog boxes for example, appear in the text like this: "In the **Action** tab of the **Field Properties** window, choose the **Submit Form** type".

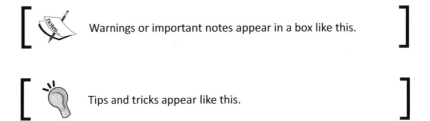

Warnings or important notes appear in a box like this.

Tips and tricks appear like this.

Reader feedback

Feedback from our readers is always welcome. Let us know what you think about this book—what you liked or may have disliked. Reader feedback is important for us to develop titles that you really get the most out of.

To send us general feedback, simply send an e-mail to feedback@packtpub.com, and mention the book title via the subject of your message.

If there is a book that you need and would like to see us publish, please send us a note in the **SUGGEST A TITLE** form on www.packtpub.com or e-mail suggest@packtpub.com.

If there is a topic that you have expertise in and you are interested in either writing or contributing to a book, see our author guide on www.packtpub.com/authors.

Customer support

Now that you are the proud owner of a Packt book, we have a number of things to help you to get the most from your purchase.

Downloading the example code for this book

You can download the example code files for all Packt books you have purchased from your account at http://www.PacktPub.com. If you purchased this book elsewhere, you can visit http://www.PacktPub.com/support and register to have the files e-mailed directly to you.

Errata

Although we have taken every care to ensure the accuracy of our content, mistakes do happen. If you find a mistake in one of our books—maybe a mistake in the text or the code— we would be grateful if you would report this to us. By doing so, you can save other readers from frustration and help us improve subsequent versions of this book. If you find any errata, please report them by visiting http://www.packtpub.com/support, selecting your book, clicking on the **errata submission form** link, and entering the details of your errata. Once your errata are verified, your submission will be accepted and the errata will be uploaded on our website, or added to any list of existing errata, under the Errata section of that title. Any existing errata can be viewed by selecting your title from http://www.packtpub.com/support.

Piracy

Piracy of copyright material on the Internet is an ongoing problem across all media. At Packt, we take the protection of our copyright and licenses very seriously. If you come across any illegal copies of our works, in any form, on the Internet, please provide us with the location address or website name immediately so that we can pursue a remedy.

Please contact us at copyright@packtpub.com with a link to the suspected pirated material.

We appreciate your help in protecting our authors, and our ability to bring you valuable content.

Questions

You can contact us at questions@packtpub.com if you are having a problem with any aspect of the book, and we will do our best to address it.

1
Getting Started with Scribus

If you are reading this book, you have surely decided to use a new software called Scribus. I would like to congratulate you on your choice. However, what I find more interesting is to understand why you opted to use Scribus.

You might be fully interested in free software, may be running Linux or any other system except Apple Mac OS or Microsoft Windows, and in this case, you don't have much choice except for Scribus, Scribus, or Scribus. This is mostly because proprietary equivalent software such as Adobe InDesign or Quark Xpress is not available for Linux-based platforms.

If you are not interested in "free" software, the first piece of advice I would give you would be to take a look at its principles. Scribus is licensed as General Public License and a lot of software that you use everyday is certainly based on such a license. But again, why Scribus? Is it because you don't need to spend a penny for what InDesign is worth based on a human month of work? Is it because you were looking for software that would let you explore your creativity? Or is it just because you've heard of it as a good application?

The answer to all of these, and many other questions, will give good reasons. In fact, to be honest, Scribus is not as complete as InDesign or Xpress. The latter is nearly twenty years old and mature, and the first is made by the most important company in the printing world that is at the center of each step of the printing process. However, Scribus will provide you with all you need to be productive at creating nice documents (which will print perfectly) and some things that you may find in other software too.

What Scribus mainly does is to simply:

- Be respectful to century-old habits of the print world
- Be as accessible as possible to new users
- Give a perfect print result

That's the point. As I travel a lot to teach Scribus, I'm always surprised at how many people show me documents that were already created using Scribus, and that I didn't even think could be. When I began using Scribus six years ago, at the very beginning, it was hard to imagine that it would become so popular. At that time Inkscape appeared too, and they have both completely changed the free software world—even if not the graphic world yet.

Laying out with Scribus will mean that you will create brochures, catalogs, business cards, books, magazines, or newsletters—in a way any kind of document with which one can communicate. A layout design job generally takes information from different sources, and places them on a page in a way that will improve readability as well as be a pleasure to look at—sometimes it also improves efficiency. Laying out is the process of arranging elements with respect to some rules on various types of content that can be single or multi column, with or without pictures, and printed in black, color, or varnished. Well, a layout is a creation that helps the reader read by adapting itself to the content. This is particularly true in magazines where the layout changes very often in a single issue—and always gives the best printed result to the reader, of course. To be honest, how easy would it be to create an exact copy of your favorite magazine in a text processor? Just have a try, and you'll see that they will certainly not be optimal for the task.

Desktop publishing software versus text processors

If you have already used layout software before, these arguments are not new to you. However, if you come from any other computer-assisted profession, you may be surprised at the way such software is organized. Especially, most of you would have certainly used text processors such as Microsoft Word, OpenOffice.org Writer, and maybe Microsoft Publisher. Once you go deeper into the details, you'll see how Scribus is different.

I've heard many people explain that they were trying Scribus, because they thought or heard it was a better piece of software. I would suggest not to begin reading this book with this idea in mind. Text processors are very qualitative when it's time to handle text (and this is an important point) but not when there is a need to customize a document. Just take a look around: you can identify any magazine or any book collection because of their visual identity, which is made possible by the Desktop Publishing set of software. Could you identify as easily the origin of a Microsoft Word or OpenOffice document? I'm not sure, because all of these documents will be very similar.

Generally, you won't use a layout program if you need to save time and work very quickly, because it is not intended to save time, but to let you be as free as possible to create a unique document: the one that will make you change the world, or the one that will help you improve the communication of your company and make it more efficient. Scribus will give you everything to be as productive as possible. However, every time you need to choose a color, every time you need to add a shape, or every time you need to change the text settings, every single little task that you will find yourself doing to get the best graphically designed final document will add to the time taken. This is a very important point if you want your layout project to succeed. I have experienced many projects where people really underestimated the time taken to perform these tasks.

To help you create your document, remember that a layout program is not based on text handling, but on the page. In Scribus, the page is an object that you'll be able to manipulate. On the page, you'll add shapes or frames that you'll place precisely, one by one, and each of these will have their own properties. Especially in a layout program, images are drastically apart from the text, whereas in a text processor both will be in the same flow. This again results in a different way of considering the elements you will have and may change the way you work. This is for the best, and once you get used to this, once you have the major but quite simple software possibilities integrated, and once you have the print process specificities in your work, you'll be more free than you've ever been to create a unique document. This document will be the result of your own creativity and not only the default settings defined by a product or another.

The graphic workflow

I would advise you to keep your text processor open. You should use it as often with or without Scribus. A layout program is not made for text processing, so use a software that is. Scribus will be the software you'll use to mix the different documents (texts, photos, and drawings) that you will want to use. However, each of these elements will be created or modified with a particular, and dedicated, application because it is aimed to be used in a particular environment: print companies. So, when you use Scribus, you will mainly use four pieces of software:

- Scribus itself to do the layout.
- GIMP, Adobe Photoshop, or any other photo editing software.
- Inkscape, Sk1, or Adobe Illustrator to draw logos, maps, and custom shapes.
- OpenOffice.org Writer, Microsoft Word, or any other text processor to write and spell check the text.

A lot of other software can be included in the list, but this is the basis. Of course, you can manage all of these tasks within a single Writer document, but this is not the way a layout program works. Moreover, it is not the result that you have on your screen that is important, but the result that you'll get in print when the document is passed through many hands and computers.

This is not the way a layout program works because photos are the job of photographers, drawing is the job of an artist, and writing is the job of either a journalist or an author. Each of these people wouldn't really need to know what the other does and how. Of course, nowadays, one single person is often enough to do all this: not due to a real wish to improve quality but due to more of a human resource necessity. Anyway, it makes it a more interesting and less boring job, but in the same time, it requires much more knowledge.

As a first step, you should work in **WYSIWYM (What You See Is What You Mean)** mode. It might be surprising if I told you that Scribus was a graphic software. But most layouts are made to enhance the readability, by graphical means. So it seems very important to know as soon as possible how the text will be structured (how many titles and sub-title types, large paragraphs or not), how often pictures will be needed, and of course who the document is made for. A book or a magazine about Elvis Presley will certainly not be similar to one dealing with peanuts of the Babuyan Isles (if these peanuts really do exist, please send me some!).

The second step is to analyze the visual code that your reader will be used to, and to decide how you will behave with them. What will you follow or not follow? Look at the aspects where you can incorporate your own creativity without being considered out of context. This will guide you to some criteria such as color, fonts and font properties, and some page layout structures.

Next, it is time to know what you are allowed to do, taking into consideration economical (ask your client or boss) and technical (ask your print company) needs. Will you be printing in black only, with two colors, or with four or more? What kind of paper, paper size, and printing type (digital, offset, and so on) will you need? All these things will help you to define the basis of your work. You can, however, consider these as constraints, or as a wonderful challenge to deal with. I like the second option. There will be enough possibilities to express your genius. The standard use of software in a layout workflow is shown in the following diagram:

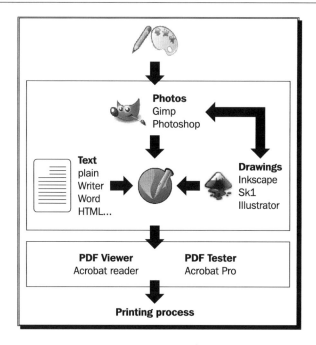

Then it's time to sketch. Begin with papers and color pencils. Work at **100%** scale. So if you use a special paper size, get it cut if needed. Once you've found something nice, plug your computer in and launch Inkscape, which will be a more practical, reactive tool to go deeper into the details. You'll then get a mockup, which you'll alternatively be able to use directly in Scribus after an import, or will have to redraw depending on the way you'll want it done. In this mockup, try to simulate as precisely as possible what a standard page will look like: add sample text, sample images, and so on. Show it to important or confident people and listen to them. If they say without an argument that it is really good and that you're stupefying, kick them and tell them that you'll ask them the day after or to come back after they find something else to say (Ah! yes, if they kicked you back, maybe you can stop right there and go to the next person you've thought of).

The next step will be to work on the real content. Once Scribus has everything such as custom swatches, master pages, and styles set, there's nothing else left to do other than filling the pages. If you have only one display, buy two new ones, or deal with virtual displays (Linux has had it since prehistoric times, so it might be cheaper than a big 24'' screen). Launch GIMP, Inkscape, and Scribus. Here, some will work with these three pieces of software at once and improve each single picture before importing and some will, alternatively, prefer to improve all the pictures first and then import them. Find your way, and find good collaborators who work in the same way (the most difficult task).

Do regular proof reading. Use all of your friends for that: a graphic designer must have many friends if he wants to be a must see. Use PDFs for this. There are many tools that can annotate PDFs; for example, Whyteboard is an easy and lightweight software that can be run on Linux, Windows, or Mac. Once everything is perfect, create your best PDF using Scribus and use its **Preflight Verifier**. Using Adobe Acrobat Pro is also nice to check the quality of your PDF and detect any errors that you could have made. Unfortunately, there is actually no equivalent in the free world. Finally, your PDF is ready to be sent to your print company, which will lead to the end of the process, unless there is a problem.

In this book we will help you in improving one part of this simplified workflow. But it is a major part. You can have the best idea, but if it is badly implemented in the software, or you don't take the print process into account, it won't work well at the end. Scribus is not the fastest software one can imagine, and not the most stable too. However, it is extremely powerful and will give you the result that matches exactly what you have set. So you can trust it as much as one of your old friends.

It's time to understand how to talk to it.

Understanding the workspace

Once you've launched Scribus, you'll be prompted to create a new document or open a previous one. We'll go deeply into the secrets of this dialog in the beginning of Chapter 2. For now, just go through by validating so that we can see the basics of this software.

This book has been written using a development 1.3.5+ version of Scribus, taking care that the menus and windows will be kept similar in a future stable release. Scribus follows a slow release scheme and there has not been a new stable release for a long time. If you're not used to free software development, stable means that the software is considered to have been tested, that most of the important bugs have been corrected, and that it shouldn't crash. Whereas, development means the developers are still working deeply on improvements and might at the same time cause errors.

By using such a version, we hope to give you the best of the new professional Scribus functions. On a Debian-like distribution, installing Scribus-ng will be better than the standard Scribus version to follow this book. If you have any other OS, download Scribus from here:

`http://sourceforge.net/projects/scribus/files`

or

`http://www.scribus.net/?q=downloads`

The official Scribus download site is the best place to go to get a package to install. However, when you'll have this book in hand, there might be some new 1.4 stable version available that should look the same and be better to use than any development version.

The layout of Scribus, as shown in the following screenshot, is similar to other software that you might know:

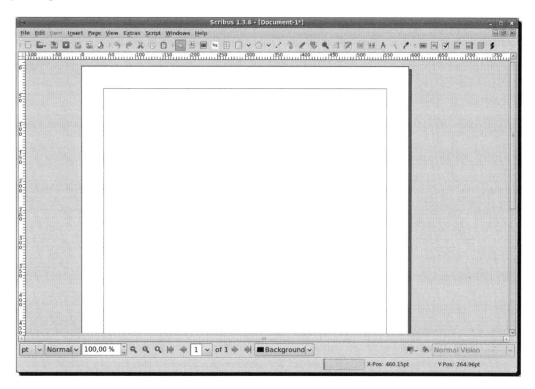

The topmost is a title bar that contains the name of the active document. If the name has no extension, it is because you never did save the document, and it might be time to do so. If there's a star after the document name, it's because the document has changed since the last time you saved it and that it might be the time to save too. Scribus can automatically save your document: we'll describe how in the *Customizing Scribus a bit* section of this chapter.

The menu bar gives you the ability to access most of the Scribus functionalities. Some menus are well known, such as the **File** menu in which you'll find the entries to create a new document or to save the actual document, but other menus such as **Page**, or **Item** may relate to specific Scribus tasks. Remember that while working on a document, Scribus will show a context menu on right-clicking. This menu will often be different and related to the object that is selected when you right-click. Contextual menus are most of the time a good reminder when you don't exactly remember where to find something related to an object type. In this document we will give the context menu entry whenever it's possible, as well as shortcuts when available.

Under the menu bar, you'll get, by default, another bar filled with many icons. These icons are the quick access to some menu entries. The ones on the left-hand side are related to **File** or **Edit** entries. Those at the center are **Insert** tools or transformation tools. On the right, PDF options are displayed. Once you get used to Scribus, none of these will be necessary because they can nearly all be accessed using keyboard shortcuts. We describe some of these tools in the next pages, and, of course, these make up the major part of the content of this book.

The main area not only contains the page at the center but a workspace too. If there are many ways to manipulate a document in Scribus, there are no other ways of displaying pages. Especially if you use a Text processor, you're certainly used to some custom display. OpenOffice.org Writer has a Web display that shows the text as a single flow, without displaying the page border and margins. In a layout program where most part of the job is to place an object precisely on page, this would be a nonsensical feature. However, this is interesting because the so-called workspace, which is the area placed outside the page, can be used to manipulate an object before inserting it or an object that you've made but not sure you'll use. In this way, you don't need to delete them, and you keep them available. It's evident that the workspace should not itself become a shambles, and should be cleaned— especially, once you're happy with your page. Some final PDF process can give errors if there are objects outside pages. Under this main area, we have some information that will help in many cases, as shown in the following screenshot:

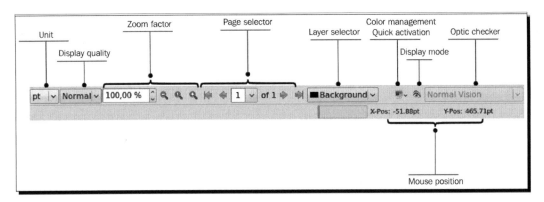

From left to right:

1. The **Unit** list changes the default unit that will be used for every placement and calculation in some windows, and for the rulers placed around the workspace. The default unit of the document is the one you've set in the **New Document** window.

2. The **Display quality** list lets you modify the way the photo will appear, from a rough render to the most precise. This doesn't affect the final PDF and is just a display setting. We'll deal with these options and explain them in the Chapter 8.

3. The **Zoom factor** and some buttons to quickly change the size of the object that will appear on screen.

4. The arrows and the list between the arrows are a quick access to browse between pages because scrolling is not always the best way when you have tens or hundreds of pages.

5. The list where the text **Background** appears is a layer selector. Some people use it often, some never do. You'll prefer your own choice once we'll have seen those functionalities.

6. The right most button changes the way all the colors of the pages will be displayed. Most of them are very advanced options. But you can already remember that when the "eye" icon is clicked, all the helper strokes on the page aren't displayed: you could consider this button as a shortcut to some kind of print preview because only real elements that will be printed are still displayed.

7. Finally, under all these you have the **X** and **Y** values that give real-time information of the mouse pointer position on the page.

This is a good amount of buttons and lists, but since they are quickly available with the help of the mouse, they provide very handy ways to manipulate the document and give you a lot of comfort. It's a good thing to get used to them as soon as possible.

Time for action – using the main status bar options

To help you get used to the status bar options, let's do a simple and common task such as inserting a photo in a shape and see how the User Interface can help us easily get the result.

1. Set the unit to **mm** by choosing this option in the first left-hand side list on the status bar.

2. In the **Insert** menu, choose **Insert Shape | Specials | Heart**.

3. The mouse cursor changes to a rectangle with a cross at its top-left corner. A label should display the position of the cross on the active page. When moving the mouse, you see in the ruler that red bars are moving along too, which helps you find the right placement. Try to reach X:100 and Y:100, then press the left mouse button.

4. Drag the mouse to the right-hand side and the bottom of the page so that the new label information of the width and height tooltips read 70, and release.

5. Click on the – button in the status bar then decrease the zoom factor to **50%** and see how your shape fits on the page.

6. There should be a red rectangle around the heart showing that it is selected. If not, click on it.

7. Then right-click and choose **Convert to | Image Frame**. This changes the status of this shape so that it can be filled with a photo.

8. Get the photo of your beloved (whoever or whatever it is) by pressing *Ctrl + D*. Navigate through your directories to get it and validate. Of course, the size of your photo might not match the size of the heart—this is a sum up of life in general.

9. But, you can immediately right-click and choose **Adjust Frame to Image** and that will be better.

10. If the picture doesn't look good and you think that he or she is much prettier than as seen, just modify the display quality by choosing **High** in the second list on the left-hand side of the status bar.

11. You still have some red and blue lines around the page, so click on the eye button of the status bar to make these helpers disappear.

What just happened?

We have inserted a shape and have converted it to a frame in which we could place a picture. Then the context menu and status bar have helped us to choose the place or aspect of what is on the page and the way it is displayed. Remember that what you have on screen is just a preview that doesn't always exactly match what will be printed because many objects that won't print are set in the page to help you, and other objects that you add might change with some display or print options. Knowing these options will be key to the success of the layout process.

The toolbar

The toolbar is one of the most important places of the Scribus graphical user interface. Anything you can add to your page can be found here. So it's easy to say that every single button has to get your respect. Tools are every function that you'll use to act directly with your mouse on an object. Tools help you create and manipulate just like in the real world when you use your hands, pen, scissors, and so on. In the previous exercise we used the shape tool.

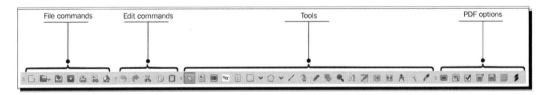

The Scribus toolbar doesn't include only tools, but some common functionality shortcuts too, especially the traditional **Save** or **Undo** button. So it is divided into several parts. Let's have a quick look at these buttons.

You can grab each part of this toolbar and dock it to another side of the workspace, usually the left one, vertically. To do this, place the mouse over the drag area at the beginning of each toolset and then press the left mouse button and drag. When you reach a side, you'll see the rulers move to make the nearest placeholder available.

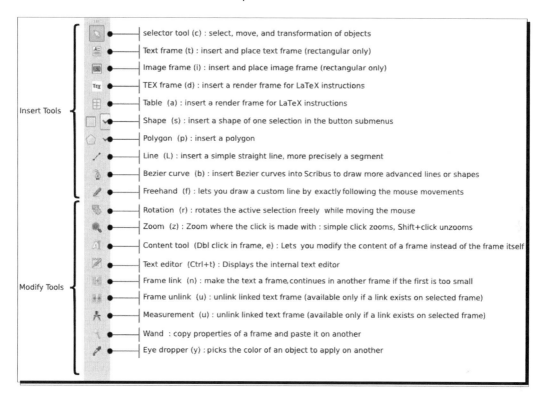

Insert Tools:
- selector tool (c) : select, move, and transformation of objects
- Text frame (t) : insert and place text frame (rectangular only)
- Image frame (i) : insert and place image frame (rectangular only)
- TEX frame (d) : insert a render frame for LaTeX instructions
- Table (a) : insert a render frame for LaTeX instructions
- Shape (s) : insert a shape of one selection in the button submenus
- Polygon (p) : insert a polygon
- Line (L) : insert a simple straight line, more precisely a segment
- Bezier curve (b) : insert Bezier curves into Scribus to draw more advanced lines or shapes
- Freehand (f) : lets you draw a custom line by exactly following the mouse movements

Modify Tools:
- Rotation (r) : rotates the active selection freely while moving the mouse
- Zoom (z) : Zoom where the click is made with : simple click zooms, Shift+click unzooms
- Content tool (Dbl click in frame, e) : Lets you modify the content of a frame instead of the frame itself
- Text editor (Ctrl+t) : Displays the internal text editor
- Frame link (n) : make the text a frame, continues in another frame if the first is too small
- Frame unlink (u) : unlink linked text frame (available only if a link exists on selected frame)
- Measurement (u) : unlink linked text frame (available only if a link exists on selected frame)
- Wand : copy properties of a frame and paste it on another
- Eye dropper (y) : picks the color of an object to apply on another

Menus, buttons, or shortcuts

Most of these tools can be used from the **Insert** menu too. But you'll certainly adopt the fastest way: using the toolbar or the shortcuts.

Properties Palette: The main place

It won't be enough to add frames, write text, or add pictures. You'll certainly have to set their aspect, such as changing colors, fonts, and many other things. Since a layout has to be an attractive and nicely designed document, we need to have quick access to the properties that let you customize those objects.

The Scribus team has decided to put all these options in one single window: the Properties Palette, often called PP (we'll call it this in this book). The Properties Palette can be opened or closed with the **Windows | Properties** menu or the *F2* key. There are so many options in the Properties Palette that it has been divided into several parts. The following are the most important ones:

- **XYZ**: Gives options to manipulate the position and size of the selected object.

- **Shape**: Allows you to redefine a frame shape (for example, a square to a circle) and the relationship between text frames and others.

- **Text**: You'll be able to set the text aspect here as naturally as in a text processor but with many more options available at a single click.

- **Image**: Defines how an image fits in its frame and some extended options, depending on the file type in which it is saved.

- **Line**: Lets you modify the width and general aspect of lines, Bezier curves, and freehand lines, as well as frame borders.

- **Color**: Is used to change the fill or stroke color of a frame or shape. There are some precise and print-specific options here that will need some explanation in Chapter 9.

And the groups!

The **Group** tab is new and not yet stabilized. It has mainly the same options as the **Shape** tab but can be applied only on grouped objects.

The most complex and important of these tabs is certainly the **Text** tab. It includes several expanders that give access to more or sometimes less advanced settings. Less because you'll get many common options such as the font size or color of the text. But you'll see optical margins, and kerning or baseline adjustments, which are very often used in layout programs and more rarely used in text processors. Of course, we'll go through these options in a later chapter.

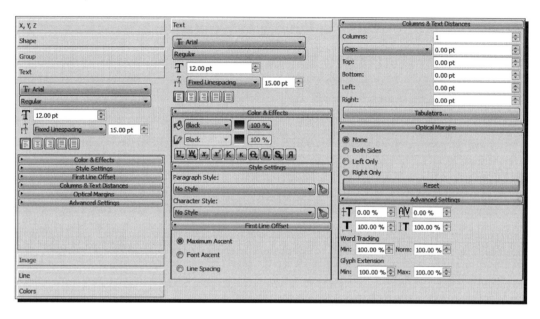

When considering the **Image** tab with the extra advanced settings and the effects windows, it can also be important to spend some time on them. Image management is an entire part of this book too. But don't be trustful to pictures. Except in some specialized fashion or travel magazines, where very good photographers are involved, pictures are usually used to illustrate and are not the most important feature. So they might not be the basis of the layout either. However, every time you'll use a picture you'll have to pass through several steps in a photo retouching program and manage as finely as possible the relation with your layout if you want to get the best results. This part of the Properties Palette can help you but cannot do everything:

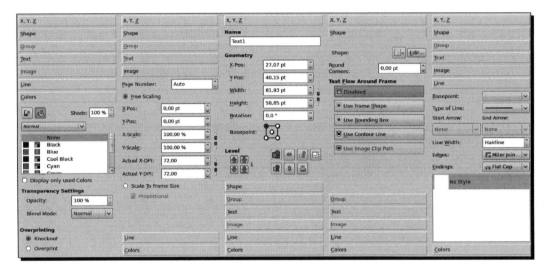

The **Nodes** window available from the **Edit** button of the **Shape** tab or by double-clicking a shape, could be considered as another important part. However, it is less commonly used simply because in a layout, shape and frames are mostly rectangles. It seems then that it is more important to spend time on text and picture settings than on shapes (except for some special actions, especially a nice one: making text flow around a picture).

Layout and story editor

In Scribus there are two ways to help you work. Of course, the layout mode is considered more natural for such software. It is activated by default—the one in which you enter automatically when you launch the software. But the layout mode is not always the easiest to work with, especially when you have a large quantity of text placed in many frames, on tens or hundreds of pages.

Add to this the fact that Scribus is still quite slow with text handling and display and you'll understand why it is getting important to leave this mode and use the Text Editor. The Story or Text Editor is an inner simple window with which you'll be able to write text as easily as in a simple text editor (gedit, Kate, TextEdit, or Notepad) with some extra features that make it useful for layout purposes. Once you've modified the text, the modifications are applied to the frames where the text is placed.

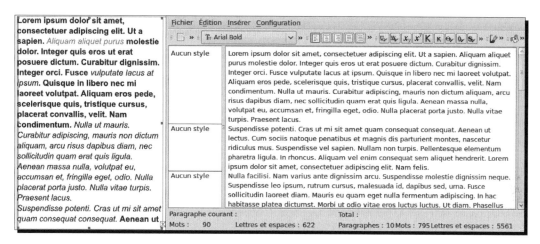

Software and per-document preferences

When you work daily on Scribus you'll like that the software behaves more comfortably for you, which might not be the same as the default behavior. Some software don't really use preferences. Scribus is very different. There are so many things in those Scribus windows that it'll take a while before you know them all.

The left-hand part shows you the settings categories. Clicking on one will display everything you can change in the right-hand part. You can understand easily how many settings there are and how tricky it can be to find the one you need.

The thing you should remember above all is that the Scribus **Preferences** window and the **Document Setup** window that you find in the **File** menu, are both very similar (20 parts for the preferences and 14 for the document setup). There are some more settings in **Preferences**, but the real difference between them is that the settings of **Document Setup** apply only to the current document.

Time for action – how Scribus applies changes

To test the difference between **Preferences** and **Document Setup**, let's follow some simple steps, in which we will change the document size and language and see how it reacts:

1. You have an empty, new A4 document in Scribus.

2. Go to **File** menu and choose **Preferences**.

3. In the **General** category, which should be the current category, look for the **Language** list and change it to **Chinese** or any other language that you prefer.

4. Click on the **Apply** button at the bottom of the window and you should see the changes. You'll now be able to follow any of the tutorials you'll find on the Web, or nearly all. Unless you're comfortable with the Confucius language, set the language back to **English** and apply.

5. Go to the **Document** category, the next one, and change the **Units** to **Millimeters(mm)** and eventually the page size to **A5**.

6. Click on **Apply** again and you will see that nothing changes. For units, it is really easy to look at the left-hand part of the status bar. It should display **pt** or any other option that you have chosen in the new document window. Close the **Preferences** window by clicking on **OK** and choose the units list of the status bar. Your choice will still have an A4 page.

7. Go to **Page | Insert** and you'll see that **A4** is still the default.

8. On the other hand, you can now choose **Document Setup** in the **File** menu and change the **Document** category in the same way you did before. Click on **OK**.

9. Nothing changes right now. But once you go to **Page | Insert**, you should see that the new page is set as **A5**. Just test it.

What just happened?

The **Preferences** will apply in two ways, mainly depending on the settings you have changed:

◆ The settings that change a document behavior will be applied to any new document that is created after the modifications

◆ The settings that only adapt Scribus behavior can be applied immediately by clicking on the **Apply** button

When changing a document property, Scribus won't adapt the existing pages by itself. If it did, you would have to make a new layout, so it lets you define whether the old pages need to be changed. It is very safe and having several page sizes in a document is made easy. It doesn't mean that it has to be done everytime, but it's easy because everything can be set separately.

Working comfortably in Scribus

The Scribus user interface is so simple that there are not many things that you can change with the mouse. But as you may have seen, **Preferences** or **Document Setup** can be the right place for this task. But to begin with, there are some simple things you can do.

Zooming

Some good advice for you would be to use zoom as often as possible. Printers are much more precise than any standard display devices. Usually, you should consider that viewing your page at an average of **100%** (real size) will not fit the quality it might have when printed—especially the little spaces between objects that won't be displayed on your monitor. **400%** is a better zoom factor to evaluate preciseness.

You can zoom using the Zoom tool (*Z* key) from the toolbar. By clicking on an area, you will see it progressively larger, so that it gets more convenient to see the defaults. But the Zoom tool (*Z* key) is very useful when you draw a virtual rectangle around an object. In this case, the area in the rectangle you've drawn will fit the screen. The Zoom tool will be active until you activate another object, and each click will modify the zoom factor. Consider pressing the *C* key or activating the selector window as soon as you've looked at what you want.

A very good alternative method is to use the mouse wheel while pressing the *Ctrl* key. This way, Scribus will incrementally zoom in or out, depending on the scrolling of the wheel. At the same time, the center of the zoom area will be the point where the mouse is placed, so that it is made very easy to look precisely at an object and then immediately at another.

Of course, it is as important to have a good overview of your page. Any time you perform an important change in your document, such as creating a shape, applying a color, or inserting a picture, you should estimate the global aspect of your page and be sure that what you've done really improves the result. The **View | Fit to Height** menu or the *Ctrl + 0* shortcut will help you in doing this.

Panning

There are two ways to consider when navigating a document: moving through the pages and moving in a page.

The first one, as we have already seen, can be easily done by selecting another page in the page list in the status bar or by clicking on an arrow. We'll of course learn later how to use the **Arrange Pages** window, which can help you in this too.

But when you've zoomed in, you will sometimes need to keep this zoom factor and look at some other place in a document. For example, think of adding a picture in a column; you will need to verify that the picture position is perfect on both sides of the column. If the zoom factor is very high, you will be able to see only one side of the picture and will need to change the area that is displayed. Do it simply by pressing the mouse wheel, dragging to the area of interest, and then releasing the wheel.

Panning with the zoom tool

It's not really intended for this, but you will like it very much: you can consider zooming out and zooming in with the *Ctrl* + mouse wheel option we have talked about previously.

Changing values in fields

If you followed what we've already done, you certainly had a glance at the Properties Palette. This one is really full of fields, spinboxes, with which you'll set precisely as many options. You can modify the values of these fields by following one of these possibilities:

- Simply use the little buttons on the right-hand side of the spinbox. The top one will increase the value of one unit and the bottom one will decrease in the same range.

- If you know exactly the value that it should be set to, simply enter the value and press *Enter*. This is usually evident for text size or frame position if your layout is based on a precise grid so that you know exactly where any object can be placed. This is a very convenient way to do it: precise, quick, and trustful at the same time. Especially if you aim to be lazy, Scribus can do calculations for you. For example, if you have a frame place at X=5mm and need to move it right by a character size of 12pt you would have to do some tricky tests; just enter 5mm+12pt in the field and Scribus will do the job by converting what needs to be.

- However, if you need to look for the best value (for example, to adapt the text so that it fits a column width or a color shade), you can scroll the mouse wheel.

- Just scrolling will increase or decrease the values by one unit.

- Scrolling the mouse wheel with the *Ctrl* key pressed will change them by increments of ten units (+10 or -10) increments.
- Pressing the *Shift* key will be more precise (or slow) by changing in a 0, 10 range.

Modifications are automatically applied when they are done in the Properties Palette. The units are usually the one set in the **New Document** window or in the status bar. But some fields have their own, like text size that is always in **pt**. Don't forget this: many people make mistakes by not verifying the units, which is as important as the value itself. A text of 10pt is not the same as one of 10mm. It's evident, but as you can zoom in your page, you can feel less sensitive to real sizes.

Customizing Scribus a bit

Generally, you'll work on very similar documents so that you'll have your very own ways of handling the software. There are some simple options you can modify at the beginning of your work that will really improve and ease your work process. Most of the options here will be available in the **Document Setup** window (**File** menu) and **Preferences** as well. Choose the one that fits your needs best as explained in *Software and per-document preferences*.

Generally, remember that each second you lose, added to another one, and further to some more, will result in days or weeks by the end of the year. You can consider keeping those days to do something else, such as going skating or surfing (I'm sure you'll prefer your own choice while on the subject).

Some quick maths

Just count how much a second lost per minute sums up to in a year:

60 sec / hour => *8 = 480 / day => * 260 days worked = 124800 seconds = 35 hours = about 1 week

As a teacher I always give advice to optimize the working process. It makes it much more comfortable, and leaves your mind free for the main task: being creative, and it also helps you save time— there are only benefits.

Changing the toolbars

Depending on the type of layout you create, it can be a good idea to modify the position of the toolbars. Especially when working on a portrait document on a normal widescreen, you'll certainly feel that viewing the whole page will not be very precise. You can improve this a bit by moving the toolbars to the right-hand side or left-hand side of the Scribus window.

If you want to save space, it's not a bad idea to keep the **Insert** tools on the left-hand side and hide the others. Or if you follow our advice to use shortcuts as often as possible, you can hide all the bars by unselecting the following:

- **Windows | Tools**, which acts on the **Insert** tools
- **Windows | PDF Tools**, which hides PDF options that are not very important for a print document and are more useful for a Web one

Document handling

If you need to work on many documents at once, it's a good idea to check the **Use tabs for document** option (if available) in the **General** part of the **Preferences**. Alternatively, the opened document will be listed at the bottom of the **Windows** menu. You can go there to get a document activated and work on it. But as it is not as handy as tabs, if you have to do it frequently, it's worth changing the option unless you have a small screen.

Once you're here you can increase the **Recent document** option. This number is the reference value of the **File | Open Recent** file list, and the same tab in the startup dialog.

Lower in the dialog, you can change the **Documents** fields to set the default directory to be displayed in the save dialog. This is a good and simple way to get organized and not lose time looking for your documents just because you forgot to set it at the time of saving. If you don't change it, remember it is set to the home user directory by default.

If you're used to a text processor's automatic save, you will certainly appreciate that Scribus can do it too. In the **Document** category of the **Preferences** or **Document Setup**, you can select the **Autosave** checkbox and modify the **Interval** value, which is set to 10 minutes. Personally, I never use autosave because it is sometimes slow and does not always happen at the best moment. Sometimes it even makes the software crash (as I was not aware of the autosave and kept on working), which makes it unstable. I really prefer saving frequently by pressing *Ctrl + S* and protecting my document from a partial save that could be fatal to the whole. This way I save when I feel it's time too, when something nice or important is done.

Using versioned directories

If you run a Linux flavor, you can easily use CVS, SVN, or such type of version management tools to easily come back to a previous state of your work. On Ubuntu, just right-click on a folder and choose **Make directory versioned**. Scribus .sla files are pure text and they work perfectly with such tools that allow many actions to secure the file manipulations even when several people need to work on the file. If you want to know more about this, just begin with http://en.wikipedia.org/wiki/Revision_control.

Default document setting

If you always have the same kind of document to create (newsletter, flyers, or business cards), it's a good idea to set the preferences so that you immediately get the right size each time you create a document.

In the **Preferences** menu, click on the **Document** setup button on the left-hand column to reach the properties. Here you will mostly set the paper size by using a standard from the main list or a custom size by entering the dimensions in the **Width** and **Height** fields.

If you always lay out the same document or print on the same desktop printer, consider applying the default margin too. The **Preset Layouts** are available when another layout than **Single Page** is selected. But more than that, if you use a printer connected to your computer with the right driver installed, clicking on the **Printer Margins** button will show a dialog in which you can choose between the available devices and get the value from the device itself. You can then trust the inner area of the margin and everything within will be printed correctly.

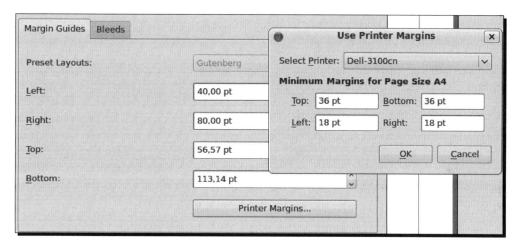

Finally, this is less-commonly used but can be useful if you print on different paper qualities. Nowadays, there are many types of paper, especially ecological paper that can be more brown or yellowish. What happens if you decide to print on a colored (orange, green, blue, or any other) paper? Changing the **Fill Color** of the **Pages** section in the **Colors** tab of the **Display** category (one of the last of the category columns), will help you get on screen an average of the color of the paper that helps you evaluate how the color of your document will fit it.

Default tool settings / zoom factor

Each tool can have a default setting that will be used by Scribus each time it is used. For example, if you want any text to be written in Arial, 10pt, go to the **Tools** category, click on the Text Frame icon, and set the value.

For the Image Frame, if your computer is a bit slow, you can change the on-screen **Preview Settings** to **Low Resolution**. This won't affect the way the pictures will be printed, but they will look ugly on the screen.

Finally, if you've used the zoom tool previously or the *Ctrl* + mouse wheel interface, you may have seen that it is zooming very fast. It doubles the factor each time. By modifying the stepping value of this tool to **120%** or so, it will be more progressive and helps you to be more precise in your manipulations.

External tools

Scribus interacts with external tools such as Ghostscript. However, it can interact with many other tools that you may prefer. The **External Tools** category is the right place to tell it how to interact with other tools.

Ghostscript is one of the most important tools because some very nice Scribus features are "imported" from it. In particular, Scribus will need Ghostscript to interpret, import, or export any kind of postscript (`.ps` or `.eps`) file. On Linux, it will certainly be already installed because it is commonly used. But on Microsoft Windows or on Mac OS you'll have to download it from the official download Ghostscript website (`http://sourceforge. net/projects/ghostscript/files/`). Since the install software of Ghostscript lets you define where to install, if Scribus still says it can't find it, you'll have to tell it where you've installed it by browsing the directory tree via the **Change** button.

If you use GIMP or Photoshop or any other photo retouching program, modify the path to the executable of your software so that Scribus knows what you want it to do.

To InDesign and Xpress users

If you've already used a layout program, you will certainly have questions such as:

* Is this software as good as mine?
* Can I import what I've done with my actual software so that I won't have to do everything again?
* Will I have many things to learn to be as productive as I actually am?

For the first question I've already provided an answer. Scribus is in some ways very good and has very original features but in some other ways it is less than perfect. The real question is: what do you already use in the software you have and does Scribus have it? I used to be an Xpress teacher and I've often met graphic designers who don't even use styles or master page and Scribus has it. Scribus can use spot color, set bleeds, and many other features required. Have a look at the table of contents, which can help you decide if Scribus matches your needs.

As an answer to the second question I could simply say "No"—mainly "No". As far as I know, it's always the tricky part in whatever software you use. Scribus will soon be able to import Xpress tags and IDXML, but it is still in development and is actually not usable; if you use Microsoft Publisher, there is really no way.

As for the last question, I don't think there are so many things to learn. Scribus has an original user interface but can be inspired by some de facto standards. And mainly, the principles are the same in Scribus and in InDesign or Xpress. Of course, you will use some of your habits, but in two or three days of Scribus testing, everything will be perfect again and you'll feel comfortable with it.

Shortcuts will certainly be the most difficult to learn. Xpress users, especially, use them a lot and even InDesign users use them for text handling. Scribus shortcut defaults are much simpler. You can use the **Keyboard Shortcuts** category of **Preferences** to change them.

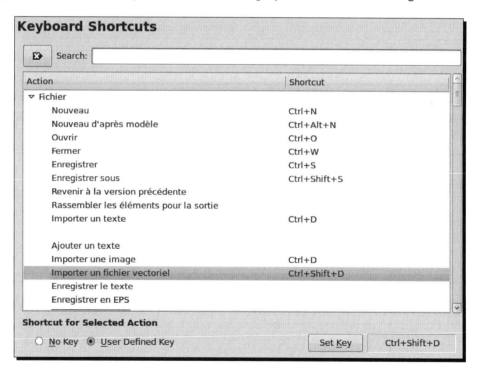

Simply select the function for the shortcut you want to change in the **Action** list, click on the **User Defined Key** option, click on the **Set Key** button, and perform the shortcut you'd like to assign. If it is already being used, you won't be able to assign it unless you find where it is assigned and erase it.

Summary

In this chapter we have defined the basis of a layout to be sure we are talking about the same thing.

Specifically, we covered:

◆ What we mean by laying out

◆ What Scribus is and how it covers some particular tasks and needs

◆ How Scribus is part of a more complete workflow, especially for print products

◆ How Scribus is organized to help you reach the result you're looking for

◆ How to improve the way you'll work by using some tips and customizing the behavior of the software

Now we're ready to go on with our first layout, which will help you to get an overview of Scribus's basic actions.

2
Creating a First Layout

Layouts can be visualized in our minds, but doing it with Scribus will be a manual job, and it's time to practice. This chapter will lead you through several design steps and will show some of the Scribus workflow basics in action. As an example, we'll design one of the simplest documents in terms of functionality: a business card.

In this chapter we shall:

- Create a document
- Create and transform frames
- Import text and images
- Format text and images with simple options
- Save the document

These are the features everyone should know to produce Scribus documents. We will certainly not describe each single option right now, but concentrate on the process.

Creating a new layout

Creating a layout in Scribus means dealing with the **New Document** window. It is not a complex window but be aware that many things you'll set here will be considered definitive. If these settings look simple or evident, you should consider all these settings as important. Some of them like the page size mean that you already have an idea of the final document, or atleast that you've already made some choices that won't change after it is created. Of course, Scribus will let you change this later if you change your mind, but many things you will have done in the meantime will simply have to be done again.

Time for action – setting page size and paper size and margins

This window is the first that opens when you launch Scribus or when you go to the **File | New** menu. It contains several options that need to be set.

1.   First among these options will certainly be the page size. In our case, people usually use 54x85mm (USA: 51×89mm). When you type the measurements in the **Width** and **Height** fields, the **Size** option, which contains the common size presets, is automatically switched to **Custom**.

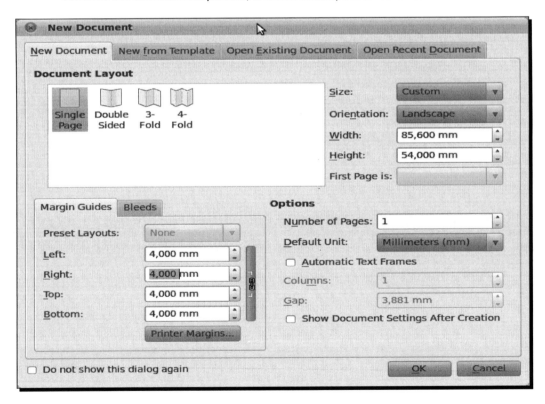

2.   If you want to use a different system unit, just change the **Default Unit** value placed below. Usually, we prefer **Millimeters (mm)**, which is quite precise without having too many significant decimals.

3.   Then, you can set the margin for your document. Professional printers are very different from desktop printers as they can print without margins. In fact, consider margins as helpers to place objects. For a small document like a business card, having small 4mm margins will be good.

What just happened?

Some common page sizes are: the series (the ISO standards biggest starting with A0 841x1189, that is 1m², and halving at each half step), the US formats, especially letter (216x279mm), legal (216x356mm), and tabloid (approximately 279x432mm, 11x17in), commonly used in the UK for newspapers.

The best business card size

When choosing the size for the business card, you'll consider the existing size often used. Is ISO 54x85.6mm better than the US 2x3.5in, or the European 55x85mm, or the Australian 55x90mm, when only a few millimeters divide them? Best is certainly to match the most commonly-used size in your country. Remember one thing: a business card must have to be easily stored and sorted. Grabbing an uncommon format can just lead to the fact that no one will be able to put your card in their wallet.

Presets will be useful if you want to print locally, but don't forget that your print company crops the paper to the size you want. So don't mind being creative and do some testing. For example, you might print on an A3 size paper for your final document or in an A3+ real printing size so that you'll be able to use bleeds, as we'll explain in the following sections.

Here we're talking about the page size and not the paper size, which can be double if the **Document Layout** is set to any option but **Single Page**. For all the folded documents, the page size differs from the paper size—keep that in mind.

For now choose 54x85.6 in landscape: just set 54 as the height or change the orientation button if you haven't.

The other setting that might interest you is the **margin**. In Scribus, consider the **margin** as a helper. In fact nobody in the professional print process will need margins. It is useful for desktop printers, which can't print up to the sheet border. As our example is much smaller than the usual paper size, we won't have any trouble with it.

Scribus has some presets for margins that are available only when a layout other than **Single Page** is selected. For our model, 4mm to each side will be fine. If you want to set all the fields at once, just click on the chain button at the right-hand side of the margin fields. But actually, we can consider that we won't have much to write and that it would be nice if our margins could help position the text. So let's define the margins as follows:

- **Left**: 10mm
- **Right**: 40mm
- **Top**: 30mm
- **Bottom**: 2mm

Choosing a layout

We've already talked about this option several times but here we are again. What kind of layout would you choose? Single page will simulate what you might have in a text processor. You can have as many pages as you want but it will be printed page after page. You'll get its result when printing with your desktop printer:

- Double-sided will be the option you'll use when you'll need a folded document. This is useful for magazines, newsletters, books, or such documents. In this layout, the reader will see two pages side by side at once, and you can easily manage elements that will overlap both pages. The fold will be in the exact middle. Usually, unless you have a small document size like A5 or smaller, this layout is intended to be printed by a professional.

- 3-Fold and 4-Fold are more for commercial little brochures. Usually, you won't use it in Scribus and will prefer a **Single Page** layout that you'll divide later into three or four parts. Why? Because with the folded layout, Scribus will consider each "fold" as a page and will print each of them on a separate sheet—a bit tricky.

You can see that for a business card, where no fold is needed, the **Single Page** layout will be our choice.

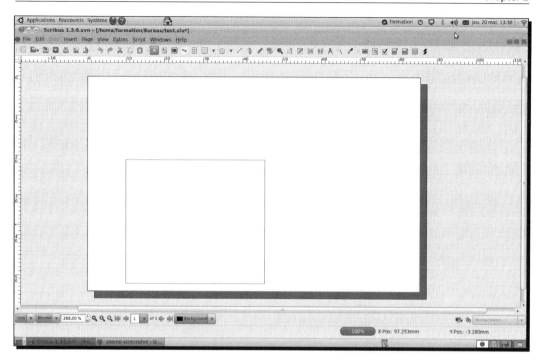

For the moment we won't need other options, so you can click on **OK**. You'll get a white rectangle on a greyish workspace. The red outline is the selection indicator for the selected page. It shows the borders of the page. The blue rectangle shows where the margins are placed.

Save the document as often as possible

"Save the document as often as possible"—this is the first commandment of a software user, but in Scribus this is much more important for several reasons:

- ◆ First of all, apologies, Scribus is a very nice piece of software but still not perfect (but which one is?). It can crash sometimes, slightly more than you'd wish, and never at a time you would expect or appreciate. Saving often will help you save a lot of time doing again what you've already achieved during the day.

- ◆ The Scribus undo system acts on layout options but not on text manipulations. Saving often can be helpful if you make mistakes that you can't undo.

In Scribus, we will use **File | Save As** (or *Ctrl + Shift + S*) to set the document name and format. It's very simple because you have no other choice than Scribus **Documents *.sla**. In the list, you will see **sla.gz** that will be used when the **Compress File** checkbox will be selected. Usually, a Scribus file is not that large in size and there is no real need to compress it. Of course, if the file already exists, Scribus asks whether you want to overwrite the previous one.

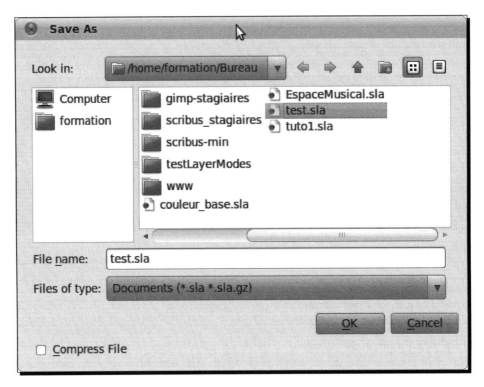

Scribus file version

Each Scribus release has enhanced the file format to be able to store the new possibilities in the file. But when saving, you cannot choose a version: Scribus will always use the current one. Every document can be opened in future Scribus releases but not in the older ones. So be careful when you need to send the file to someone or else when you're working on several computers.

Once you've used **Saved As**, you'll just have to simply save (**File | Save**) or more magically use *Ctrl + S*, and the modifications will automatically be added to the saved document. The extra **Save as Template** menu will store the actual file in a special Scribus folder. When you want to create a new document with the same global aspect, you can go to the **New from Template** menu and grab it from the list. There are some default templates available here, but yours might be better. Saving as a template might not be the usual saving process; this is done at the end when the basics of your layout have been made. Saving as template must happen only once for a template. So we'll use it at the end of our tutorial.

Basic frames for text and images

The biggest part of a design job is adding frames, setting their visual aspect, and importing content into them. In our business card we'll need a logo, name, and other information. You may add a photo.

Time for action – adding the logo

They are several types of graphic elements in a layout. The logo is of course one of the most important. Generally, we prefer using vector logos in SVG or EPS. Let's import a logo.

1. In the **File** menu choose **File | Import | Get Vector File**.

2. The cursor has now been changed, and you can click on the page where you want to place the logo. Try to click at the upper-left corner of the margins. It will certainly not be correctly placed and the logo may be too big. We'll soon see how to change it.

3. A warning will appear and inform you that some **SVG** features will not be supported. There is no option other than clicking on **OK**, and everything should be good.

What just happened?

The logo is the master piece of the card. It helps recognize the origin of the contact. In some ways, it is the most important recognition for a company. Usually, a logo is the only graphical element on the card. It can be put anywhere you want, but generally the upper left-hand side corner is the place of choice.

Time for action – adding the text

For now, let's add the text. Since there is not much to write, we will do it directly in the frame. But if you're working for a big company, you would consider writing a script that gets the names of each employee and produces the corresponding card.

1. Let's pick the **Insert Text Frame** tool in the toolbar (or *T* shortcut), place the mouse at the top-left corner of the margins, press the left button of the mouse, drag the cursor and draw a rectangle area that will contain the text. Release it when you've reached the bottom-right corner.

Automatic frame size

If you press the *Shift* key while clicking in an area, Scribus will automatically create a frame filling this area. An area is defined by the surrounding page borders, guides, and margins. So it should work here. Once the frame is created, double-click on it and you'll see the text insertion beam blinking on top left of the frame.

2. Type some text, as follows:

What just happened?

It's important to remember here that you cannot enter text immediately. In Scribus, two kinds of action are done: importing and setting content (that is, text, photos, or graphical elements) and placing them onto the pages. Just clicking on a frame will enable you to change the frame position and setting (what we call the Layout mode). Double-clicking on a frame activates the "Content mode" and sets the text or the picture's properties.

The little square at the bottom right of the Text Frame indicates that the content is fully displayed. The size of the frame does not match the current text content; we'll work on it soon.

Maybe you have noticed that the text is displayed above the logo. Scribus places every new object on top of the existing ones.

Time for action – adding and setting the color of a shape

You'll use shapes when you need a decorative graphical element that is simple enough and is not worth using specific software for, and when this shape doesn't have to receive any content.

The basic **shape** element of a layout is the rectangle. Chapter 7 will show you how to add more advanced shapes: in most cases simple shapes like rectangles and circles will be enough.

1. Pick the **Insert Shape tool** in the toolbar or press the *S* key. Draw a rectangle so that it covers the bottom half of the card. You can draw on the card if you want —remember the card will be cropped.

Shortcuts and Text Frame

Scribus uses simple keys (such as *T*, *S*, and *I*) when not in Edit mode.

When you're using keyboard shortcuts, verify that you're not in Content Edit mode. Otherwise, the key you'll press will be added to the frame content. One simple tip is to click on an empty place of the layout to **deselect** everything or pick the **Select Item tool** (arrow in the toolbar) before performing the shortcut key sequence.

2. Select the shape by clicking on it with the **Select Item** tool.

3. Open the Properties Palette by pressing *F2* (or going to **Windows | Properties**).

4. Go to the **Colors** tab at the bottom of the palette.

5. Click on the "bucket fill" button to specify that you want to set the internal color of the shape.

6. Click on the color named **FromSVG#FF8080** from the list.

7. Every shape is drawn with a thin black border that we don't need. Click on the **Edit Line Color Properties** button (the pencil icon) next to the bucket, and choose the color **None** in the list.

What just happened?

In this case, changing the color is very simple because we will use one of the logo colors so that we won't have to define it or look for it. The easiest way to do it is to use the Properties Palette (*F2*). The colors of a vector drawing are automatically added to color list when being imported. It really helps us reuse the color very easily even if the color name is not really meaningful. But for those who have already worked on websites, the hexadecimal notation that follows the # should be clear: two numbers for the amount of each primary Red, Blue, and Green.

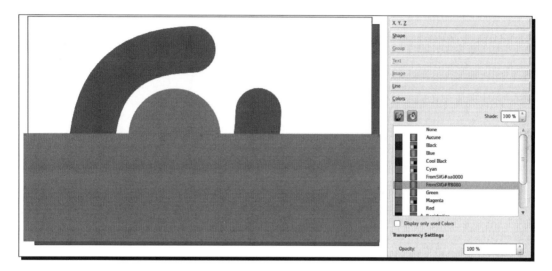

Changing the stack of objects

The pink shape is the last object that we've added, so it has been placed on top of the others. We will need to change the stack and move this object to the background.

Activate the Properties Palette by pressing *F2* and have a look at the **XYZ** tab. This tab has some interesting information: we will go through some of them right now. Presently, the most interesting information is the little number displayed at the right-hand side of the green bold arrows in the **Level** category. If inline icons are inactive, click on the shape to be sure that you have the right information.

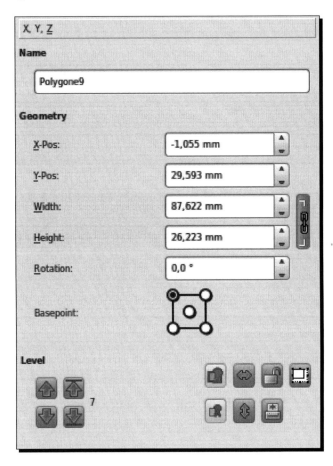

The number **7** means that there are six objects below this one. Since we have only three objects on the business card (logo, Text Frame, and this shape), you may wonder where this **7** comes from. The logo is composed of four shapes, which Scribus keeps grouped together.

How can we send the shape to the background? We have four actions and three ways to apply them: the buttons in the Properties Palette, the context menu, and keyboard shortcuts.

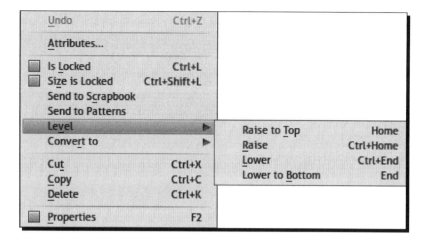

In our example, we will lower the pink rectangle to the bottom. Take a look at the difference:

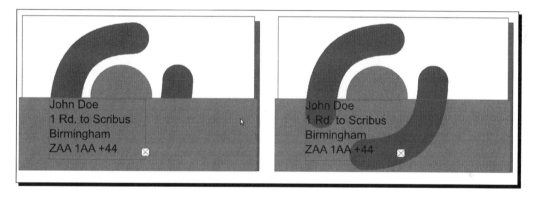

The left-hand side of the rectangle has been lowered only by one level. The example on the right-hand side shows the correct result with the rectangle lowered to the bottom.

Moving objects and exact positioning

Now that each object has been imported, drawn, or written we still need to work on the graphical aspect of the card. As of now:

- The logo is too big and overlaps the shape
- The text is not nicely formatted
- Shapes and frames have been manually placed: the missing precision is bad for such an important document that may get printed in the thousands

Placing with snapping options

Basically, moving an object is as easy as selecting it with the **Select Item** tool *C*, and dragging it by keeping the left mouse button pressed. But once again the position will be quite approximated. For more precision we will use the **Page | Snap to Guides** menu. Now move the pink shape again and try to make the top border of it match the top margin. Of course, you don't see where you go so you can temporarily use the **Colors** tab of the PP (Properties Palette *F2*), click on the **Edit Fill Color** button and temporarily set **50** as the opacity of the shape. Move the shape again as described previously and you'll see that the frame will snap to the margin. Release when it's correctly placed and set the opacity back to **100%**.

The snapping works with any kind of guide. Here, we've used the margins we've defined in the **New Document** window, but we could have created a custom guide, too. To create a vertical guide, press the mouse button when you're on the ruler at the left-hand side of the workspace, and drag onto the page. A dashed vertical line will appear under the cursor. Release the mouse button when the guide is correctly placed. Once again, this method is still not precise enough. The best way to create the guides is to use the **Page | Manage Guides** option. We will present it in the *Guides* section of Chapter 3.

Setting the coordinates

Another way to place the object is by setting its coordinates. This is the most precise way. Using **coordinates** is very handy if you have a very precise idea of what you want to achieve and have already made some sketches that help you estimate the distances. Most of the time, this is one of the things that is defined in a graphic charter.

Time for action – use X and Y properties

Let's say we'd like the logo to be place exactly at 4mm from the top and 10mm from the left-hand side.

1. Select the logo by clicking on it with the **Select Item** tool *C*.

2. Display the PP if it is not active using *F2*.

3. Go to the **XYZ** tab and have a look at the X-pos and Y-pos field. X-pos is the distance from the left-hand side and Y-pos is the distance to the top border.

What just happened?

If the values don't match what you need, just type the correct value in the field. If you have selected a different unit than millimeters, there is no need for any conversion. If you write **4mm**, Scribus will convert it for you. In the current unit, if you happen to be working in **mm**, you may try to enter "0.4cm" in the Y-pos field.

Now the position is correct. Try with the Text Frame and it will be perfect.

Basic text properties

After having improved the general aspect of our business card, it already looks much nicer, and it's time to work on the text. First of all, we need to know what should be kept the most visible to our contact: probably the e-mail address or the phone number. So let's keep that in mind when we define the aspect of the text.

You can download this font at http://www.radisnoir.net or http://openfontlibrary.org and you can read the SIL license at http://scripts.sil.org/OFL. If you don't know how to make those fonts available in Scribus, read the *Managing fonts and Fontbook* section of Chapter 5.

Time for action – formatting text

Now it's time to use Scribus.

1. Select the address frame and double-click on it to enter the Edit mode.

2. Launch the PP (*F2*) if it's not active.

3. Select all the text by pressing *Ctrl + A* in the **Text** tab of the PP:

❑ Choose the font you want to use in the first select box.

❑ Reduce the font size until you can see all the text and have some extra space around it. After having set it to 8pt we notice that the line spacing has not changed. Just set it to 9pt.

❑ Click on the **Color & Effects** expander and change the fill color from **Black** to **White**.

4. The biggest part is done. Let's work on some details:

❑ Select the name and set its font size to 13pt.

❑ Increase the **Fixed Linespacing** to 12pt.

❑ Select the phone number and set it to 13pt, too, with 15pt linespacing. Leaving some space around the phone number will make it more attractive.

5. Select the first line of the address and change the linespacing to 11pt to improve the result.

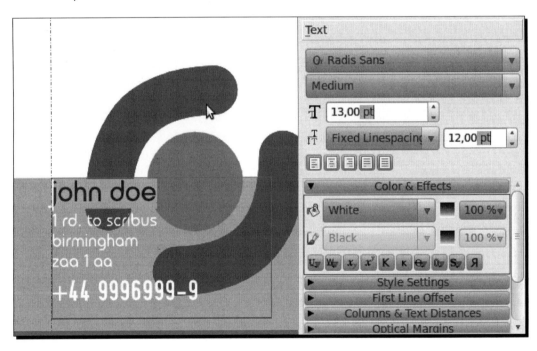

Missing glyphs

If you've used Radis Sans like I have, you can see that the numbers are replaced by squares. This is not your fault: it's due to the fact that the type designer did not make a glyph for them. Here you have three choices:

1. Choose another font for the whole business card that I have created by choosing OpenDIN, which you can download from many places including `http://scribusstuff.org/content/show.php/Open+Din +Schriften+Engschrift?content=107153`.

2. Choose another font only for numbers.

3. Edit the font in **fontforge** if you have the sources and if the license allows it.

What just happened?

Most of the settings depend on the print process. Should we print in full color, with two colors, or with only one? Which would be the cheapest? In our case, since we want to keep the colors of the logo, we will need at least two colors. If we want to stick with them, we have two choices for the text: white (the color of the paper) or dark red.

We have much more freedom for the other settings like the font family or the font size. We will try to keep the address as small as possible and play with bold for the phone number and the name. As the logo is made with round shapes, I prefer a font that resembles it, for example, Okolaks or Radis Sans, which are released under the SIL license.

Do you like it? Feel free to play with the settings until you find what you like. Try to be as simple as possible; don't use too many fonts or colors.

Resizing objects

Well it's time to work on the logo: it's really big and we would like it to be aligned the top part of the card. There are several ways to resize an object or frame.

Resizing with the mouse

When an object is selected, for example, click on the logo, and you can see a red rectangle outline. This doesn't affect the object properties but only shows that it is selected. There are little red square handles at each corner and at the middle of each side. If the mouse gets over one of these handles, the cursor will change to a double arrow. If you press the left mouse button when the pointer is on one of them and then move the pointer, you'll see the size changing according to the mouse movements. Just release the button when you're done.

While resizing the frame an information box appears near the pointer and displays the new width. You will notice that the proportions of the object are not kept, and that the logo is modified. To avoid this, just press the *Ctrl* key while dragging the handles and you'll see that the logo will be scaled proportionally.

Resizing with the Properties Palette

As an alternative, you can use the **Width** and **Height** fields of the **XYZ** tab in the Properties Palette. If you need to keep the ratio, be sure that the chain button at the right-hand side of the field is activated.

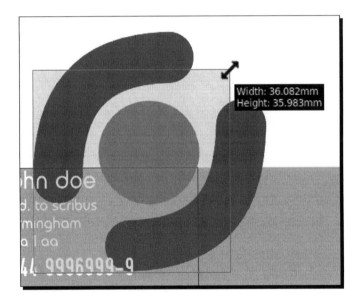

You can set the size in three ways:

◆ By scrolling the mouse wheel within the field. Pressing *Ctrl* or *Shift* while scrolling will increase or decrease the effect.

◆ If you already know the size, you can directly write it. This is mostly the case when you have a graphical charter that defines it or when you're already recreating an existing document.

◆ You can also use the small arrows at the right-hand side of the field (the same modifiers apply as described for the mouse wheel).

Resizing with the keyboard

Another way to resize objects is by using the keyboard. It's useful when you're typing and you need some extra space to put some more text, and that don't want to put your hands on the mouse. In this case, just:

- Press *Esc* to enter the Layout mode and leave the Content mode
- Press *Alt* and one of the *arrows* at the same time
- Press *E* to go back to Content Edit mode

If you do some tests, you'll find that each arrow controls a side: the left arrow affects the size by moving the left-hand side, the right arrow affects the right-hand side, and so on. You can see that with this method the shape can only grow.

Have a go hero – vector circle style

Since the past two or three years, you might have noticed that shapes are being used in their pure form. For example, check this easy sample and try to reproduce it in the best way you can: copy-paste, moving, and resizing are all you'll need to know.

Scaling objects

Scaling objects—what can be different here from resizing? Once more, it's on Text Frames that the difference is more evident. Compare the results you can get:

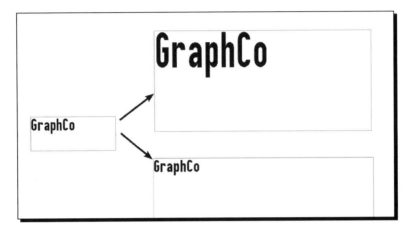

The difference is simple: in the top example the content has been scaled with the frame, and in the second only the frame is scaled. So it's scaling the content. You can scale a Text Frame (with its consent) by pressing the *Alt* key while resizing with the mouse. The *Alt* key applies, as always, while the mouse is pressed during the resizing movement.

So did you see something missing in our card?

Time for action – scaling the name of our company

Let's say that our company name is "GraphCo" as in the previous image and that we want to add it to the card.

1. Take the **Insert Text Frame** tool and draw a little frame in the page. An alternative could be clicking on the page instead of dragging.

2. Once you've clicked, the **Object Size** window is displayed and you can set 12mm or so as width, and 6mm as the height. Then click on **OK** to create the frame.

3. Double-click in the frame and type the name of the company.

4. Select the text and change the font family to one that you like (here the font is **OpenDINSchriftenEngShrift**), and decrease the size if the name is not completely visible.

5. Scale the frame until it is about 50mm wide. We can fix the width later.

What just happened?

Most of the time, you will use simple resizing instead of scaling. When you want the text to match some area and you don't want to play indefinitely with the font size setting, you may prefer to use the scaling functionality.

Using the scale options makes it very easy to resize the frame and the text visually without trying to find the best font size in pt, which can sometimes be quite long.

Rotating objects

The last important transformation tool is the **Rotate Item** tool. In our example, we'll use rotation to place the company name vertically at the right-hand side of the card. As always, you can choose among several ways of doing it.

Time for action – the quick method for rotating an object

Let's try the first method. It's certainly the easiest even if not the most precise.

1. Select the company name by clicking on its frame with the **Select Item** tool *C*.

2. In the toolbar or in the **Insert** menu, choose the **Rotate Item** tool (*R*). When the mouse cursor is over a frame, the cursor transforms into curved double arrows.

3. Press the left mouse button and move the mouse cursor without releasing. You'll see a grey rectangle previewing the place of the frame and an information tip giving the exact value for the angle.

What just happened?

The **Rotate Item** tool helps you rotate any object while moving the mouse. The more your gesture will be controlled the thinner the result you'll get.

If you want to constrain the angle, just press *Ctrl* while dragging and you'll get a rotation multiple of 15 degrees as defined in the **Other Properties** option of the **Tools** category in **Preferences**. Turn until it is 90 degrees (which means six steps of 15 degrees) and release.

But, again, there is a more precise method, which you will certainly prefer if you want to set the angle exactly to 10 degrees each time you want to reset the frame to its original horizontal position.

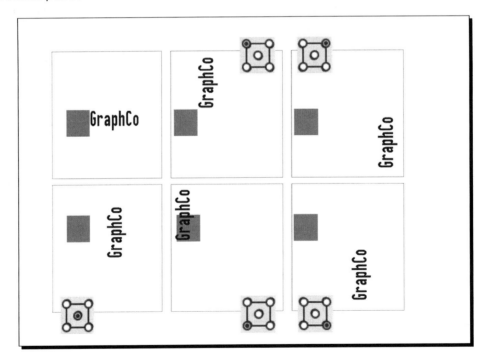

Just go to the **XYZ** tab of the PP (*F2*) and write the angle you want in the **Rotation** field. Enter **0°** if you want to reset to the original position or enter any other value that you need.

For even more control over your work, you can set the **Basepoint** for the **axis** of the rotation. The following are some examples of what it does.

The center based rotation is the one you already know from the **Rotate Item** tool. The other cannot be done with the **Rotate Item** tool. You will need them if you have precisely placed some object and want to keep some relation. In the illustration, the colored rectangle shows you how the rotated Text Frame can look more distant because of the basepoint chosen.

We will have to find a place for this frame. I suggest you to move it to the left-hand side border of the card. We may have to change some frame settings further on, but let's first have a try. Place it in a way that the name of the company hangs slightly out of the page, "Gr" should be placed above the pink shape with a white color. If you want to check whether the whole text is on the page, enable or disable the Preview mode (click on the icon with an eye at the right-hand side of the status bar) and see what the final result will be.

Preview mode

In Scribus, as in other Layout programs, the Preview mode is not a print preview, which is the default in text processors. It is simply the same layout but without helper lines and labels so that you can have a better idea of what you have created. In DTP, it is considered impossible to get an exact preview of the printed result on screen because the final printer is usually unknown.

Have a go hero – Eco power of rotation

Rotation with a basepoint can be really powerful. This illustration is really a simple drawing based on a three-ellipse shape, rotated and grouped with three circles, and so on, finishing with the rectangle. Actually, only seven shapes have been drawn. Other shapes are rotated copies. Try it out yourself!

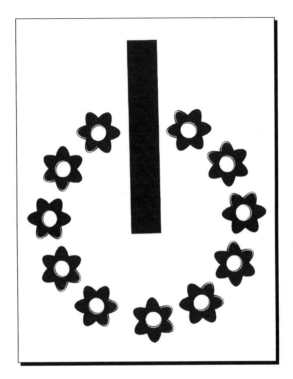

Aligning objects

Scribus has really nice and complete align options. Good alignment is really important in a layout. It helps to emphasize the structure of your layout. Aligning makes implicit relationship between elements that help the reader understand the importance of the objects on a page.

Time for action – aligning an object on another

The address and the logo aren't perfect yet: we'll push them to the right-hand side. We'll manage it by creating a guide and then aligning the frames to this **guide**.

1. Put the mouse pointer over the left-hand side ruler, press the mouse and drag to 80mm from the left-hand side page border. The tooltip with the measurement will help you.

2. Go to the **Windows** menu and choose **Align and Distribute**.

3. Click on the guide you've just created and you will see its position appearing in the **Selected Guide** field of the **Align** window.

4. In the **Relative to** list, choose **Guide**. Some of the buttons below are disabled.

5. Click on the logo and the **Align right sides** button of the **Align** window. Select the address frame and do the same. While the address frame is still selected, go to the PP, **Text** tab, and align the text to the right. You may further enhance the whole if needed.

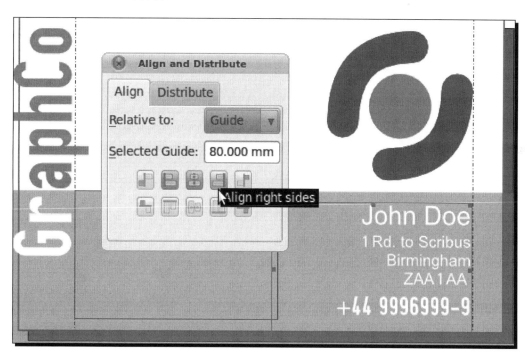

What just happened?

We have aligned two objects to each other. In this case, the object was a guide but it could have been any frame, shape, or line placed within the page. The align dialog, gives you many ways to place one object relatively by matching several criteria. For example, if you want to center an object on the page, just select it, choose **Relative to: Page** and then click on the buttons to center it horizontally and vertically.

In our case, we have chosen to align to a guide because there were no objects at the place we wanted the shape to be. So we just created this guide at the right place and aligned it. Aligning to guides is also useful because these are not printed. So you don't need to worry about them once you've used them. But if you want to align two frames to each other, you'll need to first select both.

It might take some experimenting to get used to all the options available in this window. But it's worth the effort, because the results are much more precise and quickly achieved.

Placing by using the right coordinates

We could have done this using another way, without the align window; you'll choose! Just select the frame and change the **basepoint** to a right one and specify the position of this point: here it's 80mm. Done!

There are often several ways to do a single action. It really helps to know them and choose them on purpose.

Locking objects to prevent errors

If you want to use this as a template for all the people who work at your company, we need two more things to be done:

1. Lock an object that doesn't need to be changed to prevent errors.

2. Save the card as a template.

The PP (*F2*) has several locking options depending on what you need to prevent. They are all available in the **XYZ** tab.

Icon	Menu	Description
	**Item	Size is locked**	Lock the size of the frame so that the resizing handles cannot be grabbed. **Width** and **Height** of the geometry in the PP are locked, too.
	**Item	Is locked**	Lock the size and the position of the frame or shape so that it cannot be moved. In this mode there are no handles around the selected frame. **X-Pos** and **Y-Pos** are unavailable.
		Click on this button if you want to prevent this frame from being printed. This is useful if you put a sketch in the background to help you do the layout.

The first two are really necessary in many ways because the mouse is sometimes sticky. In our business card, we could lock each frame even the one with the text, because none of the options lock the content.

When you're done, go to the **File | Save as Template** menu and choose a name. There is no need to browse to a specific directory because Scribus has its own directory for templates which is placed in the Scribus folder of your personal account. Once this is done, you're prompted to give a name to the template so that you can easily identify it. It can be a good idea to give some more detail, especially a **Category** (simply by choosing one from the list).

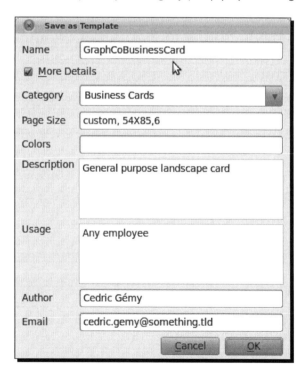

When you'll want to create a new business card, just click on the **File | New from Template** menu. In the window, choose the category in the left-hand pane, and the available template in this category will appear in the middle.

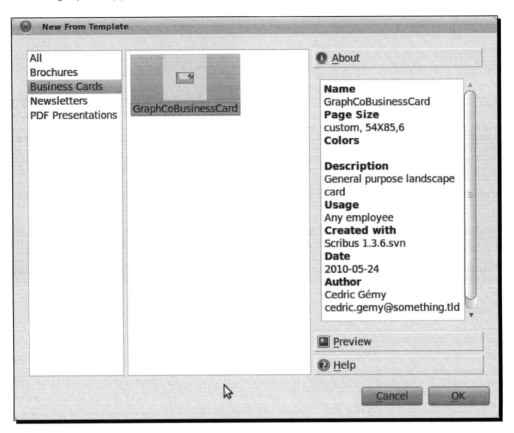

Then clicking on a template will display its details on the right-hand side pane, and its preview if you click on the **Preview** button. Open the template you need, change the information that needs to be changed, and save it as a normal Scribus document from **File | Save As**. There is no need to save it again as a template (twice) and have a second which is very similar!

Grouping objects

You have created your first business card with Scribus. Congratulations! But before we go deeper into each tool, one by one, we'd like to show you two nice features that we'll sometimes need.

The first one, and may be the most important, is the possibility to group objects. Grouping objects enables you to modify several items at the same time and in the same way. To select several objects, just click on each by pressing the *Shift* key or dragging the mouse over them.

Once they are selected you can move, rotate, or scale them without grouping them but grouping will be permanent until they are ungrouped, so that you won't have to manage each object separately unless you set it. To make them as a group, choose one of these interfaces:

- Group icon of the **XYZ** tab in PP
- Right-click and select **Group**
- *Ctrl + G*
- **Item | Group**

Unlike locking options, ungrouping is available with another button placed just below of the menus that have taken the place of the previous. Remember that when you need to ungroup, the current group has to be selected. If you don't like menus, you can use *Ctrl + Shift + G* to ungroup.

Groups exist for a long time in Scribus but they are considered as an entity with their own settings. Actually, the **Group** tab of the PP is not completely available. You just need to be patient.

Mirroring objects

We could have talked about mirroring objects a bit later. But we have seen so many transforming tools in this section that it can be the right place for this one too. Plus, you might have noticed that we have already used it. Wondering when? We used it when we were dealing with basepoints. Have a look at the screenshots. Do you see the screenshots of the basepoint options? Don't you see something strange? 3D shadows of the boxes are not oriented in the same way on each screenshot where they should.

Of course, this is just a detail. We've done it this way because we were lazy to create more screenshots (you'll later see why pictures aren't so funny to manage in a layout). But it will be useful, for example, when you'll want facing pages to be symmetrical. To apply a mirror effect on a frame or a group, you just need to click on the double arrows in the **XYZ** tab of the PP, as shown in the following screenshot. You can set a horizontal mirror (which match the example we've discussed), or a vertical one:

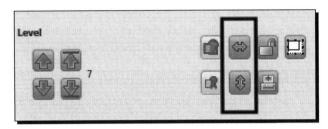

Remember that the mirror applies on the object itself. So you might need to create a copy first. You can do it:

- With the simple and common **Edit | Copy** and **Edit | Paste** options. The copy will be placed above the original, so you won't see any difference. By default, the copy is selected.

- With **Item | Duplicate**, which will move the copy according to the **File | Preferences | Tools | Miscellaneous Settings | Item Duplicate** value.

Pop quiz

1. The size setting of the new document window is made to:
   a. Define the size of the page
   b. Define the size of the paper
   c. Define the size within the margin

2. **Save as** will:
   a. Save into a .pdf file that you'll send the print office
   b. Save into a .sla file that only Scribus can open
   c. Save the document as a template

3. A font color can be applied from:
   a. **Color** part of the Properties Palette
   b. **Text** part of the Properties Palette
   c. The **Edit | Colors** window

Summary

In this chapter we've practiced a lot and have learned the basics of the Scribus tools and workflow. We have tried to show the relationship between the tools and the Properties Palette.

Specifically, we covered:

- Creating new documents and managing document properties
- Inserting and importing object and content into the document
- Transforming the objects we've inserted with resize, scale, and rotate actions
- Changing the aspect of the object and of the content

The elements in this chapter were the prerequisites for the next chapters, in which we'll go deeper and deeper into the available options. Let's begin with page handling in the next chapter.

3
Mastering Pages

In the previous chapter we have taken some time to understand how to manipulate and place objects in a layout. But we have ignored the fact that a document could contain several pages. In fact, as layout is more about laying out a page, it appears that the second most important concept of Scribus, after placing objects on a page, will be page management. Unlike in text processors, no page is created in Scribus until you ask for it.

In this chapter we will:

- Get used to page navigation
- Create, delete, and move pages
- Create and apply master pages
- Use guides to help structuring the pages

In fact, all these things are quite simple to understand. The big deal is to get used to them and really incorporate the way they work, mainly to be more productive and more creative at the same time.

Navigating in the document

Now that we will be working with some pages, sometimes lots of them, it will be very important to be able to navigate between them as comfortably as possible. Scribus lets you do this the way you prefer from several possibilities.

The first is to use the scrollbars, which is easy but not always the fastest way. The *PageUp* and *PageDn* keys are a quicker shortcut for this way.

People who love using the mouse can consider zooming out and then zooming in on another page. This can easily be done with *Ctrl* + mouse wheel scrolling. This method is really interesting when you need an overview of the content while scrolling. This way, you can have quick control of your layout.

The third is to use the page list or the green arrows of the statusbar. Consider this possibility only if you know exactly which page you want to go to, because choosing a page in the list will "jump" to that page.

The **Outline** window displays pages and all the objects included. Is a single click on one enough to reach it? This is a very precise window to manage the content of your document, sometimes too precise, especially if you have many frames. In this case, pages will be lost among all the entries.

Finally, and certainly most importantly, is the **Arrange Pages** window. We will have an overview of this window in the next section. Through this window not only can you browse your document, but also really manage the pages.

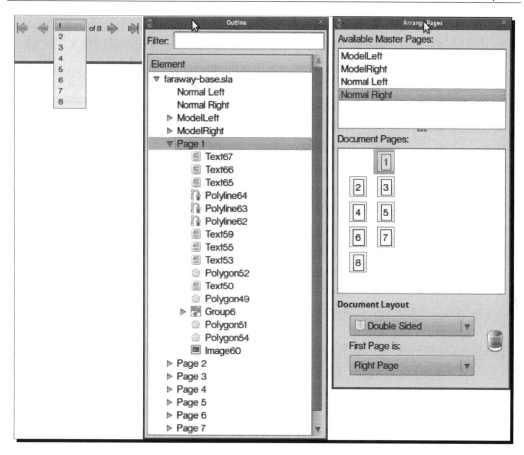

Time for action – let's surf into the document

A few steps will help you understand how the **Arrange Pages** window works and how it will be important in our layout.

1. Create a new document in Scribus. Set the **Page Number** to **8** in the **New Document** window. Or, open our sample "Far Away" document.

2. Once it is opened, you don't exactly know what the content is. Use the **View | Fit to Height** menu.

3. With *Page Up* and *Page Down* keys, or *Shift + PgUp* and *Shift + PgDn* to go page after page, browse easily through the pages, and see how the document looks, until you reach the last page, which should be Page 8.

4. Now go back to the first page by using the page list at the bottom of the Scribus window.

5. Go to **Window | Arrange Pages.** You should see your eight pages. Click on one to go there immediately.

What just happened?

Mainly, you will use the method that you like the most. But you can consider using zoom facilities when the page you want to go to is near enough. Alternatively, the page field of the status bar will be more useful to jump from a page to another, especially if this page is "far". The issue is that you need to know which page you want to get. If you work with a given table of content, it can help to find the page number and keep them in mind, or at least easily reachable.

The Arrange Pages window

Of all the Scribus windows, you should remember at least two: the Properties Palette, and the **Arrange Pages** window. The last let's you manipulate your document in the easiest way you could imagine. If it looks strange to you to manipulate pages, it is actually so handy that you'll really get used to it very fast. So let's have a look at it before using it.

The window is divided into three parts:

1. The top part shows the available master pages. You'll see in the *Applying master pages* section how practical it is to have them there.

2. The main part shows the pages of your document. Pages can be displayed in a column if you choose a single-page document or two per line if you choose a double-sided type. The number is the position of each page in your document. It doesn't necessarily refer to the page numbering but they usually match, depending on how you processed your document and if the sections have been defined.

3. At the bottom, some options are available. You will use them from time to time to do some changes in the way the pages are displayed.

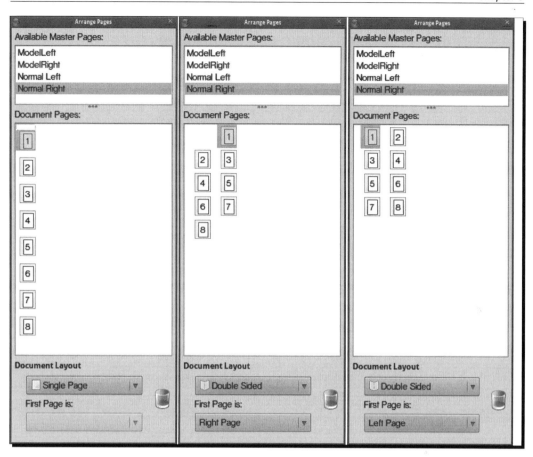

The **Document Layout** refers to the choice you've made in the **New Document** window. Did you know at this time exactly what you wanted? The best answer would be yes, but sometimes you begin a layout even if you don't have all the required answers. In this case, you can easily change the layout type from here. Changing from here is just the same as if you'd have done the changes in the **Document Properties** window, but much faster. You don't need to worry much about this layout type; just choose the one that matches most of the final printed results, so that you can get on screen a good overview of what the reader will have in hand. But basically, the print office can rearrange the page as you'd wish so that you can consider this option as a previewing option.

Layout type and first page

When a document is set to **Single Page**, you will see that you can't choose what side the first page will be. Even if it is evident, many people seem astonished by this.

Changing the **First Page** layout is another challenge. When the document is **Single Page**, no problem, this option is unavailable. But when **Double Sided** is chosen, a choice has to be made. By default, it is set to the right-hand side page. If you want to understand why, just pick any magazine you have near you and look at the first page: it is at the right-hand side of the fold and there is no page at the left-hand side of the fold. At the left-hand side, the last page of the document could be considered, but this is done by the print office and you don't need to worry about this is in Scribus. So why do we have the choice? Have a look at the following screenshot and see how Acrobat Reader displays facing pages when it is set to **View | Page Display | Two-Up**!

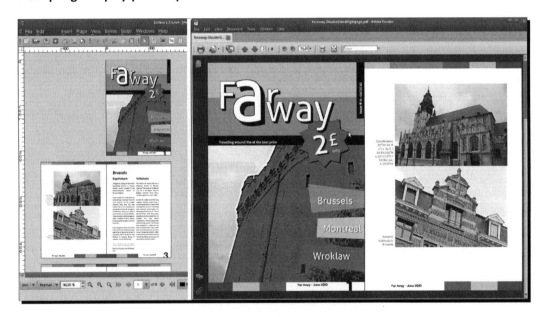

This is not so good if you compare it to the Scribus document. We can consider it as normal for reading on screen but it is not the same as reading on paper. Reproducing capabilities are different. Changing to a first **Left Page** will turn the Scribus layout model to match this Acrobat Reader setting so that you can create your document in the exact way it will be displayed. The trouble appears when you need a printed and a screen copy.

Scribus and non latin languages

We could consider this First Page option to set a document for Arabic or any another right to left languages. In fact, Scribus can hardly handle those languages.

Adding and deleting pages

Any layout program will let the user manipulate pages as any other object of the document. That means that you will be able to add or remove pages as you like but will need to take care of this too. Scribus will never add pages by itself; you'll have to do it yourself.

Adding pages one by one

Remember what we said about the difference between Scribus and Acrobat Reader in the way they display facing pages? We really need the photos nearby to the text. This will be much easier for the reader of course. How can we do this? Simply add a page after Page 1, only for the screen document.

In fact, our document has no Table of Contents, so it can be a good opportunity to add a page for this.

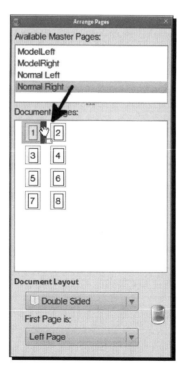

Usually, when we have several pages to add, we do it from the **Arrange Pages** window. It is very easy, with a visual feedback so that errors can be avoided. Just pick a master page in the top list of that window (you should have only one or two named Normal at the beginning) and drag it to a deposit area where you need to add the new page.

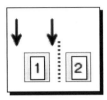

Time for action – a new page after the cover

Let's do it in our sample document.

1. Open the `faraway.sla` file in Scribus and display the **Arrange Pages** window.

2. Place the cursor on the **Normal Right** template in the top part of the window and press the left button of the mouse.

3. Drag (keep the mouse button pressed) to the space between Page 1 and Page 2 until you see a blue rectangle next to Page 1.

4. When you see it, just release the mouse button. You'll see that you have nine pages listed in the **Document Pages** as well as a blank page that is visible in the main window of Scribus.

5. What you can see here is that the shape placed on Page 1 continues on the new page, which is not too pretty.

6. Actually, the simplest is to add a white rectangle over to hide them were you want. It is much smarter to change the gap between the facing page in the **Document Setup** of the **File** menu, or use **Path Operation** to modify the shapes themselves as explained in Chapter 7.

What just happened?

The top part of the **Arrange Pages** window shows the available page template, called the master page. In Scribus, all the pages are based on a master page, and the Normal pages are the ones Scribus automatically creates for every new document. By dragging it we just tell Scribus which it should use for the new page. "Hitting" the deposit area is really important. If you release the mouse in any other place, no page will be created. Worse, you could be on another deposit area without noticing, so the other page could be added somewhere else.

Adding several pages at once

Sometimes, you need to add more pages at once. You could drag each one as described before, but if you need 20 pages or more, the task can be really boring and repetitive. A better way is to use the **Insert Page** window. You can open it from the **Page | Insert** menu. It's very easy to use. Just enter into the first field how many pages you need to add.

Then specify where you need to add them. By default, it suggests the end of the document but you can choose **before Page** or **after Page** in the drop-down list and write the page number where it should be inserted.

The other settings are default, which are usually left as is. We'll see how to deal with them in the *Creating and deleting master pages* section of this chapter.

Time for action – adding several pages

Inserting new pages is a very basic and simple task in layout programs. As we'll see in the following steps, moving the content is really apart from page management.

1. Go to **Page | Insert** to display the **Insert Page** window.

2. Enter **4** in the **Insert** field.

3. Then choose **after Page**, and enter **2** in the adjacent field.

4. You can then choose the master page that will be applied to those new pages. We selected **Normal Left** and **Normal Right** so that we can see the difference with the other pages on which **ModelLeft** and **ModelRight** are applied.

5. Then select the page size: the current document is an A5, so it's better to keep it similar but you could choose another page size if you wish.

6. Verify that the **Move Objects with their Page** checkbox is selected.

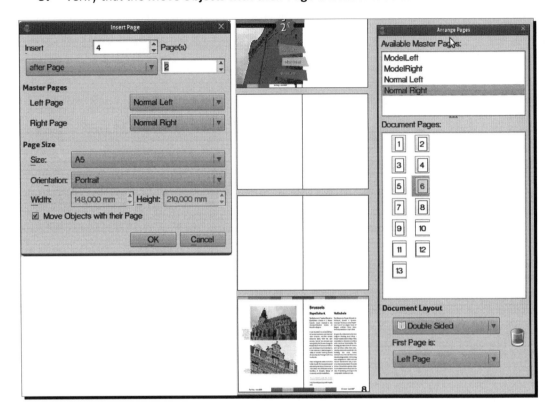

What just happened?

Here, we have added four pages after Page 2. We now have four new empty pages plus the one we added previously. The last added page is selected, that is Page 6.

You can see that the pictures and text that were on Pages 2 to 6 before are now placed on Pages 7 to 13. This is the result of the **Move Objects with their Page** option. If we had not selected it, all those frames would have remained on the original pages with the empty master page. It's very rare to do like this.

Have a go hero – where is London?

We actually have no page for London. Try to add at least two pages after the page on Brussels (London is not that far away that we need to put it at the end).

Deleting pages

Deleting pages is as easy as adding them. You can choose to **delete** pages from the **Arrange Pages** window or with the entry in the **Page** menu.

1. To delete single pages, use the **Arrange Pages** window. Just drag the page you want to delete onto the Trash icon at the bottom right-hand side of the same window.

2. To delete several pages at once, go to **Page | Delete**, and enter the range you want to delete, from the first page to the last.

An important thing to remember is that all the objects placed on that/those page(s) will be deleted at the same time. Consider a page as a top-level object on which other objects are included and linked. It seems dangerous right now, but just read a few more lines and you'll understand why it is great.

You should know what you're doing
When you are deleting pages Scribus won't ask you to confirm. If something looks strange, undo it immediately by pressing the *Ctrl + Z* keys.

Arranging pages

Consider the following:

◆ The page is an object as any other
◆ All the objects can be moved within or across the pages

It is easy to understand that pages can be moved around, too. This is one of the most powerful use cases of a layout program. Let's say you've added the pages for London at Pages 5 and 6. But you later decide that your magazine will be some kind of trip metaphor and you want to show each step of it by beginning from London. In this case, London will become the first city in your document and should be placed before the pages for Brussels.

More generally, in professional magazines, a user is mostly used to managing advertising pages. Suppose a client pays for a full page near the page for London, because he has a market there and finally decides that the last page would be a better fit. And shortly before pressing the print button (for thousands of copies) you need to change it.

You will again have two ways to make the change:

- To move the pages one by one, go to the **Arrange Pages** window, press the mouse button on the page you want to move (for example, the page for Brussels), drag and release when you reach the right deposit area. See that the page numbering is being automatically done because it is set in our example.

- If you want to move several pages, it will be much faster to use the **Page | Move** window. Here, just specify which pages you want to move and where you want them to be. This window is very similar to the **Insert Page** window.

Don't forget that the content of your page gets moved with the page itself: there's no need to do the layout again, and no need to perform any copy/paste.

Customizing page properties

When you create your documents you tell Scribus how the page should look. You set:

- A size
- An orientation
- The margins

But sometimes, you need some changes in your document. From that, you can consider several options depending on what you need.

- Do you want the changes to apply to every new page?
- Do you want to modify an existing page?
- Do you want to affect the way you'll organize the content of the page?
- Do you want to change the page itself?

We could go on with a longer list. But this will help with choosing the best Scribus method.

Mainly, if you want to change the new pages or all the pages of your document, just go to the **Document** part of the **Document Setup** (in the **File** menu). There you can change the setting you want. They are very similar to the **New Document** dialog, so no extra information is needed.

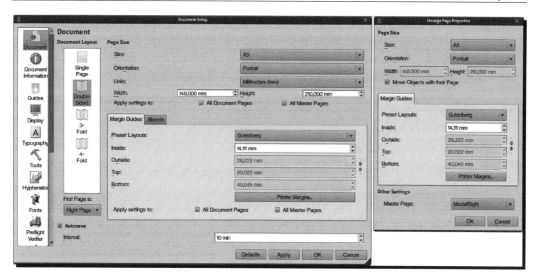

If you want the new settings to be applied to existing pages, you should think of selecting the **All Document Pages** and/or **All Master Pages** checkboxes. Otherwise, the changes will be applied only to new pages.

If you only need to change the properties of one single page, **Page | Manage Page Properties** is a better place to go. Here you will have the same settings except for the bleeds, which can only be set for the whole document. Everything else can be adapted and applied only to the current page. Keep in mind that if you change the size of the page and your document is double-sided, you should probably change the size of the other side too: Scribus won't do it for you.

Changing paper size is not so easy

To change the page size to a custom size not listed in the list, just choose **Custom** at the very bottom of the list so that the **Height** and **Width** field can be changed.

Scribus won't align folds of the modified pages either. This is only a display problem. However, remember that having several page sizes in a document can be tricky for the print shop: they need to use another printer and sometimes a different paper. If you need this, talk about it to your print provider.

Have a go hero – add a larger page

Have you already seen documents whose pages were sometimes smaller or larger than other pages? We often do it for advertising, for special content, or to get more space, too. If you have a really great landscape photo, maybe a panorama, you'd want to give it more space in your layout, but it will take the place of your text. In this case, you can consider adjusting the page size. Let's say you want a full view of Buckingham Palace on Page 4, which will need to be twice the size of the actual page. Don't forget you're working on a double-sided book!

Creating and deleting master pages

Master pages really are the Scribus killer functionality. They can be explained in just a few words because they are really easy and have just a few options. But once you know how to use them you can save hours of your precious time on each Scribus document you do. With styles (see Chapter 5) this is really where you must put some effort if you want to be more productive without losing your creativity.

The master page will help you repeat objects on several pages and keep a link between each document page and their master, so that if you change the master through **Edit | Master Pages**, pages will be automatically updated. On top of that, there is not much to say except explaining how to do it.

The default master pages

Scribus is basically built on page manipulation and adding content to those pages. Considering that good practices have to be adapted as soon as possible, there is a default master page in any Scribus document.

Time for action – using default master pages

When you create a new document, Scribus automatically creates one or more master pages: one for a single-page document, two for a double-sided, and three for three-folded and four-folded documents.

1. Create a new **Letter**, 8 pages double-sided document, with **Magazine** margins.

2. Go to **Windows | Arrange Pages** and verify that you have two master pages, **Normal Left** and **Normal Right**.

3. Double-click on the **Normal Left** page from the **Arrange Pages** top part: Scribus will show the content of the master page instead of the current page.

4. See that this master page has margins. A quick glance at **Page | Manage Page Properties** will show that **Magazine** margins are used as defined in the **New Document** window.

5. Change the margins to **Golden Mean** and validate.

6. Add a rectangle at the top of your master page and set it nicely with Properties Palette.

7. Close the **Edit Master Pages** window by pressing the *Esc* key or clicking on the close button in the header bar.

8. You should see your document pages now. Browsing through them will show you that the left-hand side page now contains the same rectangle and the page has the new **Golden Mean** margin.

What just happened?

When the document is created, Normal Left and Normal Right master pages are created and have the default margins. They get automatically applied to the existing right-hand side and left-hand side pages, respectively. If your document is of **Single Page** type, you'll get only one Normal page but the principles of using it will be similar.

You can alternatively use **Edit | Master Page** or double click on a master page in **Arrange Pages** to display the master pages. Often, as **Arrange Pages** will already be open, it will probably be the most practical to use. You know you are in a master page when:

◆ The **Edit | Master Page** window is open. When you close this window, the changes made to any master page are automatically saved and you immediately come back to the document pages.

◆ The page list in the statusbar is not available.

♦ You have only one page on screen even if your document has several (there is no need to create a master page if your document has only one page).

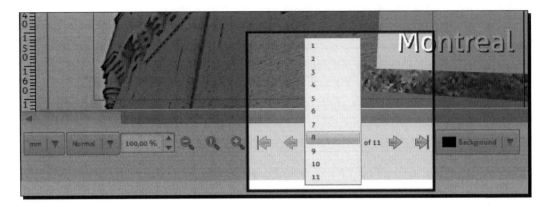

At the same time, you'll see that many menu entries are deactivated, especially those in the **Page** menu, because there is no reason to manipulate pages while you're managing the master pages.

Any changes made on a master page will immediately be applied to the related pages.

Confused with left and right?

In Scribus, unlike in InDesign, the left-hand side master page can be applied to a right-hand side page. Scribus never automates the way master pages are applied, except when creating the document. So, if you're confused by that, don't worry; you'll be able to do what you want even if you have chosen the bad side.

Managing custom master pages with the Edit Master Pages window

Sometimes it's a good idea to keep the default settings and create custom master pages as you need them. Especially, default empty master pages can be useful for pages that need no master page, such as a cover or advertising pages. Remember that all the pages are linked to a master page, even if it's an empty one.

The master page window has very few options to act on the master pages. These options are available at the top of the window in a row of buttons that let you (from left to right):

♦ Add a new master page

♦ Duplicate an existing master page

- Import a master page
- Delete a master page

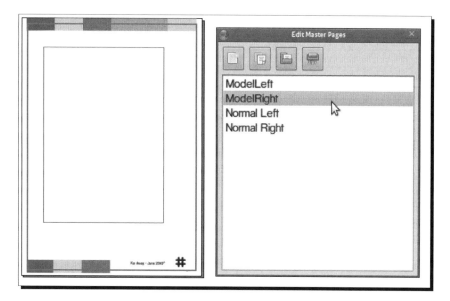

If you have a look at the master pages of our sample "Far Away" document, you'll see that two custom master pages have been defined: **ModelLeft** and **ModelRight**, which contain colored rectangles on the top and bottom, and a footer text.

Renaming a master page

Each master page needs a name. If you want to rename it, double-click on the name of the master page you want to change, in the **Edit Master Pages** window. Notice that you cannot rename the default master pages.

Creating master pages

To create a **new master page**, you need very few steps. Your master page can be a new one or built upon an existing page. If you need to create a new master page based on another one, you can just click on the **Duplicate** button of the **Edit Master Pages** window. In the other case, click on the **Add a new master page** button.

Another way is to turn a normal page of your document to a master page. We don't advise you to use it in your standard workflow, but it is useful if you forget to create a master page (this doesn't seem to be a safe method and we have experienced slowness and crashes using it). In this case simply use **Page | Convert to Master Page**. Give a name and state if it must keep the object of the master page that could eventually be applied to your current page.

Time for action – hands on master page

Creating a master page is a simple task, and should consider as soon as possible in the layout process. The number of master page you'll need will depend on your choice. Let's see how to add your new master page and have them applied.

1. Click on the first left-hand side button of the **Edit Master Pages** window.

2. You'll be prompted to give a name and reference side (we choose **Right Page**) to your master page: give a simple but explicit name like **GalleryRight** (try to avoid spaces and special characters like any é, ü, or so).

3. A new empty master page is listed in the window and the page appears in Scribus in place of the page you were on previously. It will have the default document margins and the default size.

4. Customize it with new objects. Eventually change the page properties if needed.

    ❑ Draw a small rectangle in the top-right corner (see the next illustration if you need an example). If you wish, you can go to a **ModelRight**, copy a rectangle, and paste it here. This way, you're sure they'll be the same size.

    ❑ We add a Text Frame near it and type the name of our section: let's say, "Your photos".

5. The changes will be applied when the **Edit Master Pages** window will be closed.

6. For now, click on the second button to duplicate the current and call it **GalleryLeft** and choose **Left Page**.

7. Once that is made, you can see that margins are correctly modified in your new layout thanks to the change of side. But the custom shape and the Text Frame stayed in their place.

8. Move the shape first and press the *Ctrl* key while dragging so that you can keep the alignment with the original place. Drag until you reach the other side of the page and release.

9. Modify the shape so that it matches the side needs.

10. Close the **Edit Master Page** window.

What just happened?

You've just created two master pages in two different ways. You might have noticed that a master page is quite similar to a page, and may easily confuse you. Always be sure of what you're doing and check for clues before doing so.

There is no special way to flip a page side to another. The mirroring options of the Properties Palette (**XYZ**) or the **Align and Distribute** window can help positioning, but things have to be done manually. You can create as many master pages as you want, and you can do so without closing the master page window if you wish.

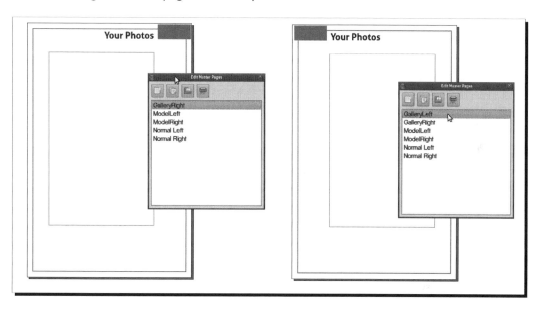

Applying master pages

You have certainly noticed that nothing has changed in your document yet. So why did we create master pages if it doesn't change anything? Simply because these are useful when they are applied. And that Scribus has no means to understand where we want to apply them. So we'll need to do it ourselves.

You may already know what we'll say: you have two ways to apply master pages, one using the **Arrange Pages** window, and another using a menu.

Applying master, page after page

You can apply master page to individual pages. You can do it:

◆ When you create a new page

◆ When you want to apply a new master page to an existing page

If you want to create a new page base on your new master page, refer to the *Adding pages one by one* section of this chapter. You may remember that dragging a master page on a deposit area will create a new page based on this master page.

So what about modifying an existing page? Perform the same process, but release the mouse when it is above the page you want to change. And it's done.

Applying masters to several pages

If you want to change several pages at once, consider using the following:

◆ **Page | Insert** menu to create the pages using your master page

◆ **Page | Apply Master Page** to change the master page of several existing pages

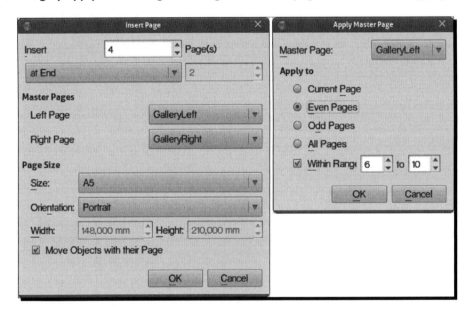

In the **Insert Page** window, you'll choose which master page you'll apply to each side. Here we have set **Left Page** to **GalleryLeft** and **Right Page** to **GalleryRight**. You cannot customize it more than that. But remember that a single master page can be applied to individual pages. So don't worry, consider this setting as the generality of this part of the document that you'll customize later.

In the **Apply Master Page** window, things are different. Firstly, it doesn't create any page. Then, you will define, on top, which master page you want to apply and on which page and side. Here we've set all the even pages from **6** to **10**.

Have a go hero – be the master of master pages!

Do you see the strangeness of our last action? Certainly, our document needs some improvement. We would like the cover pages to have an empty master page, because covers are usually very special pages. Apply the right master page on the right-hand side. And finally, change the Gallery margins so that they are similar on each side like in the **Magazine** preset. Save the precious document.

Sharing pages and master pages between documents

The power of a master page is more when you know that a master page can be easily used through documents. Once something is done, you can reuse it as often as you like. The **Page | Import** menu and **Import** button of the **Edit Master Page** window make it easy.

Time for action – reusing pages

Reusing master pages is one of the productivity tools that helps you to take advantage of a few minutes of work. Knowing how to import master pages will be very practical when you'll need to create several documents that need to have the same page design.

1. Create a new document with the same global setting: A5 size and double-sided, and eventually several empty pages.

2. Go to **Page | Import** and specify which document you want to import the page from: **FarAwayMag** seems a good choice.

3. Then specify which page you want to import. Let's say we want to reuse the cover page, so you write **1** in the **Import Page** field.

4. Depending on what you need, you can ask for new pages to be added in your new document. Validate them.

5. Then go to **Edit | Master Pages** and click on the third button **Import master pages from another document**.

6. Choose the document and then the Master Page.

7. Click on **Import** and it will be added to the Master Page list of your new document.

What just happened?

The **Import** page can take a long time because Scribus needs to open the document and copy each object one by one. The bigger the file, the longer it will take. Notice that, if you want to undo the import in your new document, you'll need to repeat undo as many times as the number of objects imported.

You can import several pages at once by giving their number separated by a comma: for example, **1,2,5,7**. They will all be inserted as the following pages. Of course, you can rearrange them later.

On the other hand, you cannot import several master pages at once. You'll need to import them one by one. If you really need to reuse many of your master pages and other settings, consider saving your base document as a template and creating new documents from it; it will be much faster and safer.

Numbering pages

Now that you know how a master page works, it's very easy to add **automatic page numbering**. In Scribus there is no such thing as a header or footer: all the elements that need to be repeated need to be put on a master page. A page number, as a number, can be considered as a kind of text (and can be typed using the keyboard).

Time for action – page numbering

That said, it will be very easy to add a master page: most will be using a Text Frame. Let's see how to use it in detail:

1. Go to your master page.

2. Add a Text Frame where you want to add the page number.

3. Double-click within the frame and activate the Content mode.

4. Go to **Insert | Character | Page Number** and you'll see a # in the frame.

5. That's good, set it nicely: you can add other text in the frame such as "page" to get something like "page #", or place shapes around or under the number.

6. Exit the Master Page mode and you'll see that the page number will be applied to all of the pages on which your master page is applied. The # has been replaced by the actual page number.

What just happened?

By adding a Text Frame, we just placed the number. We could have inserted the frame anywhere in the page, even in non-practical places. It can be the size we want too, put to the background, or have the main text of the page flowing around. If the Scribus way needs more steps than text processors, it is not very difficult because the steps really match the way layout tools work, consistently, and give much more possibilities at the same time.

When on a master page, Scribus displays a # because the master page is not a printed page; it's just a reference. So the numbers are visible only when we go back to the document page. The document automatically updates if some page is added, moved, or deleted, so that you won't have to care much about them after you've added them.

Displaying the number of pages

If you want to do something like "page 1/100", the problem is that you need to know how many pages you'll get at the end. If you don't, the risk is that you'll forget to change the value at the end (you know how one can be in a hurry at the end). If you use **Insert | Character | Number of Pages**, the number will be automatically updated.

Adding sections

Sections can be used to change the numbering scheme in some pages of the document. This is really common in books or even in some magazines where the preface or the appendices use Roman numerals, whereas the main content uses the usual Arabic numerals.

Let's say we have a 100 pages document containing a 10 page Appendix and a 3 page Preface beginning after the cover pages. Each of them will begin at 1 but the Preface and Appendix will use **Roman numerals**.

Book numbering scheme

Usually, in books, the cover page is not numbered. So, if you create a single Scribus document for a book, containing the cover, you'll certainly need to define a section beginning at Page 3.

The **Document Setup** window (File menu) has a **Section** part in which sections can be managed. Each has a default section beginning at Page 1. Just click on the **Add** button to create new sections that you will set as you like.

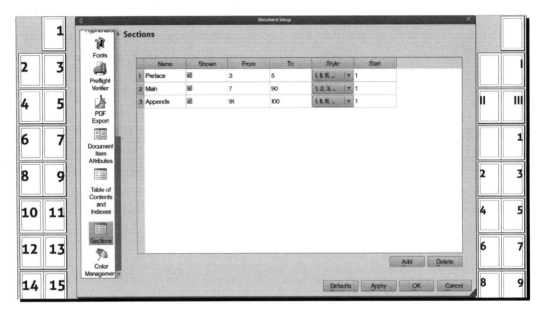

The result is a table of properties. You just need to understand what the columns mean:

1. **Name** is the name of the section. The default is named "0". You can rename it by double-clicking on it.

2. **Shown** is just to mention whether it will be displayed or not.

3. **From** displays which page of your document the section will begin on.

4. **To** displays at which page the section will end. In the example you can see that 6 is not set in the section and that the page has no number. This is very useful, for example, in empty pages between chapters or for covers that aren't set too.

5. **Type** defines how the numbering will be done: Arabic, lowercase Roman, uppercase Roman, letters, or none.

6. **Start** let's you define which should be the first page number of the section. This is useful when you split your book or magazine into several Scribus documents. Each document will begin at a specific page number that can be set here.

Guides

Guides are very different things: these are helpers which give you an easy way to place objects where you like.

Guides can be placed manually by pressing the mouse button in a ruler and dragging them onto the page. The guide is placed when the mouse button is released. It can be moved afterwards with the **Select Item** tool (C key).

Can't see the guides!
If you don't see the guides, select **View | Show Guides** or verify that the display is not in **Preview Mode** (in the **View** menu).

If a guide is placed in a master page, it will appear on each page on which the master page will be applied. It is really useful if you want to place a Text Frame or Image Frame at the same place on several pages.

The difficult part of this is that it is difficult to place a guide very precisely, for example, at the middle of the page. The **Page | Manage Guides** window helps you position guides according to a precise value (Single tab) or create several well distributed (**Column/Row** tab) guides at once.

Time for action – a simple three-folded document

When describing the **New document** window we have said not to use the 3-Fold document type but preferably a landscape A4 or similar. We will now see how we will use this A4:

1. Create a single-side A4 landscape document with two pages. Set margins to 5mm (remember Scribus converts units).

2. Go to **Page | Manage Guides**.

3. Activate the second tab and increase the vertical guide field to **2**.

4. Look at what happens in your document. Really cool!

5. Select the **Use Gap** checkbox in the same column and set the field to **5mm**.

6. Choose **Page** as a reference (otherwise the center part of the document will be smaller).

7. Go to the first tab (**Single**) and the **Horizontal** part. Click on the **Add** button to create a new guide and change the default value to **70mm** (1/3 of the page height). Add a second one and place it at **75mm**.

8. Select the **Lock Guides** checkbox so that it is easier to work on a page without the risk of moving the guides.

9. Click on the **Apply to All Pages** button and close the window.

10. You can now place the frames into your page. Remember that pressing the *Shift* key while clicking with a frame tool will create a frame at margin size. The most difficult is to fill the frame with content.

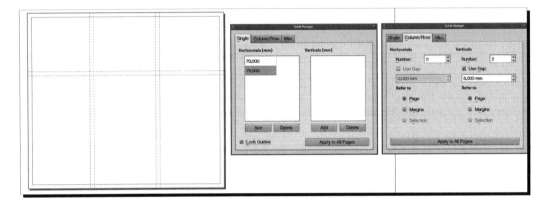

What just happened?

Instead of using the standard 3-fold template, we decided to use a simple A4 landscape document. We then needed to get some help our way to fill this page. Especially we wanted to avoid content on the fold. We used the **Manage Guides** window to automatically generate guides that are perfectly distributed all over the page, within the margin or not. Those guides represent our folds. We added a gap to these guides just as if we wanted to create a margin around each fold. Setting the **Lock Guides** option helped us work more peacefully without being afraid of moving guides, which would be unproductive or at least boring to put them back in place.

Grids

Grids are another type of helpers which is are less customizable. Grids can be displayed with **View | Show grid**. The document always has a default grid. Its color and stepping can be change in the **Document Setup | Guides**.

Major Grids are the thicker lines and Minor Grids are the thinner lines. You can set the spacing for each as they match your needs. Grids are much more regular than guides, and can really help you in object placement.

The baseline Grid refers to text positioning and will be seen in Chapter 5.

Pop quiz

1. We can delete a page by:
   a. Clicking the trash icon in the **Arrange Page** dialog
   b. Dragging the page to the Trash icon in the **Arrange Page** dialog
   c. Using the **Page | Delete** menu

2. To save a master page you need to:
   a. Do nothing
   b. Close the **Edit Master Page** window
   c. Save the document

3. A page number needs:
   a. To be inserted in a Text Frame
   b. To be inserted in a header
   c. To be set in a section

Summary

In this chapter, we've practiced a lot and have learned the basics of the most important productivity tool in Scribus, the master page, as well as managing pages.

Specifically, we covered:

- Creating, deleting, and arranging pages
- Creating, deleting, and applying master pages to pages
- Applying automatic page numbering, even through sections
- Using guides to draw a nice, structured page layout

In the next two chapters, we'll see how to handle the text in Scribus and see the properties that can make it nice without losing productivity.

4
Using Text in Scribus

Very few documents are made with pictures only. Text is always a very important part of the layout because it contains the main information. While we've mostly worked on the layout environment until now, in this chapter, we'll begin to take an interest in the content.

To begin with, in this chapter, we'll explain the relationship between the frame and its content. We won't deal with the visual aspect of the text now. If you wish, you can jump to the next chapter.

In this chapter we shall:

◆   Set the Text Frame options

◆   Set text options regarding long text (linking) or text flow

◆   Import and edit text

◆   Improve text manipulation

Creating Text Frames

No text without Text Frames: that's the rule in a layout program. Text has to be placed within areas somewhere on the page.

We have already used lots of Text Frames, especially in Chapter 2. So, you may know how to create one. But now might be a good time go deeper into the details and give you some advise and tips to help you be more efficient.

First of all remember *T* is the keyboard shortcut for the **Insert Text Frame** tool, and *C* the shortcut for the **Select Item** tool. You'll often have to manage with both.

Consider the three main ways of creating a frame (be it an Image Frame!) with the **Insert Text Frame** tool:

◆ A single-click on the page will display the **Enter Object Size** window, in which you'll be able to set the **Width** and the **Height** of the future frame as well as the placement of the basepoint from which the size will be applied. The basepoint refers to the frame corners. This is very useful if you have a very structured layout like a catalog.

◆ A press-drag-release action will give you the ability to draw a frame of any size you like, without knowing the exact size you need. This is the most widely-used way but not the most precise. Remember, placing guides can help you structure your document, and the frames will snap to them, making your frame more precise while you save precious seconds each time. By the time you've done hundreds of frames, you'll have saved hours or days only with this.

◆ Another time-saving method is to press the *Shift* key while clicking anywhere on the page. Scribus will look for margins, page borders, or guides that surround this place and which define the area. The frame will be the size of that area, automatically.

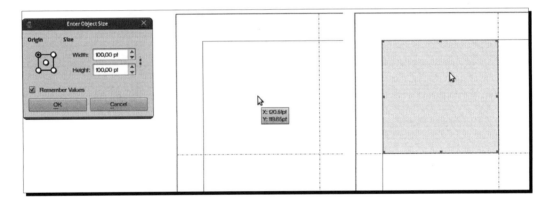

You can consider another kind of Text Frame creation method: converting a shape to a Text Frame. This will be discussed in Chapter 7. Without that, your Text Frame will always be rectangular, which is by far the most common setting anyway. So don't feel limited to this.

Setting Text Frame options

Creating a frame is one thing, but having it exactly as you want on the page is another tricky thing altogether. Half of the layout relies in the preciseness of the settings, especially the creative part. It's very difficult to say how something can look nice: if there were precise layout rules, all the documents would look the same. So knowing the frame settings and playing with them is a very basic part of our work in Scribus.

Depending on the Scribus version you use, frame options can be available in three or four parts of the Properties Palette (*F2*).

Size and position

It's evident that the main part is **XYZ**, which lets you change the position, the size, and the rotation of the frame:

◆ Horizontal positioning from left page border is made with *X-pos*

◆ Vertical positioning from top page border is made with *Y-pos*

In both, the **Basepoint** lets you choose which corner will be used for the calculations.

Positioning the object can require object stack changes. You might sometimes have some text above an image, for example, and you would want to be sure that the picture won't hide the text. In this case, the Text Frame should be placed above the Image Frame. Green **Level** arrows ⬆, ⬆, ⬇, and ⬇ of the **XYZ** tab let you change this as you wish.

Shape

If you're really fed up with rectangle frame, you can easily change it afterwards. Once your frame is on the page, just go to the **Shape** tab of the PP. Here you'll see the Shape label with a square button at its right (see the following image). Clicking on that button will display a list of default shapes that you can use as you want. But remember that keeping a layout simple is the key to success.

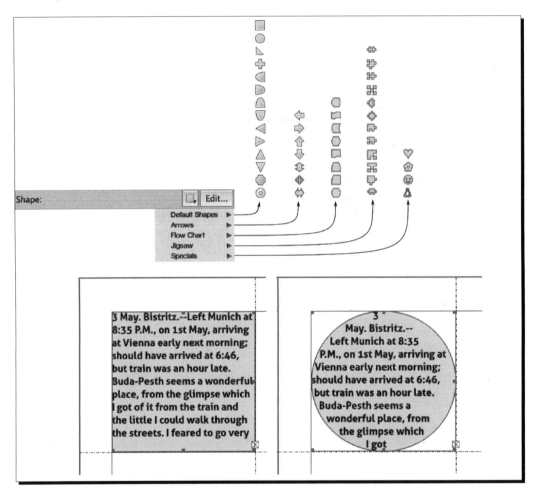

As you can see, the text (here is a sample text from the **Insert | Sample Text** menu) adapts automatically to the shape. In this example, you may notice that fewer words are visible in the second shape. We'll see how to deal with that in the next section.

Frame margins

Frame margins simply add white spaces between the text and the frame border. You don't need to set them on each frame, but it can be a good idea if you have a background color or a border to enhance readability. To change this, just go to the **Text** tab and expand the **Column and text distance** settings. **Top**, **Bottom**, **Left**, and **Right** will modify each margin while **Columns** will add columns to that frame. **Gap** is the space between the columns. After making the changes, use the eye icon at the bottom toolbar to check how the page looks and deselect the frame if you didn't want the red stroke and handles on the frame.

 Color is another part of the frame setting. To remember how to change a frame's color or border, read Chapter 2 again. Or, if you need more detail, jump to Chapter 9.

Importing simple text

Your text frames are made to incorporate texts. Until now, we have mainly used sample text or have written the text ourselves in the frames. Sample text (**Insert | Sample Text**) is great when you want to work on the layout and you don't have the final text. This way you can look for the right and nicest settings, save them, and when the final text will arrive, add it.

Most of the time, you'll import the text from another file. There are two reasons for this:

- ◆ Scribus is not the most handy tool to write text: text editors or text processors will do it faster and in a simpler way.

- ◆ You may not be the author of the text, and other people don't have to care about the layout, just the content. Only you will need to deal with Scribus and you'll receive text of other file formats. Of course, you should not modify the authors' text without their agreement.

Importing text is very simple but the procedure can be different regarding the file format you use. Some file formats will use features that we don't know of in Scribus yet. So we'll begin with simple text in a plain .txt file format written with Notepad, Notepad++, vi, gedit, Smultron, TextWrangler, or any other text editor. We'll see more advanced import features in the next chapter.

Import or append text

Appending text is very similar to importing using **Get Text**. **Get Text** will replace existing text in a frame with the new one. **Append Text** will add the new text at the end of existing text in the frame. If your frame is empty, you don't have to worry about it, just import.

Importing can be done in the following ways:

- **File | Import | Get text** (if a Text Frame is selected)
- Right-click on a frame and select **Get Text** (if a Text Frame is selected)
- *Ctrl + D* directly displays the import window.

Time for action – import it from Shakespeare land!

Let's say we have a text from Shakespeare: ALL'S WELL THAT ENDS WELL. We would like to do a little book on this famous text that we can get from the manybooks.com website, http://manybooks.net/titles/shakespeetext982ws3010.html. In the download section (the orange rectangle to the right-hand side), choose the format (.odt, .txt) and download it. We will try it in two ways just to show you the difference.

1. Begin by creating a portrait A5 double-sided document. We don't actually know how many pages we'll need; so let's say that we actually need four pages.

2. With the **Insert Text Frame** tool (*T*), *Shift* + click in the first page to create a page-wide frame.

3. *Ctrl + I* will display the import window as **File | Import** would; browse through your directories to find the text you want to use. Don't touch any other settings, and click on **OK**.

4. On the first page, you can see the title, the author's name, a reference to the website (terms of use have been moved at the end of the text so it is not visible for now), the character list, and then the story itself. Notice that the content stops at the end of the first frame.

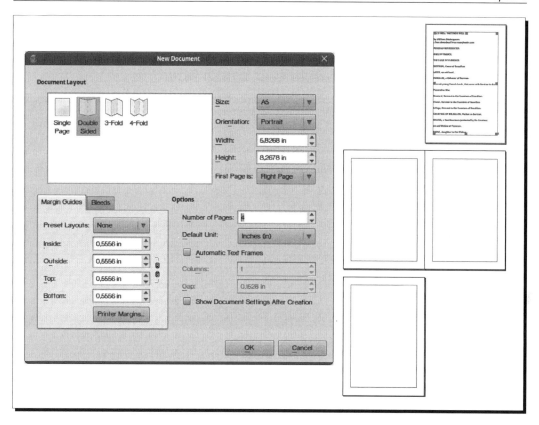

What just happened?

When importing text, it fills only the frame in which it has been imported. If we want the text to fill all the pages, we will have three possibilities:

- ◆ Do it from the original file to your new page using as many copy-paste actions needed to fill each frame one by one. You'll understand that it will be a very long process (and is not very easy) as it is hard to know in advance how many lines one might need to copy.

- ◆ Link the frames together.

- ◆ When creating the document, define that you need automatic Text Frames. But in this case, the frame will automatically fit the margin. If you need a custom frame size, you'll need to do it frame after frame anyway.

Linking and unlinking Text Frames

If, like us, you're a bit lazy, you'll ask the author to create as many files as the number of frames needed. But the trouble is that the author might be as lazy as you are and he or she might not know more than you about how much text should be imported into each frame. So the problem still prevails. In fact, a layout program can simulate some kind of text processor behavior in which the text flows from a frame to another. This is done by linking.

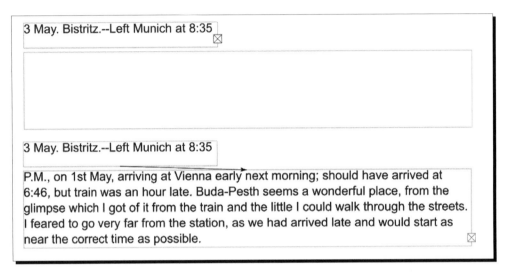

Linking is done with the **Link Text Frames** tool (*N*) or can be set at the creation of the document. The use of one method or the other depends of the layout type that you're creating. As often, you can use the following menus or icons to link or unlink:

◆ **Item | Link Text Frame** or **Item | Unlink Text Frame** menu

◆ In the toolbar, the following icons link ▦, and unlink ▦.

What you need to remember is that you need to use the **Link Text Frames** tool comfortably:

◆ You need to select the frame in which the text is actually placed, take the **Link Text Frames** tool, and click on the other frame.

◆ If you need to link several frames together, you can use the **Sticky Tools** mode from the **Insert** menu. This tool will be activated until you choose another one or deactivate the **Sticky Tools** mode. With sticky mode on, if you click anywhere or on a non-Text frame, you might get some message saying that the frame is already linked or some other message of this kind.

Notice that only Text Frames can be linked, and nothing will happen if you try to link Image Frames or shapes. If you really want the text in Image Frames or shapes, you'll need to convert it first with **Item | Convert To | Text Frame**.

Time for action – import it from Shakespeare Land, going on!

Let's say that we want to improve the first page and have the name of the document and of the author in some place and the reference to the website at another place.

1. Going back to the previous document we've made, reduce the size of the frame so that only the first two lines are visible. A little crossed square is displayed near the bottom right corner of the frame to indicate that there is more text inside the frame that can't be displayed: we call it "text overflow".

2. Draw another Text Frame (*T*) next to the bottom margin and take the **Select Item** tool (*C*) and select the first frame.

3. Take the second frame and click on it. You will see that the text will continue from the first to the second (if not, make the second bigger until you see some text in it) and that the text overflow indicator is now on the second frame.

4. You've got it if you want the text to continue in other pages; just add frames to them and link them in the same way.

5. Of course, if you have hundreds of pages (for example, the complete works of Shakespeare) it can be boring to link each page to the next.

6. Let's try it another way: create another document with the same properties and select the **Automatic Text Frames** checkbox. **Columns** and **Gaps** will be made available, but ignore them as we don't need them for now. Click on **OK** and you'll get the pages already having a frame in each page, matching the margin size.

7. Pressing *Ctrl + D* in the first page frame will display the import window. Browse through your directories to find the text you want to use. Don't touch any other settings and click on **OK**.

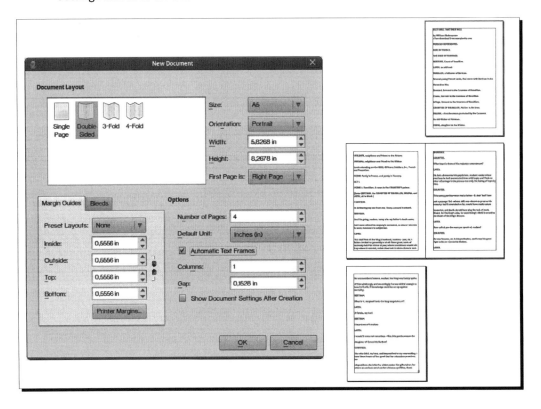

8. Generally, in books, the title is alone on a page. Reduce the height of the frame on the first page as we did in the previous document. See that the text flows automatically in the second page and that no text is missing.

9. Draw the frame for the website name just under the title frame on the first page. Take the **Unlink Text Frames** tool (*U*) from the toolbar and click on the frame of the second page. The text won't be displayed inside anymore.

10. To see links permanently, go to the **View | Show Text Chain** menu. Black arrows will be displayed between linked frames. Actually, there should be none between the frame of the first page and the one of the second.

11. Now, select the title frame, take the **Link Text Frames** tool (*N*) and click on the website frame to make the text follow inside and click on the frame of the second page too to make the text continue there. Wait for Scribus to do the calculations and you should see your text on all the pages.

12. You can add more pages and the text will go on being linked immediately.

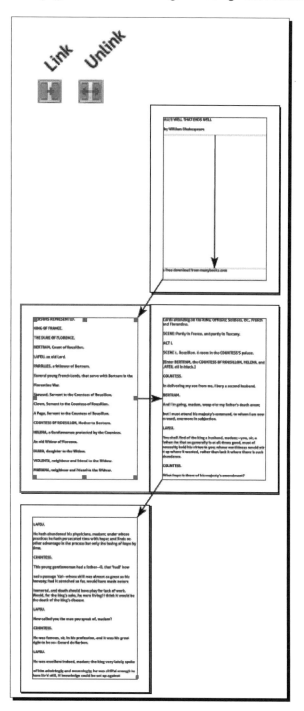

What just happened?

When importing a text, it fills only the frame in which it has been imported. If we want the text to fill all the pages, we will need to link the frames together. But now, if we have set the **Automatic Text Frame** option when we created the document, Scribus will add a default frame on each new page and link this frame to the one of the previous pages. This behavior cannot be changed, but it is important to know this behavior so that you can set the best margin for this purpose. You'll have to unlink some frames if you need to place a frame in particular place and then relink. The most important part in this process is that you don't handle text, just frames. Text is always there, if a frame is deleted, then the text will be placed in the next, or will stop in the previous frame. It is, I know, the safest to keep the text as it is.

Of course, the work on the text won't stop here and there is a real need to type it nicely. Chapter 5 will be dedicated to this part of the work. Save your file to reuse it!

From this part remember especially that:

- ◆ *N* activates the **Link Text Frame** tool
- ◆ *C* activates the **Select Item** tool
- ◆ *T* activates the **Insert Text Frame** tool
- ◆ Use the **Automatic Text Frame** option when creating the document and enable
- ◆ Using the **Insert | Sticky Tools** option can be time-saving

Have a go hero – laying out a Shakespeare biography

Of course, things are not so simple, and the editing process will demand that you add a Shakespeare biography at the beginning of the book, let's say on Page 3. This has to be done in a two column frame with a smaller text size: the same font but 10pt. The purpose of these differences is to show the difference between the original and the publisher's version. So add new content in the existing linked one! You can find a biography here: http://en.wikipedia.org/wiki/William_Shakespeare.

Flowing text

Frame links are nice to use when frames are separate in placement but share the same content. What about all those frames that contain very few pieces of text (quotes, important information, and so on) and that are often placed above? Look at the following image: what's the difference between the left-hand side and the right-hand side page?

April 1564; died 23 April 1616)[a] was an English poet and playwright, widely regarded as the greatest writer in the English language and the world's pre-eminent dramatist.[1] He is often called England's national poet and the "Bard of Avon".[2][b] His surviving works, including collaborations, consist of 38 plays,[c] 154 sonnets, two long narrative poems, and several other poems. His plays have been translated into every major living language and are performed more often than those of any other playwright.[3]

1613.[5][d] His early plays were mainly comedies and histories, genres he raised to the peak of sophistication and artistry by the then wrote mainly tragedies until 1608, including Hamlet, King of fighting finest works in the English language. In his last phase, he wrote tragicomedies, also known as romances, and collaborated with other playwrights.

Many of his plays were published in editions of varying quality and accuracy during his lifetime. In

April 1564; died 23 April 1616)[a] was an English poet and playwright, widely regarded as the greatest writer in the English language and the world's pre-eminent dramatist.[1] He is often called England's national poet and the "Bard of Avon".[2][b] His surviving works, including some collaborations, consist of 38 plays,[c] 154 sonnets, two long narrative poems, and several other poems. His plays have been translated into every major living language and are performed more

Shakespeare produced most of his known work between 1589 and 1613.[5][d] His early plays were mainly comedies and histories, genres he raised to the peak of sophistication and artistry by the end of the sixteenth century. He then wrote mainly tragedies until about 1608, including Hamlet, King Lear, and Macbeth, considered some of the finest works in the English language. In his last phase, he wrote tragicomedies, also known as romances, and collaborated with

" Sir, in my heart there was a kind of fighting"

The main text flows around the quote. This is very simple to do.

Time for action – let's jump into the flow!

Making main text flow around the quote is very simple. The basic requirement is a frame for the quote that should be placed above the main text, and then everything should work perfectly. Let's see how.

1. You have some Text Frames, containing text, and as in this example, set with two columns.

2. Draw another Text Frame above this one but smaller in size and type the quote inside.

3. Display the **Properties Palette** (*F2*) and go to the **Shape** tab.

4. In the **Text Flow Around Frame** group, click on the **Use Frame Shape** option.

5. If you want to set a margin between the quote and the main text, you can set the inner margin of the frame in the **Column & Text Distances** settings of the PP. By doing this you'll see that the text will have fewer spaces and that the frame will become too small.

6. You can, alternatively, set the **Use Contour Line** option of the **Shape** tab.

7. Nothing will change right now, but click on the **Edit** button placed at the top right of the **Shape** tab. It will display the **Nodes** window.

8. Select the **Edit Contour Line** checkbox, and just above **Absolute Coordinates** change the value of the field to **0.1in**. Click on the leftmost button to increase the size of the contour line by the value that we just changed. Click several times if needed.

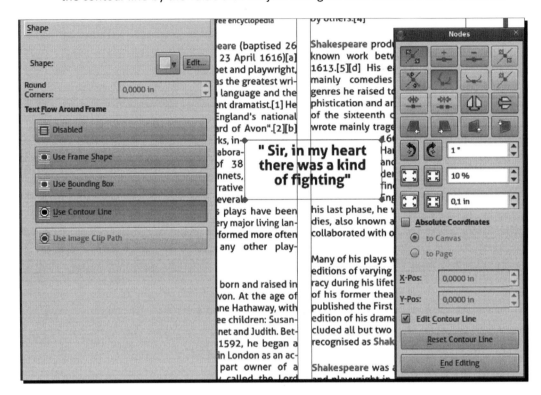

Contour line color

The contour line is invisible on the page when printed, but it is displayed in blue while you're modifying it and then in a thin grey line on the page.

What just happened?

When two frames overlap, we can make the text contained in the bottom one follow the shape of the top most. It can exactly follow the rectangular frame shape or be customized with the contour line. This is a bit more difficult to handle due to an increased number of steps to customize the shape of the contour line, but it also increases the possibilities for you. Remember only text can follow a shape.

Editing text in the layout and hyphenation

Editing text principle is very easy. The one thing to remember is that a layout program works most commonly in Layout mode (create and transform frame). To modify the text, the Content Edit mode needs to be activated. Do it by:

◆ Double-clicking in the frame that needs to be edited

◆ Activating the **Edit Contents of Frame** tool, the big "A" button ⓐ in the toolbar

Once you're in Content Edit mode, you can change the text, add new content, or select words to apply formatting to them. Actually, if you look at the image of flowing text again, you might see that the spaces between some words are really too wide. Hyphenation could help get more constant spaces, which would make the text much more appealing and easier to read. That said, we have two options:

◆ Hyphenate locally

◆ Hyphenate the whole frame

The first is much faster, but hyphenation is not always a good thing because there is sometimes too much to be done. Trying with local hyphenations can be a good thing. Let's try that first.

We'll take the frame from the beginning. If you have a look at the 5th line, you'll see two huge spaces, and at the beginning of the next line the word "dramatist", which could be cut twice: dra – ma – tist. Judging by the quantity of space to fill, "drama-tist" will certainly be good. Go into the Content Edit mode and click into the word after "drama". Go to **Insert | Character | Soft hyphen** or press *Ctrl + Shift + -* and you'll see the result. I guess that a few lines further Colla-boration could be hyphenated this way too. This paragraph will then look much better.

It seems now that there will be much more to hyphenate. Let's do it in a single click. Go to **Extras | Hyphenate Text**. All the frames are now done. You might notice that Scribus has added one on the third line so that "dramatist" is now complete in a single line: no "–" inside! This is because the smart hyphen is conditional and is displayed only if needed. That's much better than using a standard – (minus).

Saving space with hyphenation

A border effect of the hyphenation is that the use of line width is much more efficient with usually more letters so that some line might be saved on the page. It is a good idea to think of hyphenation if you have a text overflow of very few lines at the end of the article or frame. It helps to make content match the frame size and at the same time gives it a better visual appearance.

But if you don't like automatic hyphenation, select **Extras | Dehyphenate Text**, and they'll all be gone—except for the hyphenations you've made manually with the **smart hyphen** special character.

Time for action – automatic hyphenation

If you want the hyphenation to be automatically applied while you are typing, Scribus can do it for you.

1. Go to **File | Document Setup**.

2. In the **Hyphenator** settings, select the **Hyphenate Text Automatically During Typing** checkbox.

3. Now draw a Text Frame (*T*) on a page.

4. Write some text inside it and you'll see that the text will be hyphenated if needed.

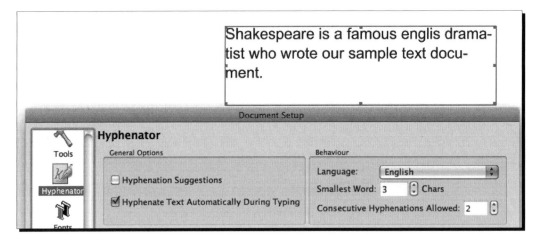

What just happened?

Some people like hyphenation in texts and some don't. If you like hyphenation, using automatic hyphenation will be very comfortable to work with. You won't have to think about it anymore. But you will reduce the control you have over text management. You can use the **Hyphenation Suggestions** box. In this case, if needed, Scribus will suggest you some hyphenations through a little window and let you decide. This window will appear for each suggestion, which we won't find very practical. Notice that even if you used automatic hyphenation, you can keep on adding your own hyphens if you don't agree with the job that Scribus does.

Story Editor

Editing text on the layout can often be frightening. Each time we move the mouse or click, we cross our fingers in hope that the frame won't move. This device can sometimes be very sticky! Compared to this, the **Story Editor** is a very convenient way to edit the text. To display the text content of a selected frame in the Story Editor, just use one of the following ways:

- Click on the **Edit Text** button in the toolbar
- Use the **Edit | Edit Text** menu
- Use the *Ctrl + T* shortcut

A new window will appear with the text of the selected frame and all the linked frames inside. In fact, the Story Editor is not really made to work on the graphical aspect. As you can see, the text is displayed roughly with no formatting applied on it. But there are several advantages to this:

- No more problems with the mouse!
- Scribus runs faster because it doesn't have to calculate the screen renderings for text and placements
- Your own actions are much faster because there is no need to select frames: you get the entire article at once
- You have the most important text features in one window
- You can easily see the defaults in your text (blank lines)
- And more (sweeties if you give me more reasons)

Technically, you can use this window to make all the changes you like: proofread, paragraph based formatting (alignment), or character based formatting (italics, bold, or colors). Your changes won't be displayed in the **Story Editor**. You might think that it's a misuse, but we think this is its real advantage. Once you know what you need to change, you don't need to see what it looks like. If quotes have to be italics, then make them italics and that's all. There is no need to have them displayed all the time. We'll have an overview of the text formatting options in the next chapter.

Of course, the **Story Editor** will not be the right place to work precisely. Working with it is more of a beginning step in which you put all the basics. In the rest of this chapter and in the following chapters, we'll try to show the possibilities of **Story Editor** when they are available.

Finally, when we want the changes to be displayed in the layout window, there are two possibilities:

◆ If you know you've done everything with this text, just click the fourth button of the **Story Editor** toolbar (**Update Text Frame and Exit**), or the same option in the **File** menu of the SE (**Story Editor**), unless you prefer the *Ctrl + W* shortcut. This will close the window and update the frame.

◆ Click on the **Update Text Frame** button (the seventh) or use **File | Save Document**. This will update the frame without closing the SE so that you might see your changes and continue working on the text—that's my favorite.

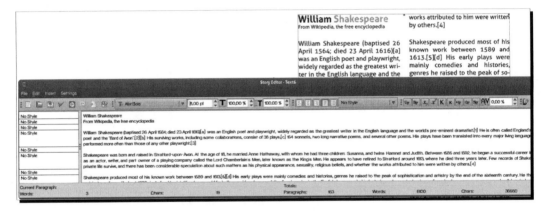

Find and change some words

In Scribus, as in any simple text editor or text processor, you can **search** for text in your document. The only difference is that it will work only on an active article, that is, the text of the selected frame and linked frames. In our Shakespeare example everything is good because we have only two **articles**: the introduction and the artwork itself.

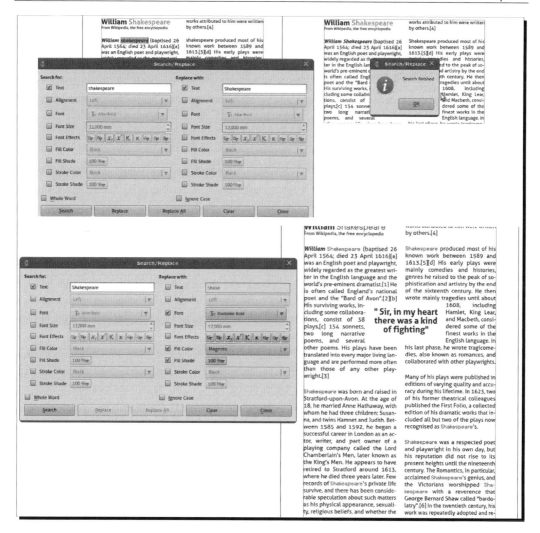

Time for action – replacing a text format overall in the document

Replacing a text format is very easy. Perform the following steps:

1. Select the frame that contains the article you want to analyze.

2. Just go to **Edit | Search/Replace** or use the *Ctrl + F* keys. You'll get a dialog divided in two parts. The left-hand side is what you're looking for and the right-hand specifies the changes that you want. Let's say we're not sure we have written Shakespeare correctly each time: it might be shakespeare, shakepeare or some other spelling.

3. On the left-hand part, select the **Text** checkbox and write "shakespeare" in the field.

4. On the right-hand side, select the same **Text** checkbox and write "Shakespeare".

5. Click on the **Search** button. If some text matches, the **Replace** and **Replace All** options will be available. The first option replaces only the selected word in the frame. Clicking on it will do the replacement and go to the next occurrence. **Replace All** just replaces every occurrence without asking you anymore.

6. Do the same for every mistake you think you might have done.

7. As an extra opportunity, you can use this window to tell Scribus you want Shakespeare's name to be emphasized in some way.

8. On the left-hand part, just write the exact name and in the right-hand part, just set the type properties you want to use. We have chosen a Dustismo Bold font, in a magenta color.

9. Click on **Search**, and then on **Replace All**.

What just happened?

There is not much to say about this very common window except that we find it really nice to perform a search based on graphical settings. On the other hand, as it seems nice it is certainly not the best way to use the software. Replacing all, every time, can be dangerous and if you have many frames with many articles, it can be very tricky to update the document if changes need to be made. We guess that using the character style, as explained in the next chapter, will be safer and much more productive with many documents.

The best way would be if Scribus could search for styles: maybe one day.

Have a go hero – emphasize the character names

Do you know how Shakespeare had to write each name? One by one—you'll say it was his job to do so, and nobody told him to use so many characters. Well, your job will be to change all the names so that they have a characteristic color that makes them very different from the spoken phrases.

Short Words

Short Words is a special kind of search and replace functionality. It is specially made to change a normal space to a non-breaking space. A non-breaking space is the space character we would use if we want two words to always be displayed together on the same line. It is useful in many situations; for example, if you would prefer that anytime you write "W. Shakespeare", "W." stays on the same line as that of Shakespeare because "W." doesn't mean anything by itself. To do this, you should add a Short Word.

Scribus is provided with some default Short Words: Mr., Mrs., Dr., and so on. But you can modify them very easily.

Time for action – automatic replacement with Short Words

Let's modify the default Short Word list to make it take our authors name into account by adding our custom wishes in a configuration file.

1. Just go to **File | Preferences** and especially in the Short Words section.

2. Look for the section dedicated to your language (certainly the en= line).

3. Add the text you want Scribus to filter: in our case, it should be "W.".

4. Don't forget to add a coma after it, as mentioned in the commented lines.

5. Click on the **Save** button and then on the **Apply** button of the **Preferences** window. If it asks to overwrite, just confirm it. And click on **OK** to close the **Preferences** window.

6. To make the changes happen, go to **Extras | Short Words**.

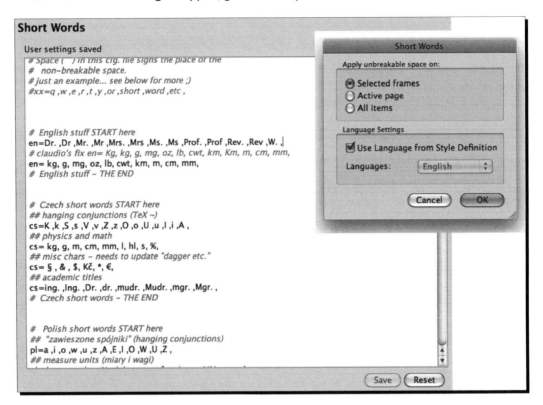

What just happened?

The window gives you the possibility to choose on which part of the file the changes will be applied. And if you select the **Use Language from Style Definition** checkbox, it will automatically choose the default settings for your text (or some setting that you will specially define in the text styles as we'll see in the next chapter). This is useful when you layout multi-lingual documents. If you don't want this feature, just deselect it and choose the language by yourself in the list below.

Unfortunately, we've experienced some trouble with this tool, and we are really cold about using automatic changes because it's hard to be sure we don't forget a special use case. If you are like us, remember that non-breaking spaces can be added one by one while typing, using the **Insert | Character | Spaces & Breaks | Non Breaking Space** menu entry or the *Ctrl + Space* shortcut.

Dealing with special characters

Special characters are really well known. Many people like to play with them because they can give a nice aspect to some character. In Scribus, special characters are really easy to add. We've already added some, such as automatic page numbers or smart hyphens. Yes, these are not the most appealing but they are special characters.

In fact we should split special characters into two categories:

◆ Characters that are being considered as typographic needs or good rules will be available in the **Insert** menu. **Character**, **Quote**, **Spaces & Breaks**, and **Ligatures** are menu entries where you can find more. Since they add a character, the frame has to be in Content Edit mode to make these menus available.

◆ If you want to add a special (somewhat funny) letter as you would do in a text processor, you can use the Scribus **Insert | Glyph** window. Some of the most common, such as copyright or trademark, are in the **Insert | Character** menu too.

Notice that you have the same **Insert** menu entries in the Story Editor, and you don't have to be in Layout mode to add special characters.

I have no special characters listed!

If you have no or very few special characters, maybe you should add some fonts for this. Scribus just lists what's available on your computer and cannot give you more. Many websites have plenty of them: try `Openfontlibrary.org` or `dafont.com`. Test the font online and download it into your system font directory to install (for example, `C:/windows/fonts/`, `/usr/share/fonts`, or `/home/username/.fonts` if you don't have admin rights, depending of your operating system).

In fact, in Scribus, you'll have to take care, because some weakness in the text engine can really give strange results with some characters. Added to that, it is difficult to deal with bad fonts in Scribus. If you see strange occurrences on your page, make a PDF and check if the problem is persistent. If this is the case, you'll have to find another solution because it would be very dangerous to keep on using this special character.

Time for action – adding glyphs on your page

Adding a character is really easy:

1. Select the Text Frame and go into Content Edit mode.

2. Once done, click where you need to add the character.

3. Go to the **Insert | Glyph** window.

4. Click on the first button on the window to show the available characters.

5. In this window select the font you want to take the character from: generally a Dingbats font or something similar.

6. You just need to browse the main part of the window to find the character you want. If there is not much, check that the **Character Class** list at the top of the dialog is set to **Full Character Set**.

7. Double-click on the character you want to add. You can choose several at once and they will be added to the field at the bottom part of the window.

8. Click on **Insert** to push them into the frame.

What just happened?

With the glyph window opened, you will be able to add any "special" character into your pages. You'll first need to choose which font contains the glyph you want to add. Then you can browse the available characters manually or use a unicode value or a character class to help you find the exact glyph you need. You can choose several at a time and insert them all at once by clicking on the insert button.

If you wish to reuse those characters, you can save the palette and open it later, even in another Scribus document. This is useful for custom bullets, for example.

Reusing a glyph in a document

If you know you'll use them in several times, you can drag them into the empty fields of the main **Character Palette**. They will be there each time you open this document. This is a convenient way to define a per-document special character list. To insert the glyph from the **Character Palette** into the document, double-click on the glyph once you've put the cursor at the right place in your frame.

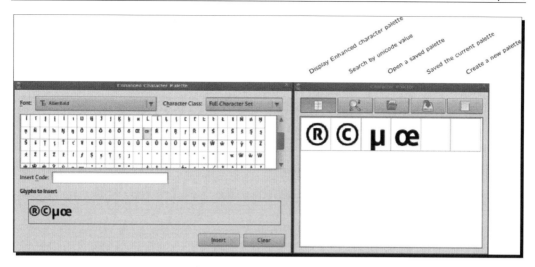

Reusing a glyph between documents

If you want to use the same glyph on every document, or want to be able to choose which glyph you'll want to use in a single document, it would be more handy to build assets. Once you've defined the glyphs, you'll use in the **Character Palette**; save it by clicking on the **Save the current palette** button, the fourth button of the palette. You'll be able then to open it whenever you like.

Manual TOC using tabs

Tabs can be considered as a special way to use a special character. You might already know the *Tab* key, which is left of the *Q*. You certainly have already used it to indent some lines. But many software provide a much more convenient way to define custom indentation using this key. Scribus is one of those.

There are several ways to define tabs in Scribus. For now, we'll see the quickest way to apply them, which is not always the best but is the most structured. If you like tabs, know that you'll get more in the *Using style* section of the next chapter, right at the beginning.

Time for action – creating a Table of Content

Let's say we want to create the Table of Content for our little Shakespeare book. We would like to add all the acts inside.

1. Type "Act I", press the *Tab* key, write a page number like "Page 5". You'll see a large space between Act I and Page 5.

2. Do the same for each act with Page 43, 100, 138, 182, or whatever matches your document. If you don't know the page number, simply use the search window.

3. Select all the lines of the TOC and have a look at the horizontal rulers at the top of the workspace. You will notice that blue brackets match the selected frame size and position, and with this the ruler begins at 0 again.

4. Place your cursor above **3.5** and click. You'll see the page number move and being placed there.

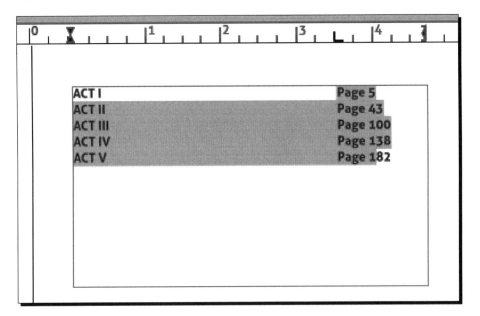

What just happened?

Scribus has a very bad built-in table of content generator. So we decided to do it our way. It is as simple as looking for the page for each text we want to add in the TOC. Then, making the table is really simple: just write the text and the page number on the same line separated by tabulation. Once everything is done, the tabulation distance can be set so that the page number can appear at the end of the line, as is commonly done.

Exporting text

Sometimes the text has to be reviewed by someone who doesn't know Scribus at all and has no wish to learn it. You will have very few options:

- Give a paper copy, but you'll have to apply the changes yourself.

- Give a PDF, and you'll have to apply changes yourself again.

- Export the article as text so that changes can be made easily by the proofreader. In this case, you'll be able to import the complete text again in your frame, but all the text properties will be lost and you'll have to do it again.

Nothing is perfect, and automatic changes from a data source to a layout program are not a very common thing. In a perfect workflow, the text is good before going to layout. But if you need to do this, just select a frame containing your article and use **File | Export | Save Text**. Give a name and specify in which directory it should be saved, and you're done. Of course, the sooner the better: the more advanced you'll be in your layout work, the more time you'll lose by importing the text again into that frame.

Pop quiz

1. Text Frames can be:

    a. Rectangles only

    b. Any kind of shape

    c. Rectangles, rounded rectangles, or circles only

2. When frames are linked, what happens to the text of following frames if the first frame is moved?

    a. The text adapts to fill the size of the frame

    b. The frame is emptied and the next fully filled

    c. Nothing at all

3. *Ctrl + F* displays the window for :

    a. Frame properties

    b. Search/replace

    c. Font management

4. Short Word is:

   a. A tool to replace abbreviation with complete text

   b. A tool to replace spaces

   c. A tool that spell checks the article

Summary

In this chapter, we've seen how to handle Text Frames and some general text manipulation tools.

Specifically, we covered:

- How to place, size, and set the frame margin
- How to import simple text
- How to set long text within several frames and frame flow
- Apply automatic changes to improve the result

The next chapter will list the Scribus text properties to make text as readable and as appealing as possible.

5
Formatting Your Text

Most of your document will need text somewhere. Importing the text is one thing but setting it nicely is another task altogether. Layout programs have a huge amount of properties that can be modified using a single click. Even if the layout process mainly deals with placing frames and managing pages, the designer who creates the page is the last stage of the production workflow before print. So he has to make the text as legible and as predictable as possible. Doing this usually takes a lot of time, and it appears to be one of the most important tasks of the layout design.

To begin in this chapter, we'll show Scribus text properties and then see how we can use them more efficiently with styles. At the end we'll try to make a book section in a few clicks by importing text.

In this chapter we shall:

- ◆ See an overview of character and paragraph properties
- ◆ Manage fonts
- ◆ Use styles made in Scribus or imported from other documents

The three ways of changing a property

In Scribus you can change the properties in several ways:

◆ Using defined text styles

◆ Using local modifications on the selected text with the text tab of the PP (*F2*)

◆ The overall frame content when the frame itself, and not the content, is selected

The third option is very practical to work very quickly on a small document, but it is certainly not the most productive in all use cases. The best workflow will be to apply paragraph styles, then apply character styles, and then local formatting. In this chapter you'll see all the advantages you can get by using styles.

In fact the third method can sometimes put your work in great danger. Think of you having set everything nicely. You do one or two changes on other frames and want to come back on this one that you had already set. You will have to double-click on that frame to go into the Content Edit mode and do the changes. But what if double-click doesn't work well? The content will not be selected, but the frame itself will. In this case, all the text of the whole frame will be changed and not only the selected characters. So what appears to be nice can sometimes be tricky. I'd say: Handle with care!

Use dynamic settings

Scribus cannot undo text formatting changes. If you apply a property locally, no problem, just put the property back to what it was, but if you did it for the whole frame, it will take very long to bring back all the changes one by one. In this case, we have two solutions:

◆ Save your document as often as possible

◆ Use dynamic settings that you can easily change and reapply, like styles

Character formatting

If you already used a text processor some day or are even using some website form to edit content, you already have some knowledge of character formatting. These are the most commonly used text graphical properties. You will have bolded some part of your text, add italics somewhere, or changed the font size and may be even the color

Scribus has grouped these options in the Properties Palette (*F2*), in its **Text** tab. It's a very good thing: this way you can get very quickly to any of these properties. However, there are so many options that they needed to be grouped into subparts: these settings are stored in several expanders of the PP.

Changing font

When you open the PP and go to the **Text** tab, you will see very basic settings at first glance. The first of them is the font selector. Scribus will list here all the fonts installed in your operating system. The list can be very long. If you'd like to get a custom list, read the *Managing fonts and Fontbook* section.

You can see that unlike in most text processors, there is no bold or italic button here. In fact, in Scribus, as in other layout programs, font variations are displayed in a list placed under the font name. You can find it strange but it's very easy to understand if you look at the following screenshot:

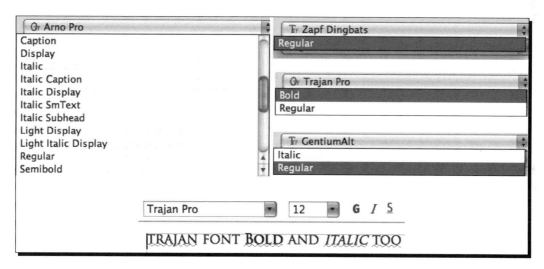

Arno Pro has many different kinds of font style; the list is even longer than we see here. Now have a look at the right-hand part and see how those fonts have very few styles, sometimes only one.

The bottom-most example is what you would get in a text processor like OpenOffice.org Writer.

I can hear your thoughts from here; "Why is this software so good if it can't even do what a text processor does?" You already think we lied about the quality of Scribus. No, let's take it from another point of view and have a look in the file system where the fonts are installed, as seen in the following screenshot:

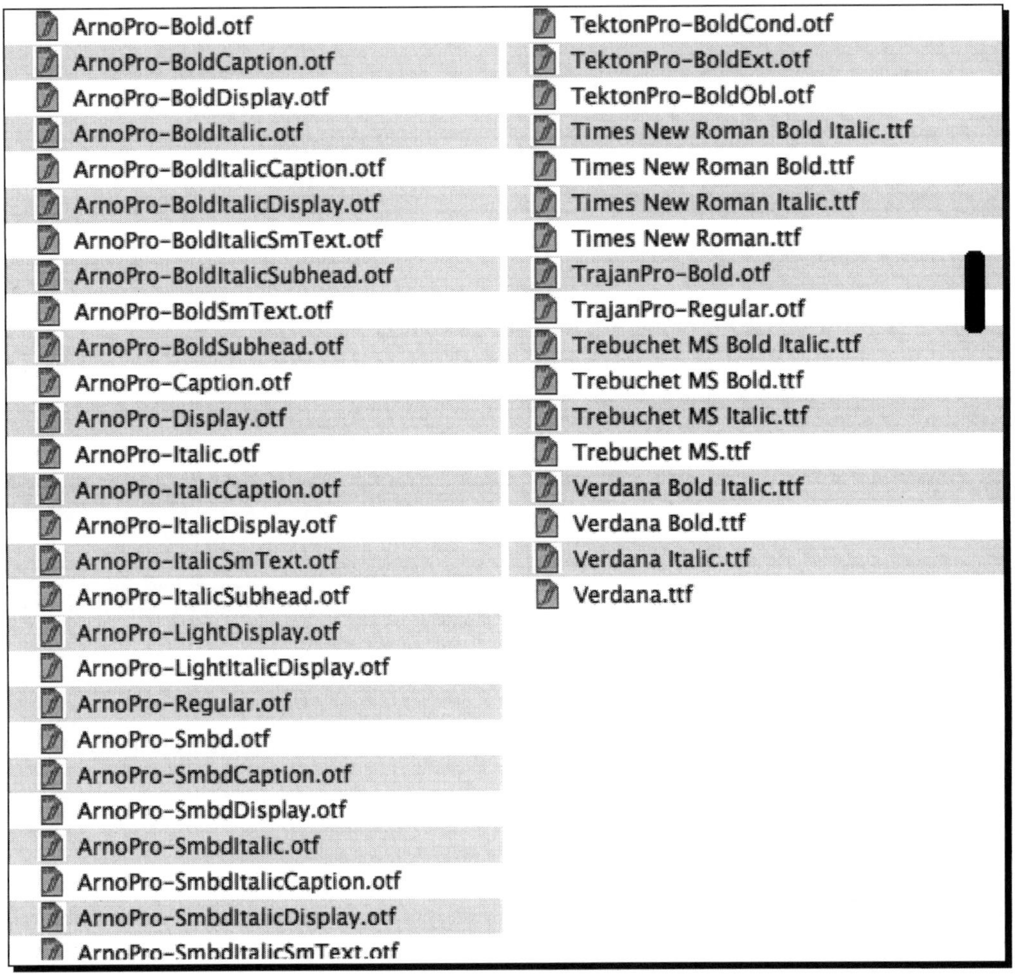

ArnoPro-Bold.otf	TektonPro-BoldCond.otf
ArnoPro-BoldCaption.otf	TektonPro-BoldExt.otf
ArnoPro-BoldDisplay.otf	TektonPro-BoldObl.otf
ArnoPro-BoldItalic.otf	Times New Roman Bold Italic.ttf
ArnoPro-BoldItalicCaption.otf	Times New Roman Bold.ttf
ArnoPro-BoldItalicDisplay.otf	Times New Roman Italic.ttf
ArnoPro-BoldItalicSmText.otf	Times New Roman.ttf
ArnoPro-BoldItalicSubhead.otf	TrajanPro-Bold.otf
ArnoPro-BoldSmText.otf	TrajanPro-Regular.otf
ArnoPro-BoldSubhead.otf	Trebuchet MS Bold Italic.ttf
ArnoPro-Caption.otf	Trebuchet MS Bold.ttf
ArnoPro-Display.otf	Trebuchet MS Italic.ttf
ArnoPro-Italic.otf	Trebuchet MS.ttf
ArnoPro-ItalicCaption.otf	Verdana Bold Italic.ttf
ArnoPro-ItalicDisplay.otf	Verdana Bold.ttf
ArnoPro-ItalicSmText.otf	Verdana Italic.ttf
ArnoPro-ItalicSubhead.otf	Verdana.ttf
ArnoPro-LightDisplay.otf	
ArnoPro-LightItalicDisplay.otf	
ArnoPro-Regular.otf	
ArnoPro-Smbd.otf	
ArnoPro-SmbdCaption.otf	
ArnoPro-SmbdDisplay.otf	
ArnoPro-SmbdItalic.otf	
ArnoPro-SmbdItalicCaption.otf	
ArnoPro-SmbdItalicDisplay.otf	
ArnoPro-SmbdItalicSmText.otf	

As you can see, the Scribus font style list is no more than what is installed on the computer. OpenOffice.org does its own font style management to make it easier for the user: there's no need to know the font; if you want italics, just use it. However, to keep it simple, you won't access more refined font styles. The OpenOffice method can look much easier, and you might wonder why Scribus tries to do it differently. In fact, the OpenOffice method can be considered as better if you like easiness. However, Scribus will be best if you like to have control on the results. The only method your print provider is very used to is the Scribus one: you should only use fonts that are installed on your computer (if there is no italic, then there is no way) and they have to be given to your print provider, by embeddeding them in the final PDF, or given as is, as .ttf or .otf. You can take from your font directory with the help of the Collect for Output feature. . This is due to the following reasons:

- The print office will need the original font file to be able to print it. They simply can't have a copy of each of the hundreds of thousands of fonts that exist. We'll see later how to be sure that the print office will have all the requested elements.

- Printing costs a lot and we try to avoid troubles. Avoiding good fonts ensures as little trouble as possible. There are many free fonts available on several websites, but most of these fonts are not really precise fonts (apart from their appearance on screen). It can takes years of work to get a really good font saved with the best letter-spacing defaults and other metrics. When you want to use such a font there is no reason to say that a single-click will be better and that the modification that you'll do will be better than the one a specialist did after months of work.

- Fonts have a communication purpose and, for example, it would be nonsensical to have an italic Trajan.

So when you want to change the font, just go to the first field of the **Text** tab of the PP and then look at the available font styles. If the one you need is not there, choose another font or install it if it exists somewhere else.

Font and copyright

Fonts are copyrighted. Usually, you can install them if you own a copy and use them as you wish without giving credit. But if you work with several people, you'll certainly need to buy a copy for each one of you. Read the license with care. If you'd like to use some free fonts, you can have a look at `http://www.openfontlibrary.org`. Some other websites will let you download many fonts for free, but most of these are not free in the "free software" meaning.

Changing the font size

Changing the font size is really simple. The field placed just below the font style is made for that.

There are a few things to remember about the font size in Scribus:

- Roughly speaking, font size doesn't say exactly how big it is
- Size can be changed by the frame
- There are other ways to manipulate sizes to get a nice result

About the size of a font

Usually, in text processors when using a 12pt font size and changing to another font, you won't be worried about the place that the text will need. But since Scribus places the text within a frame, and this frame is limited to a "restricted" area, the text will often have to fit inside. So now, you should care. One of the clues you might look for is the little red square that might be displayed at the bottom right-hand side corner of the frame: it indicates that not all of the text fits in the frame.

Time for action – the font sizes

Let's try a small exercise on font sizes and see what happens.

1. Begin a new empty document; choose the size you want.

2. Draw a first frame in a page and type "All Is Well That Ends Well".

3. Set the font to Dustismo, if you have it (it is a GPL font that you can easily find, for example, at http://www.dafont.com/dustismo.font).

4. Duplicate the frame with **Edit | Copy** and **Edit | Paste**. The new frame is placed above the previous frame and you can move it down with the down arrow key. Keep both frames aligned anyways.

5. Set the font of this new frame to any other font (choose an Arial or Helvetica or any Sans standard font)

6. Just look at the difference.

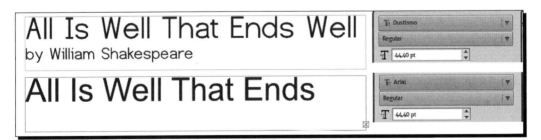

What just happened?

When you change the font as you wish, some might have the same size exactly on screen and some others won't. In fact, you don't have many solutions to know the real font size: try and try and try again. In fact, 12pt or any measure doesn't tell you exactly how big the characters will be; it depends on the font design. You have to take care of it, because as you can see, a bigger font results in a need for extra space, and here, the frame is now too small. When working on your layout, it will be better to choose the fonts as early as possible and not change your mind after that. If you do change, read your document carefully to look for potential trouble.

About the ability of a frame to change the size

We've already talked about this, but remember that you can change the font size without changing the value in the PP.

When you have a text in a frame, you can drag the frame handle while pressing *Alt*. This way, the text will be resized with the frame. You can press *Ctrl* as well if you want to keep the aspect ratio of the frame and of the text. If you don't, scaling will be applied.

About scaling and extensions

In fact, if you don't press *Ctrl* with the *Alt* key, you will apply some scaling to your font. There are two kinds of scaling: horizontal and vertical. Just remember that you should avoid scaling if you use bitmap fonts, but you should avoid bitmap fonts anyway. Most commonly, you will use TrueType fonts (`.ttf`) or OpenType fonts (`.otf`) and more rarely PostScript fonts. They are all vector fonts that support scaling and other changes quite well without getting ugly.

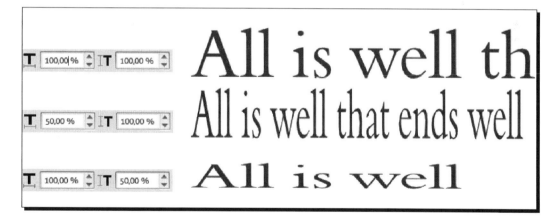

Scaling properties can be changed in the **Advanced Settings** expander. Mostly, you will use them on titles so that it can fit an area in one direction (let's say horizontal) without taking too much place in the other (because you need the rest for the main text, which should not be too small for legibility). You will more rarely use it on the main text. If you need to, you would preferably look for some condensed or extended font: it would be easier for everyone and everything.

Strangely, vertical scaling is not sensitive to frame height so that the text can go outside the container. You should be able to get some nice graphical effects from this behavior.

What's the best font size?

From all what we have said in the previous pages, you'll understand that font size is much more difficult to handle than simply changing a setting. You're the one who will know what changes need to be made to match your graphical wishes or content needs. But here are some things you should always have in mind:

- All the settings are important.
- Don't use font sizes that are too big. 12 for the press is already a big size.
- Adapt font size of your font to the content structure level.
- Adapt the font size to the available space.
- Don't keep text lines too large but don't keep them too small either: use columns if possible.
- Begin to work on the most important element, which is the main text. Set it nicely, leave empty areas for the title and illustrations, or simply keep them empty.

The first time you create a document, you'll have to find the best settings. You can use **Sample Text** to do this. But once you've found them, apply them methodically (see *Using Styles*) and just adapt at the end if needed.

Apply kerning

Kerning is the ability of Scribus to modify the white space between letters. Kerning differs from spacing in a way that while spaces are common manufacturer settings to define letter distances, kerns will be defined by pairs to improve the visual aspect of the text. A common example is to deal with the distance between A and V characters, which often look too wide. This is more evident with Serif fonts. Good fonts have hundreds of built-in, pre-defined kerning pairs that give them some personality. But layout software lets the user adapt it if necessary, and it's often necessary depending on the quality of the font.

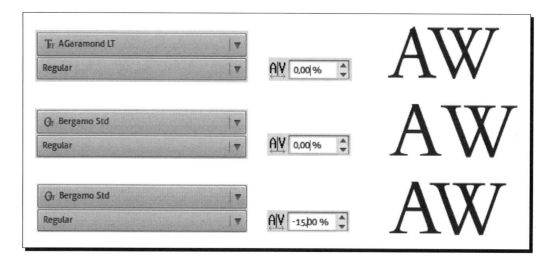

In Scribus, kerning can be applied between a pair of two characters or to a whole selection. But this is not exactly what kerning settings are made for. Here kerning is defined relatively to the font size so that the same kern property won't always display the same on all texts.

What should I use?

In the paragraph setting there will be new options that will play with the glyph size and spaces. You have the choice to use the property you like the most. Feel free to test before applying them all over a document.

Text colors and effects

It's evident that colors can be an important part of a layout job but not necessarily. Above all, text is mostly written in black because it will need a high contrast with the paper to be highly legible. But even in black, there are plenty of very nice documents. Color in a page or on a text is a bit like photography: a color photo can be very nice, but black and white is still used a lot because getting a nice photo that way can be easier. Colors are difficult to arrange and are time consuming, and working in black makes things more evident, and last but not least, cheaper.

When creating a new document, you get only primary colors and blacks. We'll show how to create custom colors in Chapter 9. But, right now, you'll see how you can apply colors to text in Scribus.

Regular letter color

First, we will see how to change the color of the characters. This is as easy as selecting the text and choosing the **color** in the **Color & Effects** expander of the **Text** tab in PP. The selector that applies to the text is the only one available and represented by a bucket fill icon.

It displays the default colors from which you can choose. If you want the color to be lighter, change the value (called **shade** or tint) as a percentage at the right-hand side of the color selector.

Adding stroke and shadow color

In Scribus, you can give a **stroke** (O button) to a letter and this stroke can have a different color than the letter itself. The stroke width can also vary as you wish. The shadow (S button) will be set the same way but you'll need to use the button (second from the right) next to the O button.

Time for action – stroking letters

To change the stroke, you just have to follow these steps:

1. Select the text you want to stroke.

2. Go to the **Text** tab of the PP and expand the **Color & Effects** properties.

3. Find the **outline** button (third from the right) and click on it to activate the stroke. You'll see the selected text get bolder, but it's not bold, it is just that the stroke is made visible.

4. Just above it, the color selector is now activated (the paintbrush icon). It is set to black but you can change it to what you want.

5. Deselect to see the result. Colors are inverted on selected text, so it is not always easy to estimate what it does.

6. To change the stroke width, you'll have to go back to the outline button, and keep the mouse pressed on it.

7. You'll see the **Linewidth** value appear. Just change it, and it is automatically applied.

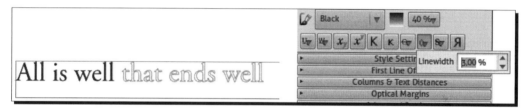

What just happened?

Character stroke, like all the properties that have a little triangle at the bottom right-hand side (such as shadow, underline, and so on) works in two steps. A click activates the property but pressing it will display one or two settings that will only be displayed if the property is on. Unfortunately, it happens that it is deactivated when trying to change something. Just be careful with that.

Uppercase and underline

Finally, you will certainly not use a lot of uppercase letters and you could use underline too much. Those effects shouldn't be set on a long paragraph. Generally, they are best used for titles or a single line (for example, at the beginning of a chapter). It's very easy to understand: uppercase letters have all the same size, so that they are difficult to differ; underline goes through the descending part of some letters (such as p, q, and so on) and diminish legibility.

You can still use them if you want in some cases. There are two possibilities for each:

- Underline words only
- Underline the letters and spaces between words
- All **capitals** with the same size
- Different capitals size

Just have a look at the samples on the right-hand side. Look how the width of the line changes between the first and the second line. Have a look at the properties and notice that the **Linewidth** is expressed in percentage. The **Displacement** tells Scribus how far the line must be from the text: 0 when the underline is on the **baseline**, and it increases when lowering down.

Background color

There is no setting to set the color for text background. Changing the frame color or adding a frame under the text is the only solution we have actually within Scribus.

Paragraph formatting

Paragraph formatting are generally less known than character properties (except alignment) but they are as practical. To begin with, it's important to understand what Scribus calls a paragraph and how you create it.

Paragraph differs from simple line break. A paragraph is created when you press the *Enter* key whereas a line break is done by using *Shift + Enter*. It's important to notice because paragraph settings are applied to the whole paragraph. For example, we'll see later, that when using paragraph styles, drop cap can be set only on first letters of this paragraph.

Scribus uses very few paragraph settings in the PP. If you want to get full options, you'll need to go into styles quite early. We guess this is a good thing even if we'd like to have more properties available in both PP and styles, just for consistency.

Paragraph settings available in the Properties Palette (*F2*) are as follows:

◆ **Linespacing**: It defines the distance between text baselines. The default is **Fixed Lineheight**, but it can be changed to **Automatic Lineheight** (the easiest) or to **Align to Baseline Grid** (the prettiest throughout the columns to keep them aligned).

◆ **Alignment**: It defines the way letters will be set regarding the frame or column margins. Generally, you can align to the left-hand side, to the right-hand side or on each side (which is called justified). Forced justification is a bit different in the way even the last line of a paragraph fills the columns where it is only left aligned with standard justification.

◆ **Word tracking** (advanced setting expander): It changes the way letter-spacing is applied within a word. You set the minimum and the maximum to help Scribus define the amount of changes it can do.

◆ **Glyph extensions** (advanced setting expander): It allows us to automatically adapt a glyph to fit to the most permanent aspect through lines of a paragraph. You set the minimum and the maximum to help Scribus define the amount of changes it can do.

◆ **Optical margins** (optical margins expander): It provides special management for "weak" or small glyphs (, . ; ...) at the margins. Optical margins can give nice results but the Scribus text engine can be improved, and sometimes optical margins give really weird placement.

Time for action – improving white spaces and alignment

Let's see these settings in action. You'll be able to make some experiments during these few steps:

1. Let's say we have an A4 page with the Shakespeare biography we used previously (get the text from the Wikipedia article).

2. The text is imported in a two-column frame and a quote is inserted at the middle of the page.

3. The first line is set to caps and has a Aller font of 15pt. The line below is simply italic with a smaller font size.

4. See how there are no empty lines between paragraphs? This is something we're used to. It really helps to get things clearer when working with paragraphs, properties, and styles.

5. Select the main frame and click on the **Justify** button in the **Text** properties. All the content of the frame should be affected. You could also have launched the story editor, selected all, and applied the same alignment from there.

6. As we can see on top of the quotation frame, lines of both columns are still not aligned. Let's go to the **View | Show baseline grid**, and see if it can help. Small horizontal lines will be displayed on the page.

7. Now in the PP, display the alignment list options and select **Align to Baseline Grid**. You'll see all the text moving down to fit the lines on both columns. Baseline increment can be changed from the **Document Setup | Grid** section. The default is **14.40pt**, which is common for a 12pt font size.

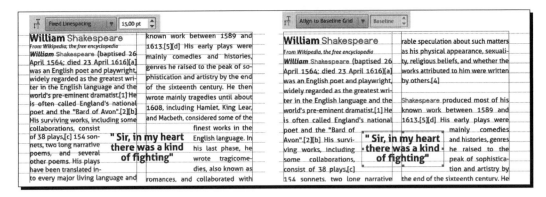

8. You might see on both sides of the quote that large white spaces are visible between words. We could hyphenate, but let's try to avoid it. Now go to the **Advanced Settings** of the **Text** properties.

9. Have a look at the first line of the first text paragraph, modify the **Min** value of **Glyph Extension** to 94% and see the difference. Text is compressed so it takes up less space. But it's still not perfect.

10. Change the **Max** value of **Glyph Extension** to 103%. Some word spacers will be made smaller.

11. Now let's add the same value to word **tracking** and you will see some letters move too.

12. Finally, let's try the **Optical Margins**. Open the dedicated expander and activate the right-hand side option. That's OK, so now, look at the real size of the document or do a test print.

Shakespeare, a successful glover and alderman originally from Snitterfield, and Mary Arden, the daughter of an affluent landowning farmer.[7] He was born in Stratford-upon-Avon and baptised on 26 April 1564. His actual birthdate is unknown, but is traditionally observed on 23 April, St George's Day.[8] This date, which

my heart
ras a kind
;hting"

and baptised on 26 April 1564. His actual birthdate is unknown, but is traditionally observed on 23 April, St George's Day.[8] This date, which can be traced back to an eighteenth-century scholar's mistake, has proved appealing because Shakespeare died on 23 April 1616.[9] He was the third child of eight and the eldest surviving son.[10]

my heart
ras a kind
;hting"

and baptised on 26 April 1564. His actual birthdate is unknown, but is traditionally observed on 23 April, St George's Day.[8] This date, which can be traced back to an eighteenth-century scholar's mistake, has proved appealing because Shakespeare died on 23 April 1616.[9] He was the third child of eight and the eldest surviving son.[10]

ny heart
as a kind
hting"

and baptised on 26 April 1564. His actual birthdate is unknown, but is traditionally observed on 23 April, St George's Day.[8] This date, which can be traced back to an eighteenth-century scholar's mistake, has proved appealing because Shakespeare died on 23 April 1616.[9] He was the third child of eight and the eldest surviving son.[10]

ny heart
as a kind
hting"

What just happened?

Glyph extension has been the most useful setting. From the beginning it had done most part of the work. We use other settings to improve partially. One thing to remember is that you shouldn't modify these values too much. Generally, they should stay between 90% and 110% or your white spaces will be replaced by other kinds of visual distortion: text and letters won't look as consistent (which was the purpose of those changes).

Optical margins have been used to modify the position of the commas and minus glyphs. When looking at them with a high zoom level, it can seem to have a weird aspect, not really aligned. But when printed at its real size, the column will look much prettier on right margins. Generally, when you have done so many changes, it is good to take a print if this is the document's final destination. The way the text is displayed on screen and on paper may have a different feel to it.

Managing fonts and Fontbook

As we have seen in the beginning of this chapter, Scribus will display all the fonts installed on your operating system. In fact, all the software you have will behave like this. But we have several possibilities to get a different list of fonts. This is important mainly because:

- When you work on a document that needs two or three fonts, you don't want to look for them all the time
- If you look for a client or have graphical charter, you want to prevent errors

Managing your font will be a time-saving operation and a help with keeping a structured layout as well.

Define a default font and deactivate font

First of all, when you create a Text Frame in a new document, the default font is automatically applied to the text you type inside. The default font can be defined in the **Tools** part of the **Document Setup**. If you always use the same, set it in the **Preferences**.

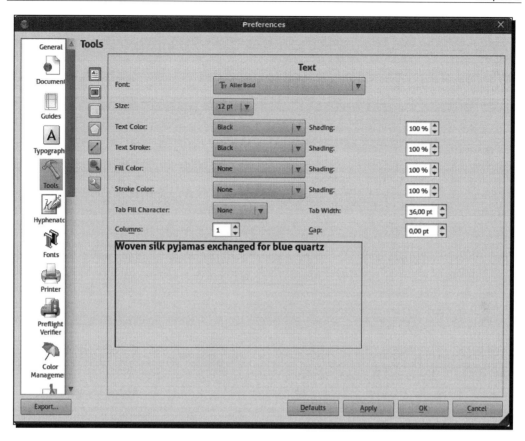

If your trouble is in the size of the font list, you should consider reducing drastically the quantity of fonts loaded into Scribus. You'll get two benefits of it: you'll find the font you need faster and Scribus will itself have fewer fonts to manage.

My font is not there!

If your font doesn't appear in the font list, Scribus found something odd in it. Generally, this happens with freely downloadable fonts that can vary in design quality, or have too many missing glyphs. The only thing you can do is improve the font if the license gives you this opportunity (you should only use such kinds of fonts) or choose another one.

To do this, go to **Preferences** or **Document Setup**. In the **Fonts** section you'll see a tab called **Available Fonts**. In the first column you have the **Font Name**, the **Style** in the fourth, and for our purposes, the **Use Font** in the second column. All unchecked fonts won't appear in the Scribus font list anymore until it is reset.

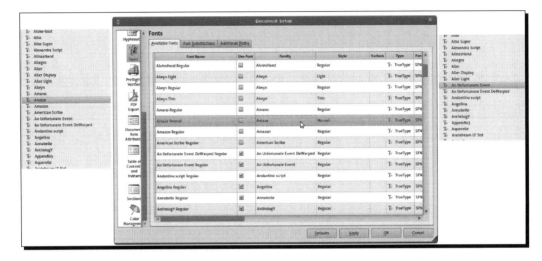

Adding new fonts in Scribus

In fact there are use cases in which we don't want to install fonts for all applications, just because the font is used in a single document and it will be inefficient to make it available for all the applications. Or you may not have write access on system files. Usually, it happens when we design for a client who has their own font set. It is more important if the fonts are not free because we're not supposed to keep them for our own needs.

It this case, the **Fonts** options of the **Preferences** will help again. **Additional Paths** is an interesting tab, but if you have a document open, you should have Scribus telling you to close it first. Once this is done, it will be very easy.

Time for action – setting a custom font directory

Basically, you'll need to have your fonts stored in a directory and have no document open in Scribus before telling Scribus where it can find the new fonts.

1. Put all your new or most used fonts in a single folder.

2. Without any document open, go to the **Preferences | Fonts** options.

3. In **Additional Paths**, just click on **Add**.

4. Browse your directories and choose the folder containing the fonts you want to add.

5. Click on **Apply** and then on **OK**. It's done.

What just happened?

Of course, the remove button will give you the means to delete a folder if you don't want to use the fonts anymore. Putting the fonts in custom directories helps you get the needed font only for a single document. It also helps you control the handling of these fonts if you need to work on several computers, need to reinstall your system, or any other critical operations.

Managing fonts with Fontmatrix

If you need more advanced font managing features, you should have a look at Fontmatrix, which is the best cross platform font manager in my opinion. Fontmatrix gives you lots of information about font, both technical (manufacturer) and graphical (glyph list, sample, font comparison, and so on). You can add tags to your font or create categories that will help you activate or deactivate the fonts for the whole system.

Using styles

Text styles are one of the most important features in Scribus. Using text styles will make text handling and formatting much more easier. As they are a way to reproduce formatting all over the document, you'll get many benefits from them, such as:

◆ There is no need to remember what the font size, color, or kerning you put on a title or so; styles do it for you

◆ A bunch of text properties can be applied at once quickly in a single click

◆ The overall aspect of your document can be easily modified if you change your mind

◆ Access to some new features such as **Drop Caps** and language settings (for check spelling in a multi-language document)

◆ A bunch of font defined properties can be shared throughout several documents

◆ There is no need to care anymore about the lack of a text undo engine in Scribus

We should find some other benefits, but using styles is like using master page. Once you're used to them you can't go back: they are easy to define, easy to apply, easy to change, and divide the working-time on a document by ten times or more. People often underestimate the importance and power of styles, because it's hard to guess how much you will earn from it when you begin a document or when you don't know them. It appears that many people think that it is a waste of time to go into a separate window to define things that they can't immediately see on the page. And as they are a way to define in advance what the text will look like, many people are scared to create them. In fact, except in the case when you have a graphical charter, you generally won't know at the beginning exactly what your document will look like. My personal approach is to create a style for each text category (title, subtitle, and so on), keep them empty, and then modify them as I need to, so that all the text formatting of my document is automatically updated.

In Scribus, you'll need to make a difference between two kinds of styles:

- **Paragraph style** will save the settings that apply to paragraphs: alignment, space before or after, and drop cap. A paragraph style will be applied to a whole paragraph (it would be tricky to have several alignments applied on a single line).

- **Character style** applies to the selected character only and will modify the formatting of the letters such as font, size, and color.

We have already seen most of the options that will be in the **Style Manager** window. So we will focus here on the process of creating or applying styles.

Creating styles

All the style management happens in the **Style Manager** window, which can be displayed by pressing *F3* or using **Edit | Styles**.

To create a style you'll have several options:

- Click on the **New** button at the bottom of the **Style Manager** window and choose the style type you want to create

- Right-click on the style category in the main list of the window and choose **New | Paragraph Style** or **New | Character Style** depending on which you're on

Once this is done, new tabs will be displayed on the right part. **Character Style** will have a **Properties** tab that will display all the available options to define the letter aspect. Paragraph will have two main tabs: a **Properties** tab which shows paragraph settings and a **Character Style** tab that will give the ability to define the aspect of the default text for this paragraph. Don't get confused by this: **Properties** can refer to two different things and **Character Style** too. Always have a look at the context.

Once you have done this, you just have to change the properties in the tabs to set the aspect of the letter or of the paragraph. Don't worry about making errors, it's easy to make changes: you'll just have to come back to this and modify it.

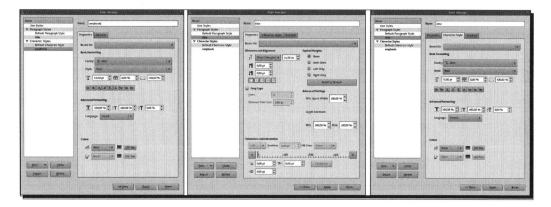

Applying styles

Once styles are defined, you can apply them on any text. Here, there will again be a difference between character and paragraph styles. The first will be applied on the selected letters only, whereas the last will be applied to the whole paragraph even if there is no selection. The good thing is that it's easier to apply a paragraph style because you'll just have to click within the paragraph.

Generally, we apply paragraph styles, which are more general settings, before character style, but you can do it your own way.

Styles can be applied in three ways:

◆ Choose the style in the **Paragraph Style** or **Character Style** list of **Style Settings** in **Text** properties of the PP (*F2*). They list all the styles that are available for this document.

◆ In the **Story Editor** the left-hand side column lists the paragraph style applied paragraph after paragraph. Just right-click on it to display a menu in which you'll get the style list. This is one of my favorite places to apply styles quickly when I begin a document. There's no need to select, no need to bother about pages; just apply. Paragraph styles are displayed at the right-hand side of alignment buttons in the button bar of this window, too. As always with the **Story Editor**, changes are displayed only when the **File | Save Document** (*Ctrl + S*) menu is used. Unfortunately, character style cannot be applied from here.

◆ Finally, if you know you'll use a style often, you can define a shortcut in the Style Manager. There is a shortcut tab for each style. Just click on **User Defined Key**, then **Set Key**, and perform the shortcut. It will be displayed in the box below. Validate the shortcut, and it should be available for your document.

Deleting styles

Deleting a style doesn't need too much explanation. In the **Style Manager**, just right-click on the style and choose **Delete** in the context menu or click on the **Delete** button to act on the selected style.

Scribus will ask for a replacement style. It will display the available styles and you have to choose between them. Click **No Style** if you don't want to apply styles on the corresponding text anymore. Just remember that deleting a style will affect all text on which this style was applied. It will be changed to the new style or the Text Frame default if set to **No Style**.

Sharing styles

Styles are saved in the document that they are created in. So if you simply launched Scribus with a new document, the style list will be empty again. If you want to reuse some styles that you've already defined, click on the **Import** button of the **Style Manager** (*F3*). Scribus will ask you which document contains the style you want to import. Browse through your directories and select the best one. This will be up to you to decide.

Scribus will then give you a list of the styles found in the document. Just select all the styles you want to import and deselect the others. By default, **Rename Existing Style** is chosen at the bottom of the window. This is the safest method. If an imported style has the same name as a style of the current document, the imported style will be renamed to "Imported", followed by the style name and the document name. You can then perform a replacement if you're sure of what you're doing. But you can tell it to **Replace Existing Styles** so that you won't have to care about this after import.

Link styles for cascading changes

The styles can be linked together so that any changes made to one can be automatically set to the others. Let's say you have two styles called S1 and S2. You want S2 to follow changes to S1. When editing S2, select S1 in the **Based On** list and it will inherit from its changes. Of course, some of the defined differences will be kept so that both styles aren't exactly similar.

Time for action – working with styles

For working with styles it will be very practical to improve the whole text formatting of our layout, so let's go back to our "All's Well That Ends Well" example.

1. Create a **Double sided** document that's 4 inches wide and 6.7 inches high. Select the **Automatic Text Frames** checkbox.

2. Import the sample text we downloaded from `http://manybooks.net/titles/` `shakespeetext982ws3010.html`. If you have a tool that can clean up blank lines, use it. The text will be much easier to set later. On Unix-like environments, it can be done using `cat original.txt | sed '/^$/d' >final.txt`.

3. Then go to **Page | Insert** and choose **150** pages **at End**.

4. We can now use the **Style Manager** from **Edit | Styles**. Right click on the **Paragraph Styles** list and choose **New Paragraph Style**.

5. In the right-hand part of the window, give it a name, (for example, **Standard**) go to **Character Style** tab and choose a 10pt font size.

6. Go back to the **Properties** tab and decrease **Fixed Linespacing** to 12.

7. Click on **Apply** and then on **OK** to go back to the document. We can now apply this style. We wish to use it on all the text as it is the basis for the document. Select a frame, launch the **Story Editor**, select all the text by pressing *Ctrl + A*, and in the toolbar of this window, choose the style we just created.

8. In the **File** menu of the **Story Editor**, choose **Update Text Frame and Exit** to go back to the layout. If you go to the end of the document, you will see that all the text fits in our specified amount of pages.

9. You can go back to the **Style Editor** (*F3*) and modify the font or the font size for the **Standard** font. You can adapt the style until you get the result you like.

What just happened?

When creating styles, it's very easy to set the first **Standard** text style in the text editor. The selection is very easy and it goes faster.

If you want to improve the result, you can go back to this style and modify it until you get a nice result. If you want to place styles on parts of text (such as titles) just select the paragraph and apply it from the **Style Settings** part of the **Text** tab in the PP.

Don't forget you can apply character style to a text selection within a paragraph.

Have a go hero – creating a book with styles

When using styles, creating a book can be done in a few clicks. Take the text again and try to use styles for the names of people, for acts, scenes, or anything that is repeated throughout the document. For such a document you will mainly use paragraph styles.

Importing styled documents

We have discussed the weakness of Scribus in editing text—especially the lack of an undo option. Generally, you will get the text from someone who will use a text processor, or may be simply a text editor. If you work alone, it can be a good idea to do so. It makes it easier in the end to separate graphical ideas from the content and to eventually begin a new document from scratch.

People who use text processors use styles everyday—sometimes without noticing it. In OpenOffice.org Writer, paragraphs styles are displayed in the first list of the **Formatting** toolbar. They are also available in the **Style** window, where character styles, page styles, and picture styles are stored too.

When using Scribus combined with OpenOffice.org Writer, you will be able to import paragraph styles when you import your text. This is very useful. If styles are correctly applied in the original document, you'll just need to edit them within Scribus and set them nicely. If you use Microsoft Word and run Linux, you'll be able to import your document too if Anti-word is installed. If not, or in other cases, just open your .doc document into Writer and save it as .odt, which Scribus can import.

New .docx word file format

Microsoft created some years ago a new file format .docx, which is very different from the previous .doc format that was used for a long time. As far as our tests have driven us, Scribus can't import those files and it often happens to crash. If you get some kind of file, save it to .doc format or better to .odt format (which is the best for Scribus).

Time for action – import a Writer document

Before importing, whatever it is, have a look at the document in the software it was made with. If there are any errors, they will be easier to correct in the text processor, first. Check some points at this time to clean the file and then import.

1. Before importing, have a look at the document. If there are any errors, they will be easier to correct in the text processor.

2. Delete all the empty lines (too many people do that but you will replace them with a space before and a space after in Scribus paragraph style).

3. Check that the styles are perfectly applied (display only applied styles), and try to remember where because it will be useful when you get them in Scribus.

4. Go back to Scribus. If you want to work on a new document, set it with automatic frames in the **New Document** window. Ours is set to A5 double-sided with six default pages, and a top margin at 20mm.

5. Then, select the frame of the first page and choose **File | Import | Get Text** or *Ctrl + D*. Select the .odt document that you want to import, but it can be a .sxw document as well.

6. In the import window, you won't have to set any options. Everything should be automatically detected. If you want to avoid style import because you prefer applying them completely from within Scribus, select the **Import Text Only** option. But for our purpose here, there is no need to select it.

7. In the **Importer Options** window, just instruct Scribus what to do. If you work on a new document, it won't do much. The first will apply Writer style settings to Scribus styles (for those which have the same name); the second compares styles and tries to avoid duplicates by merging all the similar styles into one; the third will keep styles of both documents and the import will be prefixed by the document name so that you can remember easily where it comes from.

8. If a font is missing in Scribus when compared to the original document, Scribus will ask for a replacement. Just select a font or cancel and install it (see the *Managing fonts and Fontbook* section).

9. When you validate, the text will be imported and dispatched through the linked frames.

10. Launch the **Story Editor** to have a look at how styles are applied.

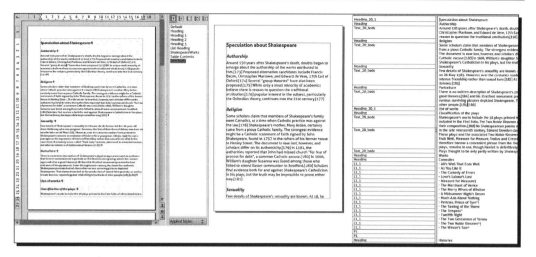

11. It looks the same except that some P1 styles appear because we forgot empty paragraphs. You can see that name doesn't exactly match, so it's important to see where they are applied.

12. Now, go to the **Style Manager** (*F3*), and do some changes. **Heading_20_1** refers to the main titles; go to its **Character Style** tab, increase the **Font Size** to 20pt, and make it bold and all caps. And in the **Properties** tab, add 0.3 in as space before and 0.2 inch as space after.

13. Then double-click on a heading and in the **Properties** tab, and change **Based On** to **Heading_20_1**. Set space before to 0.1in and in the **Character Style** tab decrease the **Font Size** to 16pt.

14. Leave **text_Body** and select **L1_1**, which comes from the original bullet list, base it on **Text_20_body**, and modify the indentation (at the bottom of the style properties) so that the left indent is set to 0.5in and the first line indent kept to 0.

15. Click on **Apply** and close the window (*F3*) and see the result. In our case, a title (**Sexuality**) is alone at the end of the frame, which is not very good. Just click at the beginning of the line and then going to **Insert | Spaces & Break | Frame Break** will throw it into the next frame.

16. Keep on adjusting. For example, a list of work could be put in a two-column frame to improve readability. If you want to customize the bullet list, just do a search/replace on "-" and replace it with a glyph that you want according to a specified font.

Importing a web page into a Scribus document

Nowadays, many documents are both printed and published as an HTML webpage. If you need to import a webpage into Scribus you won't get lost as it works exactly the same as a `.odt` file. Just save the web page to your computer, and import it. Of course, Scribus won't know where to place images and will ignore them.

What just happened ?

When importing OpenOffice files, you'll get many styles at the end, because Scribus keeps every reference it finds in the original file and doesn't decide for you if they are useful. Cleaning the file at the beginning helps importing text with fewer unnecessary styles as well as enhancing the ability to improve the text formatting later. Sometimes, you'll need to remove the property overload after an import by clicking on the brush button at the right-hand side of the styles in the Properties Palette while a text is selected. Finally, you'll certainly need to make some after-import clean up to delete unused styles. Browsing quickly through the Story Editor can help identify them by looking for their names on the left column.

Importing a structured document

Finally, some people don't use text processors. Some will do everything in the layout program, because they think text processors aren't precise enough in text formatting. On the other hand, some will prefer to avoid all the formatting part of the work to concentrate on the writing task. In this case, tell them to add some easily-recognizable code within the text.

For example, we could decide to use H1 code preceding every heading. A title like "List of Work" would then become "H1-List of Work" in text. Of course, this is incorrect if we read the text, but it won't stay like that. Every other paragraph style could to be defined with such a code.

When importing it into a Scribus frame, choose the **Text Filter Importer** option. You'll then be asked to describe your filter. Select **Apply**, and then the next settings will appear. Show Scribus the style you want to use for each structured code you have defined. Don't forget to verify that the **remove match** option is selected to make Scribus delete the code used as filter automatically.

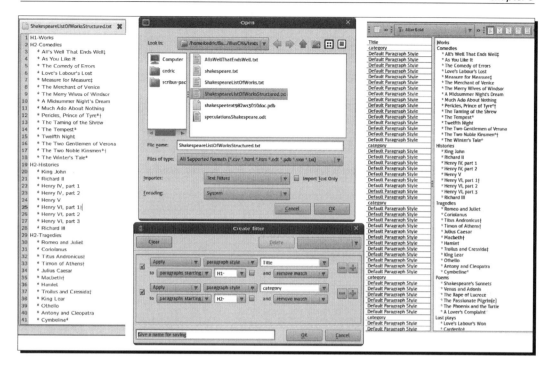

1. Who is Trajan and why is there no italic for the Trajan Font?

   a. Trajan was an emperor famous for standing straight and rigid

   b. Trajan was a Roman and they didn't write in italics

   c. Trajan was the typographer who was lazy the day he did the font

2. Paragraph style can define:

   a. Paragraph formatting only

   b. Character formatting only

   c. Both paragraph and character formatting

3. Style heritage is made by:

   a. Using the Based On option

   b. Importing a new style

   c. Linking frames

4. When importing an OpenOffice document, Scribus imports:

    a. Text, character styles, and pictures

    b. Text, paragraph styles, and pictures

    c. Text and paragraph styles

Summary

In this chapter, we've seen how to handle text itself, especially how to set it up for a pleasant read, and how to improve the workflow using styles and file import.

Specifically, we covered:

◆ A good quantity of text formatting options, for characters and paragraphs

◆ How to manage fonts

◆ How to use character and paragraph styles

◆ How to import structured or formatted text

In the next chapter, we will go deeper into Scribus text handling options to show how some specialized text can be used or imported.

6

Special Frames for Complex Content Management

The layout frames are really simple shapes (rectangles mainly) that contain only one type of content: text or an image. But there are some more complex use cases such as tables, mathematical algorithms, and many others that need some other tools to make the layout process easier.

In this chapter we shall:

- ◆ Use Scribus Table tools
- ◆ Import tables or data from a spreadsheet
- ◆ Use a frame within another
- ◆ Have an overview of Scribus LaTeX capacities

Using tables

You've certainly already seen tables. They are grids that generally contain numbers, but any content can be entered into them. They are often used in catalogs for product lists. In some ways tables are quite similar to tabulators but they might differ in some points.

- ◆ Tabulators are single-line paragraph based.
- ◆ In tabulators there is no column property, just a vertical alignment that lets the user guess it.

◆ Tabulators are generally used for short lists whereas tables can be very long and very wide.

◆ Finally, the content will not be understood in the same way if it is displayed in a table or in tabulators. You'll have the choice to use the best for your document.

Time for action – creating a table

As tables are made to display data in a structured grid, the Scribus **Insert Table** tool will require you to specify how many columns and rows you'll need.

1. Take the **Insert Table** tool by clicking on its icon in the toolbar ⊞ or pressing the *A* key.

2. Draw a rectangle on the page at the position and size you want the table to be. It is approximate and you'll be able to change it later.

3. In the window that appears, write the number of columns and rows you need. This time write the exact number you need including headers.

4. Now, your table should be laid out on the page. To add content, begin by selecting the right cell: press *Alt* and double-click on the cell you want to edit. It is now selected and ready for content inclusion.

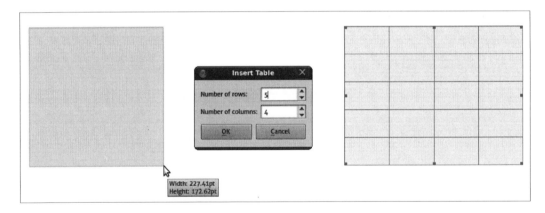

What just happened?

The Scribus **Insert Table** tool is very basic, but this is not a big issue for there are many ways to add a table in Scribus, other than with the tool. This tool will be useful for simple tables containing very little content. In any case, if your table needs calculations, you'll have to import them from a spreadsheet.

Before creating the table within Scribus, it's a good idea to draw it on paper and define how many columns or lines you'll need and what its eventual size will be. The weakness of the Scribus **Insert Table** tool stands in the difficulty to adapt the table after its creation. So beginning it perfectly will deeply help.

First of all, Scribus needs to know which size your table needs to be in. With the **Insert Table** tool, press the left button of your mouse where you want to place the top left-hand corner of the table and drag it to the place where the bottom right corner needs to be. If you use a table in a multi-column document, using guide **snapping** with **Page | Snap to Guide** can help a lot.

Once you release the mouse button, Scribus will display a dialog that asks for rows and columns. Just enter the number in each field. This way, all the columns and all the lines will be of exactly the same height or width.

A Scribus table is now added to the page. If you deselect or select it, you'll see that the table is a whole object and that cells cannot be modified just by clicking on it. In fact, Scribus tables are grouped frames, as shown in the **Name** field of the PP. You could have created such a frame by using **Item | Multiple Duplicate** too. Choosing one or the other is up to you. But you'll see that using tables will give you some new possibilities.

Time for action – formatting tables

The good thing is that formatting a table is very simple. There is no special option for this. Just because tables are frames, they can be handled like any other object we have used until now.

So you might have noticed in the preceding Time for action that *Alt* is the key of your success when using Scribus tables. Once you remember this, consider changing the color of the cell or cell-border with the **Color** tab options of the PP.

1. To change the cell border you can use the **Line** tab of the PP (*F2*). You'll see that there are new options there that let you define the border for each side. Just check the border line you want to use and change the width.

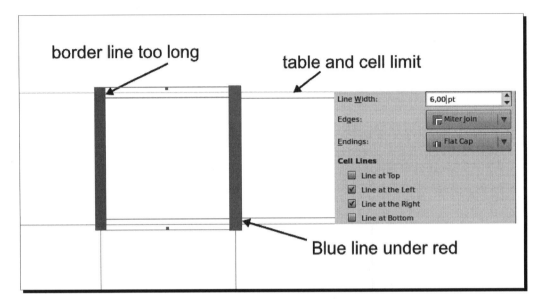

Ungrouping tables

You can ungroup tables as you wish and manipulate them as with frames. This can look simpler at first glance, but grouping those frames again won't give you the same properties. For example, when ungrouping, you won't be able to modify each side border one by one. So, don't ungroup too quickly.

2. The content of the cell can be modified with standard **Text** properties of the PP or text styles. To set the margin between text and the cell just use the **Top**, **Bottom**, **Left**, and **Right** fields of the **Columns & Text Distances** expander.

3. It will be quite impossible to change several cells at once. But you can easily reproduce cell formatting options from one to others. Just select a cell and set it nicely, then select the Wand tool (**Copy Item Properties**), press *Alt*, and click on the cell you want to modify. Remember this is not a style, just a copy of the properties, so if you change the first, the others won't be modified.

What just happened?

There are just a few but still you should remember to deal with table cells:

- ◆ Use *Alt* + click to select a cell
- ◆ Use *Alt* + double-click to change the content of the cell
- ◆ Use *Alt* + *Shift* + click to extend cell selection

If you use a Linux distribution, the *Alt* key can be captured by your window manager. You should preferably set it to use the Windows special key instead so that you can keep the advantage of the common use of the *Alt* key in not only Scribus, but also GIMP and Inkscape.

That done, the cells can be formatted as with any frame. There are some things you should remember about Scribus cell borders:

- ◆ The border is drawn equally on each side of the cell: that means a 4pt border will be displayed 2pt inside and 2pt outside
- ◆ It results that in some places the border might be too long
- ◆ It results that when you have two cells, side by side, with their border set, there will be a common border line between them
- ◆ The color and width is the same for all the sides of a cell

Have a go hero – create a game grid in a few clicks

We are sure you've already seen such kinds of game grids. You could do this by multiple duplicating but a table can be of good help for this. Just have a try.

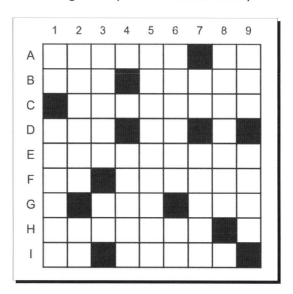

Time for action – modifying rows and columns

As Scribus tables are some kind of frame group, there is actually no real row or column concept to apply. But we can find some solutions to manage cells as if they would be.

1. If you need to change the column size or row height, you'll have to select all the cells for there is no special selection mode for those objects. You just need to press *Alt* and *Shift* while clicking on each cell: it's not very difficult but can take long if you have many cells.

2. Once this is done, drag the handle placed at the middle of a side to modify the position of this side. You will see that the adjacent column is not following so you'll have to do the same for it with the risk of not being very precise. If you want a more accurate result, you'll have to do one of the following:

   ❏ Place guides where you want to place a cell limit, activate snapping to guide (**Page | Snap to Guides**) and resize the first column and then the second.

   ❏ Use the cell x, y, width, and height properties of the **XYZ** tab in the Properties Palette. Do some calculations within the fields. If your table begins at 100 and you want your first column to be 50 units wide, the **X-pos** of the next cell will be 100 + 50. But you'll have to repeat it a lot, so the first solution might be easier.

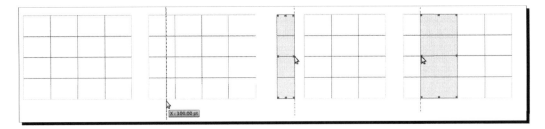

What just happened?

Multi select is the key concept to modify frames as rows and columns. It is not as practical as we would sometimes wish. In fact, if you need to extend your table, it will be quite difficult. There is no easy way to add columns or rows. There is no easy way to split or merge cells too. The best way is to take care of writing the right number in the table window setting when creating it. Generally, it is not a problem for you already know how much information needs to be inserted in the table.

Changing or importing values

We've already said that *Alt* + double click lets you enter inside the frame to change its content.

By default, the content of the frame can be text only but you can easily change this with **Item | Convert To | Image Frame**. Then by pressing *Ctrl + I* you'll be able to import an image. If you run an older Scribus version than 1.3.8, it can be *Ctrl + D*. To know more about image options in Scribus, refer to Chapter 8.

But, in some cases, you can take advantage of Scribus table handling. It can be very boring to add content cell after cell. For example, if you have ABCDEFGHI, each letter written in a single column header, it will take some time, and there's always a risk you might move a cell frame while *Alt* + double-clicking.

An easy way to do this is to link all the cells with the **Link Text Frames** tool (*N*).

Time for action – linking content through cells

The **Link Text Frames** tool is the one you would use to make the text go from one frame to another. It's a very simple Scribus tool and here's another way it can be used:

1. Create a table that is wide enough and say it will be 9 columns and 2 rows.

2. *Alt* + click on first cell to select it.

3. Go to **Insert | Sticky Tools** to be sure that the next tool will always be available.

4. Select the **Link Text Frames** tool (*N*).

5. Then click on each cell from left to right and keep pressing *Alt* while doing so.

6. You can deselect the **Sticky Tools** option and activate the **Select Item** tool (*C*).

7. Select the first cell and write directly inside or in the text editor: *A Ctrl + Return, B Ctrl + Return*, and so on until *I*. The text editor will display red vertical lines between letters in place of the frame breaks that we've made. Apply the changes to the layout.

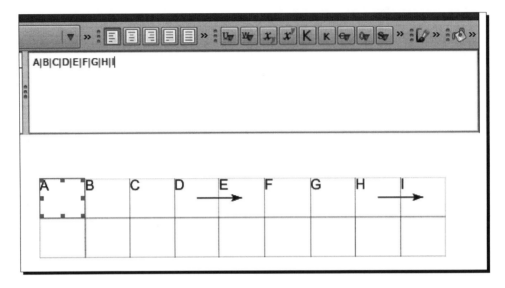

8. In the **Text** tab of the PP, set the alignment to center. It is applied to all the cells because they are all in the same paragraph.

9. In **Columns & Text Distance**, increase the **Top** value until the **A** is vertically centered in the cell.

10. Give the cell a black color in the **Color** tab.

11. In the same way, change the text to a white color in the **Text** tab. Other letters might be white on white so you can't see them but don't worry.

12. Just pick the Wand tool (**Copy Item Properties**) and *Alt* click on each cell of the row and everything is perfect.

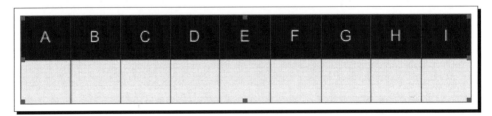

13. Open any text editor you have and write something like: 10,20,15,32,87,12,45,54,12 and save it as plain text, for example, `number.txt`.

14. Back in Scribus, select the first cell and go to **File | Import | Get Text**, in the dialog, select your file and in the **Importers** field, select **Text Filters**.

15. In the next dialog, define you want to replace commas with \n (special character for new lines). Click on **OK**.

16. Finally, set the top margins and alignment in the same way that we've done for the header line.

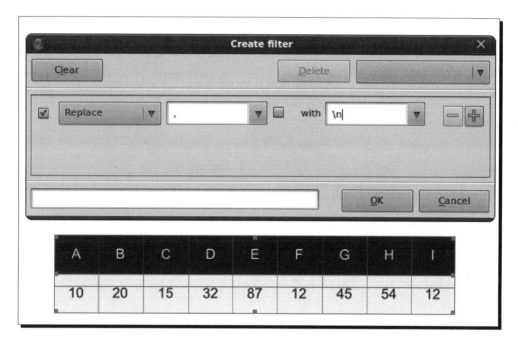

What just happened?

What we have done here can be made with any imported text. **Filtering** text can be used for a lot of actions such as automatic style applications. In this case we have used **regular expressions** to help us. Regular expressions are rules you can apply to perform text selection or **replacement**. It is often used in programming, for example, to validate an e-mail address when someone in subscribing to a website. Some useful information about **regular expression** can be found at many places such as http://www.regular-expressions. info/ or http://en.wikipedia.org/wiki/Regular_expression. If you often use the same replacement rule, you can save your rule by adding a name in the field to the left-hand side of the **OK** button.

The Wand tool (**Copy Item Properties**) is the other extraordinary functionality to get repetitive formatting, and make it faster. When used in combination with the **Link Text Frames** tool to link cells, it makes it very easy to handle a huge quantity of information in a Scribus table.

Automatically filling tables with values

In fact, the file type that we have used in the previous example is called CSV (comma separated value). It is very commonly used to exchange data from a spreadsheet like Microsoft Excel or OpenOffice.org Calc to any other kind of structured text, as well as databases.

When you have such a file, Scribus can build the table for you. Let's say you have a comparison of several layout applications with calculations and want to put it in your own layout. In your favorite spreadsheet program save it as CSV and go back to Scribus. Go to **Script | Scribus Scripts | importcsv2table** and follow the on-screen instructions.

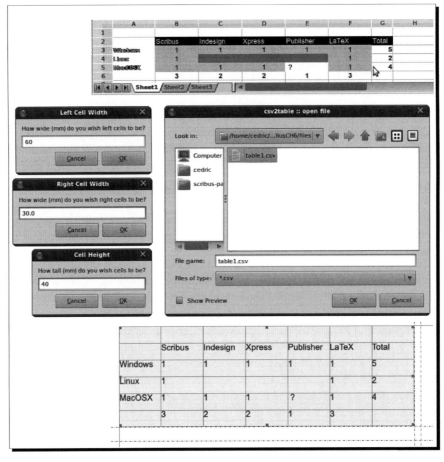

Scripts and customization

Scripts are mainly a user-defined action to help them achieve more easily the result that they want. Most of them have been made by the users themselves. The Scribus scripts menu only lists some of the most interesting scripts that the Scribus team has heard of. If you want to know more about scripts, we will tell you more at the end of the book in Chapter 11.

As you can see, the new table may need some adjustment in size and in formatting because only the content is imported.

Time for action – importing a OOCalc table

But if you need to keep the exact content of the spreadsheet, cell formatting included, we prefer to use Calc and you'll need **OpenOffice** installed. You can use the software you like to create your table but it needs to be opened in **OpenOffice.org Calc**. From here, do the last adjustments and add a chart if you want. And follow these steps:

1. In Calc, draw your table and format it, select the cells you want to add to your Scribus document and copy them (*Ctrl + C*).

2. In OpenOffice.org Calc, choose **File | New | Drawing**.

3. A new window opens and now paste with **Edit | Paste Special**, and in the window choose **Calc**.

4. Without doing anything, go to **File | Export** and save it where you want but as an EPS file by just adding `.eps` at the end of the file name. Select the **Selection** checkbox at the bottom of the dialog so that only the table and not the page is exported.

5. In the **PostScript Options** window, just verify the color settings so that you keep the colors you put on your table.

6. Go back to Scribus, unselect everything and use **File | Import | Get Vector File**.

7. Choose your EPS file, click on **OK** and then click on your page where you want to place your table.

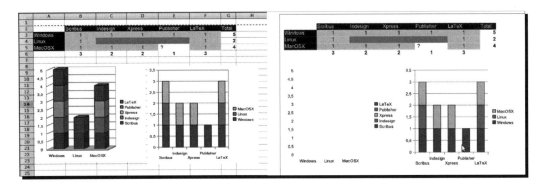

What just happened?

Comparing the original and the result in Scribus is not so bad. Just notice that the 3D part of the first chart is not here just because OpenOffice.org saved it as a bitmap within the **EPS** and that Scribus has difficulties in handling it. You'll find more information about EPS import in the chapter on images. In the near future, Scribus will be able to import PDFs, which could make this process much easier. The trouble would be to consider the OpenOffice PDF as press-ready, which it is actually not.

Bullets with inline frames

Inline frame is a frame that is put within the text of another frame so that it can be handled as a character. We often use it for bullets, logos that need to be in text, or icons in software documentation that need to be in the content to show the reader where to click. You can certainly imagine many other use cases but by doing this, you will understand how it works and you'll be able to use them in other contexts.

Inline frames and PDF export

Unfortunately, I have sometimes experienced some weaknesses in Scribus's inline frames when exporting them to PDF. It happens that they were exported empty and the content was lost. So a piece of advice would be to do a test when you've exported one or two before going on to the rest.

Time for action – using inline frames

Using an inline frame is really simple.

1. Create a frame that will be used as an **inline frame**.

2. Select it with the **Select Item** tool.

3. Copy it (*Ctrl + C*).

4. Go into the frame where you want to place it and double-click on the text to enter into it. Place the cursor where it needs to be placed; for a bullet, it will be at the beginning of the line.

5. Simply paste (*Ctrl + V*).

What just happened?

The nice thing with inline frame is that if you change the text before it, it will follow the changes like any other letters in your text. Sometimes, you'll need to adjust it more precisely with baseline or spacing. For a bullet, you would have to repeat those settings on each, so it can be a good idea to create a character style containing the adjustment values.

You should remember that the frame size cannot be modified when in inline state. So you should set it before placing it. If you need several sizes, which might be the case of a logo, create a set of duplicates and change their size so that you can easily copy-paste them later. If you want to use them in several documents, consider creating a scrapbook (see the end of this chapter).

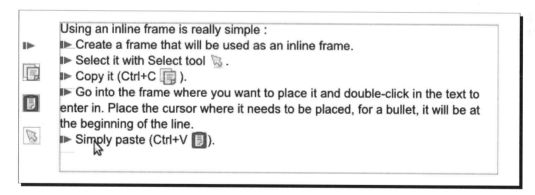

Understanding the render frame

The render frame is a Scribus frame type that calls external specialized tools such as LaTeX, GnuPlot, Lilypond, Graphviz, or PovRay and displays the result of their calculations within the frame area. The render frame is a really powerful feature of Scribus that allows you do add really advanced content into your document like no other application.

To be quick:

- With **LaTeX**, you'll add mathematical formulas to your documents.
- **GnuPlot** is used to draw **2D** or **3D graph**s.
- **Lilypond** produces professionally-engraved **musical scores**.
- **Graphviz** is mainly used for diagrams.
- **PovRay** (Persistence of Vision) is a well-known ray tracing program that gives realistic **3D** renderings. Though it is old, PovRay it is still evolving and will be really enough for basic 3D ads in a printed document.

Let's talk first about LaTeX because it's the render frame default render engine.

LaTeX (no confusion with latex please) is a free document markup language in the same way that HTML can be considered as a page markup language. But as HTML is used for websites, LaTeX is used for typeset documents.

LaTeX is quite old (30 years) now but it is still widely used. In fact, if you run a Unix-like system, you will certainly have heard about it. LaTeX is THE language used by mathematicians, physicians, and others to write and layout their document. In fact, many people already asked us why Scribus exists when LaTeX could do the same.

Personally, I don't think LaTeX and Scribus are similar. LaTeX is great because it has very powerful automation, spell checking, and many other kinds of error-checking tools. LaTeX is using one of the most powerful font description languages: **Metafont**. And LaTeX has many export tools to create .eps, .pdf, .rtf, .docbook, .html, or any other format that you'd like. A well-done LaTeX document will be very nice to read because of the quality of the rendering.

Some links

Though it s quite old, LaTeX has a very important and competent community. You will find a lot of information about it on the Web. For a graphic designer, it can be interesting to read, especially `http://www.tug.org/texshowcase/` or `http://nitens.org/taraborelli/latex`.

For GnuPlot, go to the official website `http://www.gnuplot.info/` where you will see some nice demos. The website for Lilypond is `http://lilypond.org/index.html`, Graphviz is `http://www.graphviz.org/`, and, finally, `http://www.povray.org/` for Persistence of Vision.

Scribus is more for a graphic designer or for people who want some kind of good and immediate visual control of what they are doing. LaTeX is more for structured documents whereas Scribus is simpler for communication in which the page organization is optically defined.

The Scribus render frame allows the user to add some LaTeX output within a Scribus page. You could guess why: simply to get benefits from LaTeX qualities, for example, in a mathematical expression.

In fact, you will certainly not use render frames every day, but they are a good example of the power of open source and free software code sharing.

First contact with render frames

First of all, to use the render frame you'll need some TeX tool to be installed. If you have a Unix-like system you will certainly already have them but you can check your system to see if the pdflatex executable is there. If not, you'll need it and the dependencies.

On other operating systems, you will have to install it. Just go to `http://tug.org` and download MacTeX if you run a Mac or proTeXt if you're on Windows. Once you've downloaded the file, follow the instructions to install it.

You'll need to install dependencies for each of the rendering engines you'll want to use. Just check the websites of each project to get the package and install them.

Time for action – creating your first render frame

Once this is done, you can launch Scribus and have a first try.

1. Activate the **Insert Render Frame** tool (fourth icon in the toolbar or use the *D* key) and draw a frame on the page, in the same way that you would do for any other frame. After a little "rendering" time, you will get a sample content in the frame.

2. This content tells you what to do: right-click and select **Edit Source**.

3. You'll have to then choose which render engine to use by selecting form the available engines in the **Program** list.

4. And finally, feed the render engine with some lines of code, according to the program chosen. This can be done in the **Editor** window.

What just happened?

The source window will display the code used to generate the content of the frame. This source code is specific to each external render engine. The one we see first is LaTeX, but if you change the selected program in the **Program** list, you'll see samples for each. On the right-hand side of the **Editor** window, you have tabs with options that help you modify the source or the rendering options. LaTeX is the more complete section of the window.

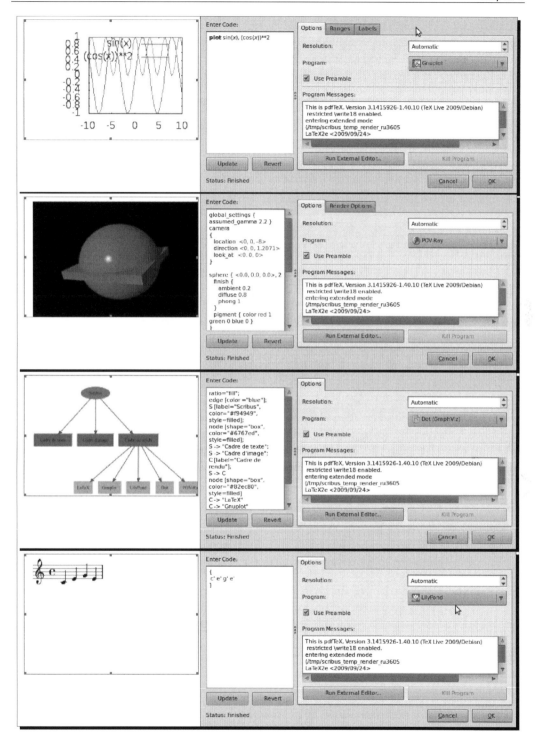

Of course, it will be impossible to learn each of these languages in this book. But we can do some tests, just to see the interaction between this window and the render frame. In fact, it will take very long to learn LaTeX, or any other language. And the Scribus source editor is certainly not the handiest. The **Run External Editor** button allows you to launch your favorite editor from within Scribus:

- For LaTeX, it can be Kile, TexnicCenter, or Texshop

- For Lilypond, it can be Denemo

- Using Art of Illusion for PovRay files seems a good and cross-platform solution, but consider Blender with the additional Povanim exporter script available at `http://jmsoler.free.fr/util/blenderfile/fr/povanim_en.htm`

Modifying a render frame LaTeX source

The principle of modifying the source code is to write your custom code within the text area in the left-hand side of the window. This area displays colored text. The coloration is syntactical and helps you understand what is written and to work more efficiently. For example, LaTeX commands are displayed in red and the text content in black.

Time for action – e=mc2

Let's write some simple formula right now and see how render frame behaves.

1. First of all, you might find the rendering very bad. Don't worry, it's just an overview you have on your page, and the result will be much better in the final PDF document. But if you want to improve all that, go to **File | Preferences**, click on **External Tools** category, and increase the resolution value placed at the bottom right-hand side of the window. But again, there is no need for a high resolution here.

2. Let's modify some graphical option first. Edit the current render frame source code and go to the **Fonts/Headers** tab. Change the **Fontsize** to one of the preset values. Click on the **Update** button. You'll see that all the text of the frame is modified.

3. The code in the source below `\usepackage{amsmath}` just tells the render engine to use the American Mathematical Society package. There are many packages made for LaTeX: `graphicx` will manipulate images, `psfrag` will generate curves and graphs from LaTeX commands, and many more.

4. In fact we'd prefer to modify only the size of some lines. Replace the sentence beginning by "Your" with "Let's write a well-known formula in LaTeX!" keep the double anti-slash at the end of the line to keep the line break. You should have something like this:

```
Let's write a famous formula in LaTeX !\\
```

5. If you want LaTeX to be written perfectly, just add an anti-slash just before LaTeX:

```
Let's write a famous formula in \LaTeX !\\
```

6. Now, add \Large at the beginning of the line and update to see that the text will be bigger from here to the end. To keep only this sentence Large, add \normalsize at the beginning of the next line:

```
\Large Let's write a famous formula in \LaTeX !\\
\normalsize Placing formulas is very easy:\\
```

7. If you want the text to be displayed in Helvetica, just specify it: add \sf after \ Large and update. \sf is a shortcut and of course LaTeX has much more advanced font selection options:

```
\Large \sf Let's write a famous formula in \LaTeX !\\
\normalsize Placing formulas is very easy:\\
```

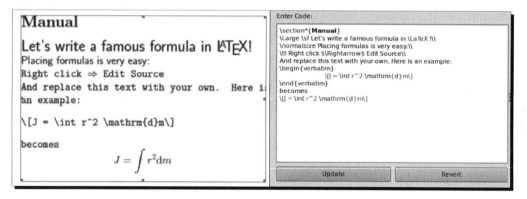

8. Delete some lines to get the following result:

```
\section*{Manual}
\Large \sf Let's write a famous formula in \LaTeX !\\
\normalsize Placing formulas is very easy:\\
\begin{verbatim}
\[J = \int r^2 \mathrm{d}m\]
\end{verbatim}
```

9. Change Manual to Introduction to Render Frame. Here, the curly braces contain the text that will be affected.

10. \begin will define that the formula is there, and \end the verbatim value just specifies that the text will be displayed in typewriter style. To be more precise, \begin specifies that a verbatim section begins there whatever the content will be. If you write "E=mc2" between \begin and \end and update, you'll have the text appear inside.

11. If you want "2" to be superscript just add ^ after c and update. Yes, it should not work, of course, because the verbatim section will not interpret the commands so just delete \begin and \end lines and update again.

12. Once again it will not work and you'll get a rendering error because our LaTeX code is not good. Just add a $ at the beginning and at the end and update again.

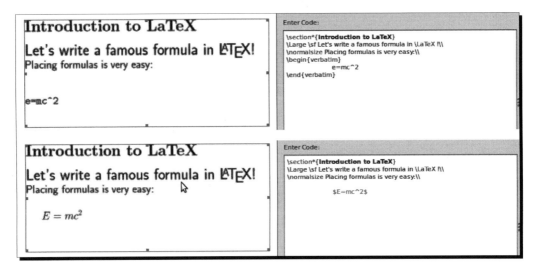

What just happened?

By modifying the source code in the editor window, and updating, we have asked Scribus to call LaTeX engines. Scribus grabbed the result of those engines and put it in the render frame as an image with a given resolution. Knowing LaTeX commands is the key; of course, nothing can be done without that. You can get many examples of LaTeX formulas on the Internet like in this link: http://www.hamline.edu/~arundquist/equationeditor/.

It may seem difficult if you never wrote LaTeX before. But before giving it away consider a few things:

- We showed the functionalities with incremental process, and we didn't try to avoid errors to show what happens when an error occurs: nothing. Errors aren't fatal, so it's worth a try.

- We could have used other tabs of the source editor to help us because they give shortcuts to many characters often used in formulas.

- Look at the typographic render: how long would it take to you to get the right "E", the right "=", the right space between them, and the right baseline modification for the 2? Consider that learning mathematical rules is quite difficult too and LaTeX will do most part of the job for you. If scientists created and use it, it is really because they were fed up of guessing how to respect the rules in any software they'd use.

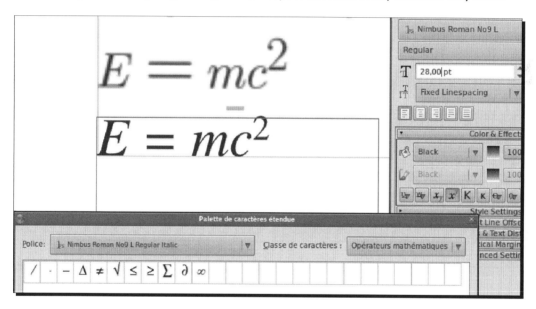

In fact, trying to do it manually with PP options will be very difficult. For example, for a given "E" size, the "2" size will be bad and will need adaptations as well as regular font setting. Here we chose Nimbus, which is quite a good font, and the right spaces were missing, and we could only add standard non-breaking space. And when we wanted to replace the "=" with the real long mathematical one, we would need to open the Glyph window for our font. But the sign was not there, even in the mathematical operators category. We can keep the standard "=" glyph, of course, but it is too low and the baseline needs to be adjusted and so on. In fact, it took some minutes, to try, and the result is not good.

Such formulas cannot be written without some special knowledge and material, and LaTeX can really help.

Getting help for render frames

Of course, nobody can know all the programming languages in the world. In fact, once you have tested one, you'll see they all have common rules, and getting to a second will be much easier. There are many documentations on the Web and even on the official website of each external rendering tool, which can help you begin or help you find sample code to work with. Don't reinvent the wheel!

The energy that you'll give in learning LaTeX, Lilypond, or Pov language will certainly depend on the quantity of the files you'll have to write with. In any case, you can use a specialized editor for each of these languages. For example, Texmaker is a nice and cross-platform user interface to write Tex documents, and we already told about Denemo or Frescobaldi for Lilypond files, or Art of illusion for Pov. You can instruct Scribus that you prefer those editors instead of the simple built-in code editor. Go to **File | Preferences**; in the **External Tools** category, you'll see the list of called rendering engines at the bottom. Just select the one you need and give the path to the external editor you prefer. When you edit the source code, you'll be able to click on the **Run External Editor** button and it will automatically be launched.

For example, download the file `http://www.mutopiaproject.org/ftp/BachJS/BWV903/bwv903fan/bwv903fan.ly`. If you're interested in music publishing, remember this website; it has many scores of public domain artwork.

You can open this `.ly` file in Frescobaldi, which is an independent `.ly` editor, and generate the score from it. But `.ly` files are simple text so you can open them in any text editor you have (Notepad, Smultron, gedit, and vi), and copy the document. Then paste the content into the Scribus source editor after specifying that you want to use Lilypond files.

Many tools will exist to help you produce the source code and just copy paste it into Scribus render frame. Just use your favorite tool.

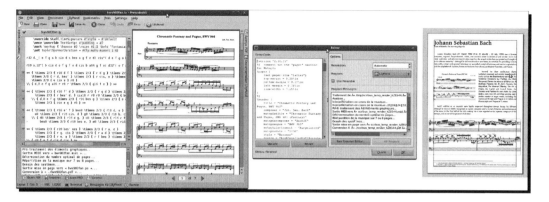

Time for action – Scribus scrapbooking

If you often use some custom frame settings or layout, you certainly won't like redoing them each time. For example, if you're doing a book about LaTeX, you'd like to show sample code. In the margin of the code, it would be nice to say it is LaTeX and have some nice setup.

Let's say you have some render frame, at its left-hand side a black and long rectangle frame, and at the left-hand side of it a render frame containing \LaTeX and a simple Text Frame containing "Formula 1". The latest are 90° rotated.

1. Select them all and use **Send to Scrapbook** from the context menu (right-click).

2. You will be asked to choose a name for your object: for example, type LaTeX.

3. Now go to the **Windows** menu and display the **Scrapbook** from there and you'll see your frames inside.

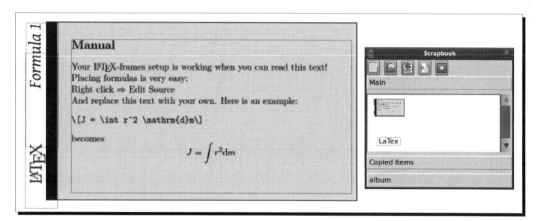

4. If you want to reuse them later, just drag them from the **Scrapbook** window into your page, and you'll just have to change the content of each frame.

What just happened?

It is very easy to reuse elements within the document. More than that, Scribus doesn't save the scrapbook within your document itself but as an external resource. So you just have to click on the third button of the Scrapbook window to save it. You'll just have to remember where you have stored it. Scribus will add two files in the directory you have chosen:

- ◆ A `.png` file that is used to display the aspect of the object within the window
- ◆ A `.sce` file that remembers the structure of your object

You can send them to anyone you want, or to your other computers if you work on several machines. When you need to use them again, go to the scrapbook window and click on the second button, which will help you choose the directory where you saved your elements. They will be available again.

Scrapbook and patterns

Patterns are different from scrapbooks. Patterns (made with the **Send to Patterns** context menu) will be used to fill a shape instead of a color or a gradient and cannot be used as single objects.

Pop quiz

1. The shortcut for the **Insert Table** tool is:
    a. *T*
    b. *A*
    c. *B*

2. The keyboard modifier to use to access a table cell is:
    a. *Shift*
    b. *Alt*
    c. *Ctrl*

3. Rows can be selected by:
    a. *Alt + Shift* + click on each cell
    b. Clicking on the border of the left-most cell
    c. Clicking on the border of the right-most cell

4. Cells can be formatted using:

   a. Table window

   b. **Table** tab of the PP

   c. **Line** and **Color** tab of the PP

5. To import a Calc formatted table, we can use:

   a. EPS format

   b. CSV format

   c. OpenDocument spreadsheet format

6. Render Frame is a:

   a. Text Frame

   b. Image Frame

   c. Frame that uses an external engine

7. To write maths or physics formulas into Scribus, we'll use:

   a. Lilypond

   b. LaTeX

   c. GnuPlot

Summary

In this chapter, we've seen how to add special content and how it can sometimes take advantage of an external file format or render engine to get the best result as possible.

Specifically, we covered:

- How to add tables, form simple text content, CSV content, and OpenOffice.org Calc spreadsheet
- How to write mathematical or physics formulas using LaTeX engines
- How to insert music scores using Lilypond engines
- How to reuse our graphical elements using scrapbook

In the next chapter, we will go deeper into Scribus drawing tools and shapes so that not only can the content be advanced and customized, but the graphical elements too.

7
Drawing Advanced Frames and Shapes

Drawing shapes will be the most common action that you'll do in Scribus. Every other action will be setting the frame properties and frame content properties. Your frames will mostly be rectangles because traditionally a text stands in pages that are themselves rectangles. However, sometimes you might need or may be interested in getting some different results, especially if you're using pictures that can support other frame shapes more easily without losing readability.

In this chapter, we will spend some time on using some frame options, and will be able to get more custom shapes when needed. Specifically, we shall:

- ◆ Recall basic options
- ◆ Use shape distortion
- ◆ Draw lines and curves
- ◆ Modify shapes as we wish with the Points window
- ◆ Mix and convert frames

Frame conversion and text to outlines

Anytime you have to test a new software, the first things you'll see are the defaults. You have to work for some time with them to adapt your workflow to the available tools and take advantage of the specificities.

In Scribus, frames are central. Adobe InDesign, in some ways tries to avoid them by using a single tool for text edit and text frame, and at the same time it can import pictures without requiring a frame. But in any case, a frame is made even if automatically. We've also seen in Scribus that tables are a kind of group of generated frames. The easy part is that there is nothing special to learn to use and format tables.

Another good feature with Scribus frames is that they can easily be converted to any other kind of frame. So, if you created a Text Frame and want to put an image into it, you can still do so without deleting and drawing a new frame. This is very important because the default frame shape is set to rectangle and cannot be changed.

You can:

- ◆ Convert a Text Frame to an Image Frame
- ◆ Convert an Image Frame to a Text Frame
- ◆ Convert a shape or polygon to a Text or Image Frame
- ◆ Convert a frame to a polygon
- ◆ Convert any polygon to a single line
- ◆ Convert any frame to a single line
- ◆ Convert a line to a polygon

Here when talking about lines, we include outlines and Bezier curves. The trick is that a shape or a frame can have a fill, and not a line. Or the fill will not be closed. The need of using Bezier curves in Scribus is not very common as it is more of a drawing program feature, but there are some nice use cases as we will see later in this chapter.

The available convert options for the current selected objects are listed in:

- ◆ **Item | Convert To**
- ◆ The right-click context menu as **Convert to**

As it seems interesting, you will think you'll need to use frame conversion a lot. In fact, not so much because the frame shape can easily be changed from the **Shape** tab of the PP. There is no real need to create a shape and then convert it.

Time for action – images in a text shape

Putting text in any shape can really affect readability, so we will work more with image frames. We will try to create a book cover that will be filled with a bright image and then have over it the same colored image in a text shape.

1. Draw the first image frame covering the whole page and import your photo inside. Import a picture from **File | Import** and choose your image.

2. With this frame selected, go to **Edit | Contents | Copy**. We'll need it later.

3. Then draw a large Text Frame and write a word inside it.

4. Format it with a bold font and increase the font size so that it fills the frame.

5. We have now reached the main part of our tutorial. Right-click on the Text Frame and use **Convert to | Outlines**.

6. Then use **Convert to | Image Frame**.

7. Now ungroup using *Ctrl + Shift + G* or **Item | Ungroup**.

8. Select the first letter frame and use **Edit | Contents | Paste (Absolute)**. Do the same for all the letters.

9. We'll then change the first Image Frame with effects to make it differ from the letters. Right-click on it and choose **Image Effects**. Click on **Grayscale** and on **>>** to apply it.

10. Then choose **Brightness** and apply it. Under the preview image on the left, you can drag the slider to the right-hand side to increase the brightness. Click on **OK** to apply.

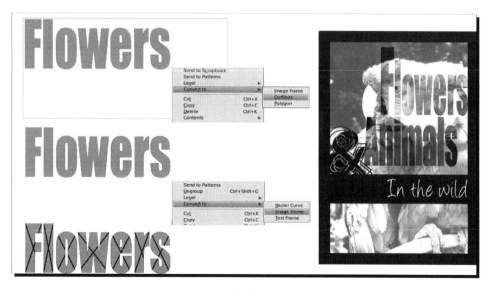

What just happened?

We used a basic Image Frame to place the background and have some basic coordinates for the pictures. The image has been modified to be lighter and gray. When we copied with the **Contents** menu, we copied the image itself, not the frame, which would have been copied with a normal copy command. We then pasted this image as content in other frames. When pasted it in **Absolute** mode, the image is placed with the exact similar page coordinates. So the position of the grey one and those new instances give the effect of continuation.

To draw the frame for the colored pictures, we used letters. Images are copied within the title letters. We just draw a Text Frame and type text inside. Converting immediately to an Image Frame would have just converted the rectangular Text Frame to a rectangular Image Frame. To keep the text aspect, converting to **Outlines** is useful. And then apply what we need: a conversion to **Image Frame** so that we can put our picture inside.

Have a go hero – create a magazine cover with frame conversion

By converting any shape to an Image Frame it is possible to put pictures in any kind of shape. Try to extract the best of this and create a nice magazine cover using these functionalities.

Drawing basic shapes

Converting text to a frame was on how to get a custom frame shape from something we already knew perfectly, that is, text inserted or typed in a frame, and without having to draw anything manually. There are tools specifically dedicated to that part of the work. Shapes and Polygons are really made for this purpose. In the toolbar, the **Insert Shape** icon is the white shadowed rectangle placed to the right-hand side of the **Insert Table** tool and the **Insert Polygon** tool (the pentagon).

You can see there are black arrows next to them. The arrows will display a menu that will give you many choices to get a nice result.

As a first step, click on the arrow to the right-hand side of the **Insert Shape** tool. It will display a list of predefined shapes, organized into **Default Shapes**, **Arrows**, **Flow Chart**, **Jigsaw**, and **Specials** categories. Click on the shape you need to use.

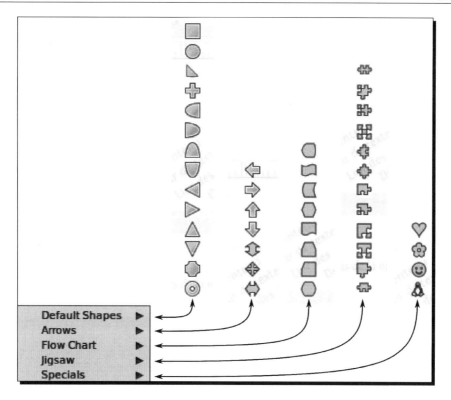

The chosen shape is now displayed in place of the rectangle icon and will be available until you choose another one.

To draw with it, you'll just have to press the **Insert Shape** tool icon or the *S* key and press-drag-release the left mouse button.

The shape's default color will be black for both the stroke and the fill. You can modify it in the **Colors** tab of the PP. This is nearly everything you need to know about shapes: they can't contain text nor images. But you can convert them as seen previously. They can also be customized with the **Nodes** window as we will see later in this chapter.

One simple thing you can add to a basic rectangle shape is rounded corners. The radius can be set in the **Shape** tab of the PP. It can be a positive or negative value depending on the result you need.

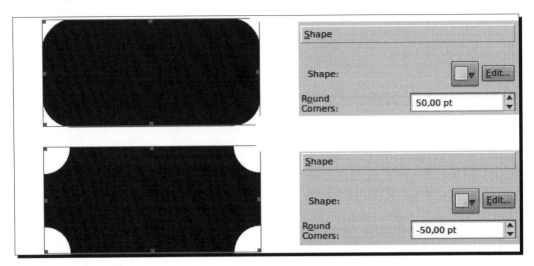

Drawing polygons

The **Insert Polygon** tool (P) will add shapes too. But instead of having a predefined list of elements, you'll create your own thanks to some settings. Polygons can be defined when using the **Polygon Properties**. Click on the arrow to the right-hand side of the **Insert Polygon** tool icon and then choose **Properties** in the menu that appears.

- **Corners** specifies how many sides you need. The default is **4** but can be increased to **999** (having so many sides is unnecessary for your polygon and will look like a circle at this point).

- **Rotation** will turn your shape. It's the less important setting of this window because the rotation can be done afterwards, on the page, with the **Rotation** value in the PP or using the **Rotate Item** tool.

- The **Apply Factor** checkbox just activates the last few options. It's interesting when you want to deactivate them all and come back to your regular polygon.

- **Factor** will divide the sides in the middle and increase or decrease the radius at this point so that you can get a star when it's minored and a more complex polygon when majored.

- With **Curvature**, sides will be rounded. The curvature is related to the factor value. In this case, **Factor** gives the curvature radius so that the sides keep on going through it.

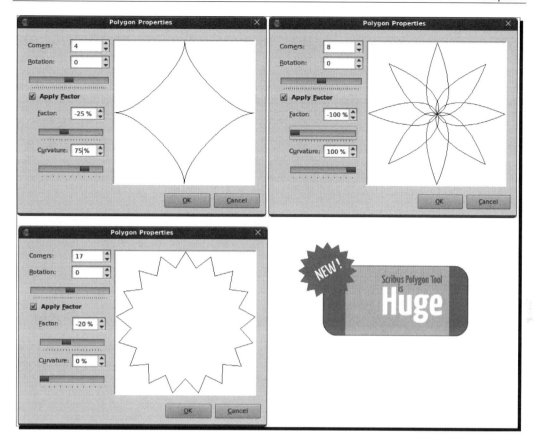

Mesh distortion

Mesh distortion is one of the tools you can use to modify the shape you've drawn. Basically, you'll also use path operations or **Nodes** window. Both will be considered later in this chapter.

Time for action – distorting a shape

Mesh distortion is a nice and easy feature that let's you interact with your frame's sides with the help of some special handles.

1. To modify a frame or a shape, just select it and go to **Item | Path Tools | Mesh Distortion**.

2. A window will appear. The selected frame or shape is displayed inside a grid too and has some circle handles.

3. Dragging those handles will distort the grid and the shape as well. Take the third handle of the second row and drag it down.

4. Take the third handle of the third row and drag it down too.

5. You then just have to adapt other handles to make them nicer and smoother.

What just happened?

Dragging handles just distorts the shape by the same amount as the grid. The current active handle is displayed with a red fill, whereas the inactive handles are kept with a single red stroke.

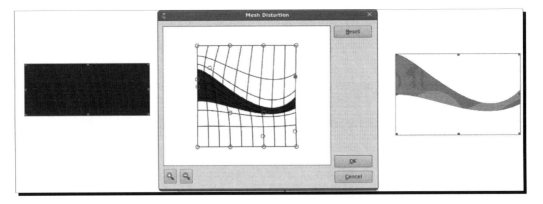

By watching the position of the handles or the shape of the grid, one can see what changes have been made. In the example, we have mostly moved the two middle handles of the second line, one to the left-hand side and one at the very bottom of the grid on the right-hand side. The second handle from top has been slightly moved up and the next slightly down. The shape has then been converted to an Image Frame and a picture is imported at the end.

This window has no value that could be saved for a future reuse. The best we can do it is by saving the shape into the scrapbook.

Free to share

As a nice example of the free software philosophy, the source code used by Scribus for **mesh distortion**, Boolean operations, and other geometrical commands is based on the Inkscape **lib2geom** library.

Have a go hero – import a photo in a flag

The Scribus mesh distort tool can help you draw custom and smooth shapes: it's really common. Try to use this technique to modify a rectangular image frame and give it the shape of a flag. Try to do this with a text too to simulate the floating text on the flag. An example is shown in the following screenshot:

Mixing shapes with path operations

Path operations are sometimes called Boolean operations because they are based on Boole's maths. They are really well known in graphical applications. Adobe Illustrator knows them as Pathfinder and Inkscape has much more choice than Scribus in its Path menu. In Scribus they are not so easily accessible because they are rarely used. But they can sometimes be very useful.

You will use them when you need to have a more complex shape than a rectangle or a circle. Generally, you will use two or three basic shapes to make a new one by combining or subtracting them in a certain way and then using them as a background shape, text, or Image Frame.

The principle is really simple:

1. Draw two shapes.

2. Make them more or less overlap.

3. Use the Path operation window to combine them into one resulting shape.

4. Do what you need with that shape.

In Scribus, path operations will be available in a window that you can call from **Item | Path Tools | Path Operations**. Here, you will have several possibilities, such as:

◆ **Union**

◆ **Subtraction**

◆ **Intersection**

◆ **Exclusion**

◆ **Break apart**

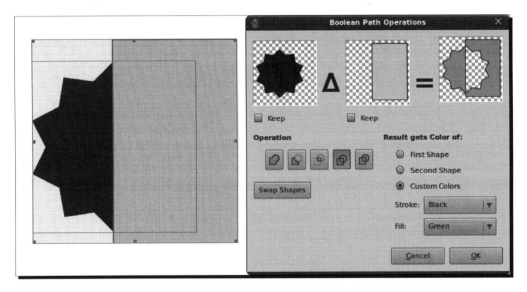

This Scribus window is really rich in features. You can see the result in the window before you validate. It makes it a lot easier to choose the right option. You can swap the shapes if you draw them in a bad order, or decide which color will be kept. Just remember that, at the end, you'll have only one shape, so only one color left, even if the shape you use has different colors. One thing you should notice is that Path Operations work only with shapes and polygons, and not with frames, so you might need to convert them afterwards.

Have a go hero – let's create a mix!

Creating new shapes with path operations is most commonly used in advertising, where the purpose is to show a difference among products of the same category. Let's assume you'd have to create a model for one of these. The following example is similar to what you'd get:

Lines

Lines are other elements of the layout. They can be used to:

- Separate areas, for example, between columns
- Highlight or underline something, as for titles
- Join or link elements, for example, when set with arrows or other kinds of ending
- Give a custom graphical design
- Be used as guides to place objects, especially because Scribus can't have built-in rotated guides, so lines can be used instead
- Make technical drawings

Some years ago it was very common to see documents using lines as the most important graphical element of the layout. It has now virtually disappeared, maybe because those kinds of elements are hard to use, and it really calls for some different kind of creative approach. But they are still used in many other cases.

You can count on three Scribus tools to help you create lines and a window to customize them as you wish. They all have common settings, share line styles, and can be defined in the **Line** tab of the PP and the stroke color can be applied to them, whereas fill color won't do anything.

Drawing straight lines

The **Insert Line** tool (*L*), placed just after the **Insert Polygon** tool (*P*) in the toolbar will draw straight lines.

Line and border

Don't get confused with lines and borders. Borders, also called frame lines, are always all around a frame. They can be set with the **Colors** and **Line** tab of the PP or with styles. But they cannot be placed or customized apart from the frame. Lines based on the **Line** tool are single objects.

Drawing lines is as simple as pressing the left mouse button where the line should begin, dragging, and releasing where it should stop. If you want a perfect horizontal line, press *Ctrl* while dragging and try to move horizontally.

In fact, *Ctrl* will snap the line to 15 degree increments so that you can move quite easily without seeing your line take a bad direction. If 15 degrees doesn't suit your needs, you can change it in the **Miscellaneous** settings of **Preferences** or in the **Tools** section of **Document Setup**.

Plus, if you look at the **XYZ** tab of the PP, you'll see that **X-pos**, **Y-pos**, **Width**, and **Height** can be turned to **X1** and **Y1** (for the position of the first point) and **X2** and **Y2** (for the position of the last) if the **Basepoint** drop-down list of the **Line** tab is set to **End Points**.

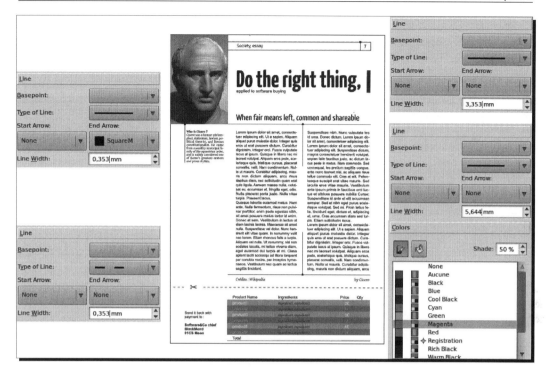

Time for action – drawing lines with the Pen tool

With the **Insert Freehand Line** tool (*F*), also called the **Pen** tool, you'll be able to draw any line type you wish. This tool is made to simulate the behavior of a real pen, so it is hard to get a pure straight line or nice curve with it. You will use it when the final result doesn't need to be very precise. It can be used if you like to give a hand-made effect. We sometimes use it to annotate: it happens when I have to report or correct things on a layout.

1. Go back to a document we've already made. Open the **Layers** window from the **Windows** menu.

2. Create a **layer** by clicking on the + button at the bottom left-hand of the layer window. Double-click on its name and enter **Comments**.

3. Deactivate printing for this layer by deselecting the second box on its line.

4. Now activate the **Insert Freehand Line** tool (*F*)

5. Sketching with this tool is really nice and fast: press the left mouse button and drag. Release when you want to stop. Of course, it's easier when done with a pen tablet. You can quickly write text too, but it might be easier with a Text Frame.

6. Then, open the PP (*F2*) and go to the **Line** tab. Play with the **Line Width**, and with the **Start Arrow** list, apply a **TriangleInM** or any other shape fits your line.

7. Go to the **Colors** tab, activate the **Edit Line Color Properties**, and choose **Red**. We could have created a line style too and just chosen it in the **Line** tab.

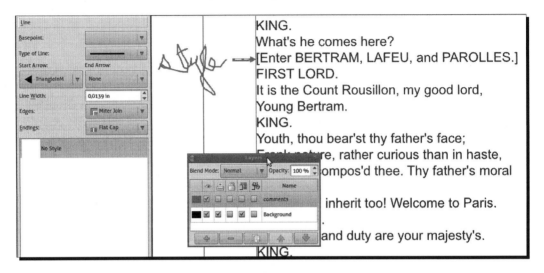

KING.
What's he comes here?
[Enter BERTRAM, LAFEU, and PAROLLES.]
FIRST LORD.
It is the Count Rousillon, my good lord,
Young Bertram.
KING.
Youth, thou bear'st thy father's face;
Frank nature, rather curious than in haste,
compos'd thee. Thy father's moral
inherit too! Welcome to Paris.
and duty are your majesty's.
KING.

What just happened?

We can use the **Pen** tool in two ways:

◆   The most common way is to simply press the left mouse button, drag, and release. This way, you'll be drawing joined segments.

◆   The other way is nearly the same in practice, just that the *Ctrl* key has to be pressed from the beginning to the end of the process. You'll get smoother results with much prettier curves this way.

Scribus or Inkscape?

Straight line, freehand, Bezier, and so on are tools that Inkscape or even GIMP can have. If you just have a line, Scribus can be enough, but if you need a more advanced curve feature or need to create a complex drawing, have a look at Inkscape. Make your lines and shapes there and import them into Scribus. You'll save time in the end.

Like any other line, the color can be set in the **Colors** tab of the PP with the stroke color, and the thickness in the **Line** tab.

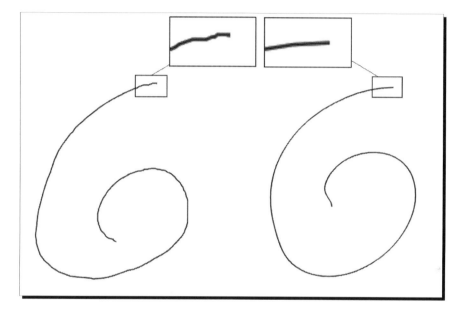

Options to customize line aspect with arrows or dots

We have several times talked about the **Line** tab of the PP. It would be good to have a complete overview of what's inside.

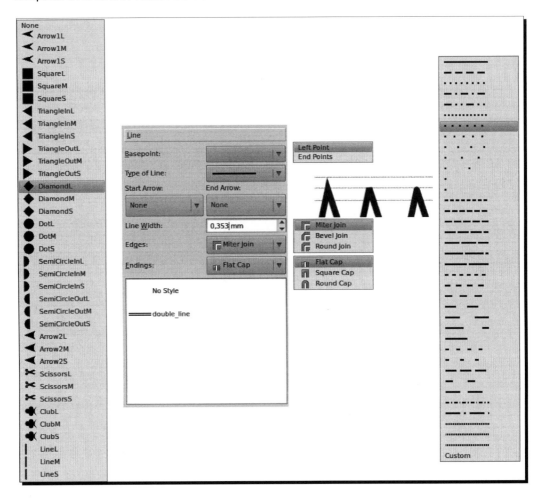

The options seen in the previous screenshot are as follows:

◆ **Basepoint** on **Left Point**, will display the length of the line as the **Width** in the **XYZ** tab, whereas on **End Points** will show the position of the beginning and ending points.

- **Type of Line** gives a list of plain, dashed, or dotted samples. You just have to choose one to apply to the selected line. The default is a plain line. You can consider creating your own type by choosing **Custom**. A new area will appear under the list with a sample dash. Just click under the line to place a new marker and use the **Value** setting to give its position relative to the preceding marker. You will this way define dash or dot length and the space between too, alternatively. You can immediately see the result on your line.

- **Start Arrow** and **End Arrow** show a list of default built-in arrows that can be placed at the beginning of the line (**Start**) or the end. Arrows are given in three sizes: L (large), M (medium), and S (small). But once you've chose one, remember that the arrow is relative to the thickness of the line, so it can be adapted if the setting has changed.

- **Edges** define what is happening in the line corners when edges meet, typically when they are done with Bezier curves. **Miter Join**, the default selection, keeps it acute and projected; **Bevel Join** makes it truncated, whereas **Round Join** gives a rounded result at the same place than **Bevel Join**. **Endings** just tell how the border of the dash segment need to be set: you'll generally use **Flat Cap**, the default, or **Rounded Cap**.

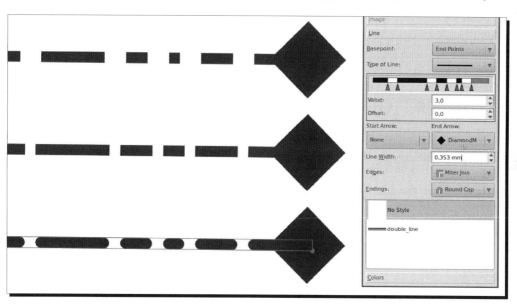

The last part of the **Line** tab refers to the list of defined styles. In the **Style Manager** (**Edit | Styles**) or *F3*, the same place where we've set character and paragraph styles, contains some line options. In some ways it completes the line capacity not only by defining custom lines that we'll use several times in a document, but also because it is possible to have more complex lines with nearly all these options but arrows. Choose **New | Line Style** in the **Style Manager** and give a name to your line. There is a default line inside. Set it as you want with the options on the right-hand side. If you want another line in your line style, click on the + button above the line list and set it. Remember that lines are all centered. So, you should begin with the thicker one and finish with the thinnest (top of the list). An overview of the result is displayed at the right-hand side below the other options.

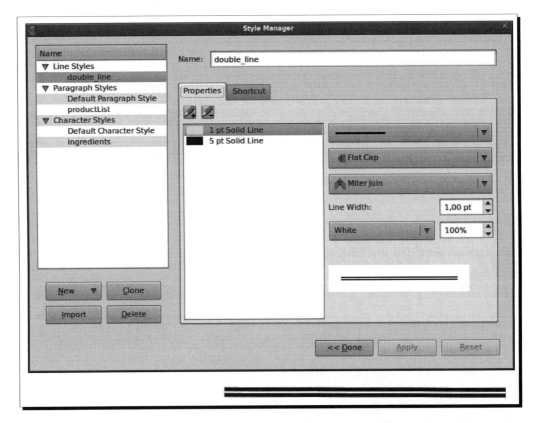

Time for action – attach text to a line

If you're not really interested in drawing a line or prefer using a real vector drawing program like Inkscape instead of Scribus for this, you might also consider this tip that many people ask for: make a text follow a line. There are no tools for this in Scribus so don't look for it in the toolbar. Of course, it is still possible and here are some steps to follow:

1. First of all draw a line (with the **Insert Freehand Line** tool, for example) or a shape.

2. Then add a Text Frame, write your text inside, and set it nicely if you already know what you want.

3. Select them both.

4. Go to **Item | Attach Text to Path**.

What just happened?

You can see that the line is now hidden, but it is still there. If you then want to separate the text and the line, just go to **Item | Detach Text from Path**. By selecting the line and the text at the same time, Scribus understands what needs to be joined. Just take care of selecting only one line.

If you want to modify the text, double-clicking on it will have no interesting result. You'll get some blue points that we will manipulate in the next section. **Columns & Text Distances** has disappeared from the **Text** tab of the PP but a new **Path Text Properties** option has appeared. Here, you can change the way the text adapts to the line and set the whole text. If you want to do some formatting on some part of the text, just use the **Story Editor** (**Edit | Edit Text**), make the changes, and apply them by pressing the *Ctrl + U* keys until you get what you want.

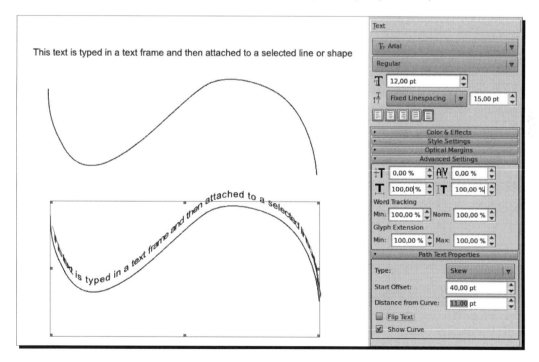

The options provided in the **Path Text Properties** are as follows:

- **Type** will change the way the text follows the line. **Default** puts the letters perpendicular to the line. With **Stair Step**, all the letters will be kept vertical. **Skew** will do the same, except that the letters will be distorted to follow the line's curvature as the baseline. The last gives very odd results if the line has two vertical parts.

- **Start Offset** specifies how far from the line start point the text will be placed. It doesn't extend the text, just moves it along. If you want the text to fill the line, you can use **Forced Justify** alignment and eventually **Horizontal scaling** or letter spacing/tracking.

- **Distance from Curve** specifies how much the text has to be taken away from the line, as any baseline offset would do.

- **Flip Text** puts the text under the line, mirrored on line axis. It is more interesting when the text is around a shape, a circle, for example, and you want it to be placed inside the shape.

- **Show Curve** simply displays the line which was used in the attachment.

Have a go hero – make a stamp-like shape with curved text

All these settings are quite simple and once you know what you need to do, it is very easy to get the expected result. But sometimes, it is important to define in advance some of the basic actions that you need to take. In the example here, there's a little trick for the way the bigger text is written in both directions. It's quite simple, but worth a try.

Point to modify existing lines and shapes

When double-clicking on a text attached to a path, we have seen that some strange color points were made visible. All the Scribus shapes and lines can do so, and you may have experienced it when we were working with shapes.

These points are handles that can be used to modify the shape or the line. They are related to a window called **Nodes**. This window can be opened at any time with the **Edit** button of the **Shape** tab in the PP. We have already been in there when dealing with text flowing around frames as a contour line, which was in fact a special use of this window.

This window is complex in the way that it has many options. There is no need to know them all by heart. The **Nodes** window is helpful but sometimes too much for a layout program, as manipulating nodes will be much easier in a vector drawing program such as Inkscape. Nodes are the point through which the line will go, start, or end. **X-Pos** and **Y-Pos** of this window give the node position.

If you draw a curve, you should see two pink handles for each node. These are control points that will modify the curvature of the line, one for each side, so each curve will have four handles available. When a node or a control point is selected, it turns red. You can select several points by *Shift* clicking on each point that you want to modify.

The most important are the first two lines:

- The first line lists the node actions:
    - Move nodes by dragging (enables the next options)
    - Add a node
    - Delete a node
    - Reset this node control points

- The second line lists the control point actions:
    - Enable control point buttons
    - Move control points separately
    - Move control points together, makes them symmetrical on the node
    - Reset the selected control point

The other options perform mirroring, skewing, or scaling as we have seen earlier for contour lines. All these options act on the selected point, depending on the dragging of your mouse, so it is very hard to explain the movement in this book. The best method is to have a few tries and see how it reacts. It can take some time to get used to it.

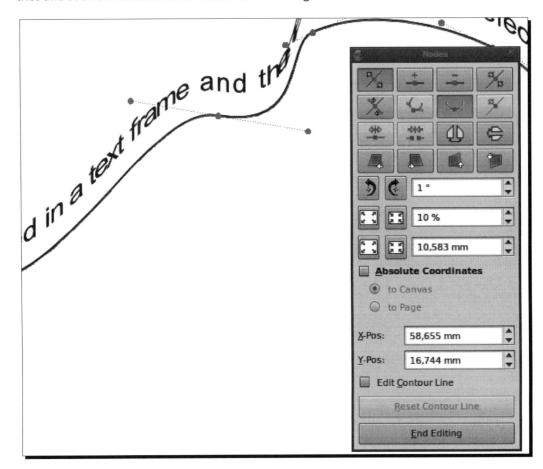

Drawing paths with the Bezier tool

Drawing Bezier curves or paths is going deeper into the vector drawing options of Scribus. Bezier curves have been made popular by the PostScript printing language. We have already manipulated Bezier curves with the **Line** or **Nodes** window. But in the former, we didn't have much control on the line, and in the latter we could just modify an existing one. The **Insert Bezier Curve** tool lets you draw a path with a high level of control. It results in really nice and smooth curves. And if you succeed, there is no need to go into the **Nodes** window anymore, because most part of the node and control point options can be used directly with this tool while drawing on the page.

Unfortunately, it is at the expense of the complexity and the need for a good practice and foresight. It's feasible, of course, but at the beginning, you will still need the **Nodes** window to improve your path. Especially because the Scribus Bezier tool is now quite old and would gain from an improvement.

Scribus and drawing

Drawing Bezier curves is considered an advanced tool in photo editing or layout. But it is the basis of vector drawing so that once again, paths can be easier to manipulate or draw from a vector application. Remember that most graphic designers use at least three pieces of software: the photo editing program, the vector one, and the layout application.

The **Insert Bezier Curve** tool (*B*) is available in the toolbar, between the **Insert Line** tool and the **Pen** tool, and in the **Insert | Insert Bezier Curve** menu.

Time for action – creating custom paths with the Bezier tool

It's time to have a try. Our purpose is to draw some kind of "B" letter. We will need straight lines on the left-hand part and curves on the right-hand part. We will then import a picture inside, and use these frames with a text flowing around.

1. In a new blank page, activate the **Insert Bezier Curve** tool by pressing *B*.

2. Click where you want in the page, let's say left of the middle so that you have enough space to go on.

3. Move the mouse above this node to make the vertical line of the B, click again, and go to the left to begin the first curve.

4. Place your mouse right to the middle of the first segment and press the mouse button. Drag towards the top right at an angle of around 45 degrees and you'll see two dotted lines. The straight one shows the control line (the mouse position gives the position of a control point) and a curved one, which is the actual curve state.

5. Drag until you find the perfect curve and release.

6. Then at the half of the next curve, do the same.

7. Finally, go back to the first point and click.

8. Press *Esc* to deactivate the drawing process and go back to **Select Item** tool.

9. You can now customize your path with the **Nodes** window by double-clicking on it.

10. Adjust some control points and nodes.

11. Select the first and last point that should be really near and click on the Close Bezier curve button of the **Nodes** window.

12. Then activate the **Delete Nodes** button and click on one of these nodes.

13. Close the **Nodes** window by clicking on **End Editing** at the bottom.

14. Right-click on the path and choose **Convert to | Image Frame** in the contextual menu.

15. Import an image into it and set it as you wish.

16. Draw a Text Frame partially above the Image Frame and add some text in it.

17. Change the stack of object so that the Text Frame is placed below the Image Frame. Press the *End* key.

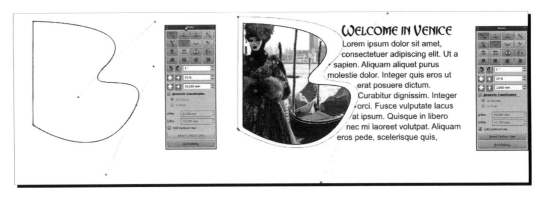

18. Select the Image Frame and in the **Shape** tab of the PP, activate the **Use Contour Line** option.

19. Click on the **Edit** button at the top part of the tab and in the **Nodes** window, select **Edit Contour Line.**

20. Manipulate the nodes and control points that define the margin between the image and the text. Validate when you're happy with the result.

What just happened?

Using the **Bezier** tool gave the basis of the shape. If we wanted to have a shape that looks more like a B, we could just have written the letter, set it, and then converted it to a **Bezier** curve. By clicking we created straight paths and by dragging we created curves. As it is hard to foresee the shape of the curve, we kept our rough trials and improved it with the **Nodes** window.

We went back to the **Nodes** window to make the text flow around the shape. We selected the **Edit Contour Line** option so that it matched the option we used in the PP. If we hadn't selected this checkbox, we would have changed the frame shape and not modified the margin.

Pop quiz

1. When converting a text to outline:
    a. We can still edit the text as is
    b. We cannot edit the text anymore
    c. We need to convert it back to make it editable

2. When copying a frame content:
    a. The frame is copied with the content
    b. Only the content is copied
    c. They are both copied

3. If you intersect a rectangle and a circle that is over it, what default result will you get?
    a. The rectangle with the circle color
    b. A similar rectangle only
    c. The circle with the color of the rectangle

4. To customize your dash line, you can:
    a. Draw it with shapes and save it as a pattern
    b. Draw it with shapes and save it in the scrapbook
    c. Use the custom option of the Arrowhead drop down
    d. Create a line style

5. How do you import an image into letters?

    a. Draw letters with Bezier paths

    b. Convert the text to an Image Frame

    c. Convert the text to outline and then to Image Frame

6. To create more complex shapes from basics, you would:

    a. Create a group of the shapes

    b. Combine the shapes

    c. Perform Boolean operations on them.

7. Node window can:

    a. Modify a shape

    b. Modify a line

    c. Modify the margin around a shape

Summary

In this chapter we've seen how to draw more advanced kind of shapes, lines, and frames.

Specifically, we covered:

- How to use the basic shapes and polygons
- How to mix shapes to get more complex frames
- How to draw a line and write text on it
- How to convert a line, shape, polygon, and frame to any other object type
- How to distort an object with Mesh distortion or the Node window

In the next chapter, we will see in detail how to use and manipulate images within Scribus.

8
Importing Images

If you were asked for the subject of a previously published document without images, which you've read, would you have an answer? I'm not sure you would. Most of the documents now-a-days contain pictures, and computer assisted layout has really made photo placement and handling easy. So you will certainly need to import pictures, either one per day or may be several each day.

It's certainly one of the features that you are waiting to explore, and you may be wondering why we waited so long to talk about it. This is because it is not as simple as it may seem.

In this chapter, we'll provide you with the information that will help you secure the formatting and printing of your photos. We will see:

◆ How to import photos, keep them where we place them, and make sure that they are always where they have been placed, especially in relation to your layout and your original photos

◆ How to set the photos to make them match the printing needs

◆ How to apply effects to the photos

◆ How to improve the workflow between the image editing software that you have and Scribus

◆ How to use and import vector drawings

Importing and exporting: The concepts

We have already used some pictures in this book. But before we begin to go deeper into the subject and see what the possibilities are, it seems important that we clarify some conceptual points. If you are used to DTP software, you won't learn much here and may want to go directly to the next chapter. If you're not, read the following paragraphs carefully. It will help you to understand some of the functionality that we will talk about in this chapter.

To begin with, remember that there are two kinds of graphics you can add to your layout. You can have photos, generally taken from a digital camera, downloaded, or bought on some website. Photos will generally be stored in JPEG files, but you can also find PNG, TIFF, or many other file formats. The second kind of graphics is vector drawings such as logos and maps. They are computer-made drawings and are stored as EPS or SVG files. You will certainly need to work with both in most of your documents.

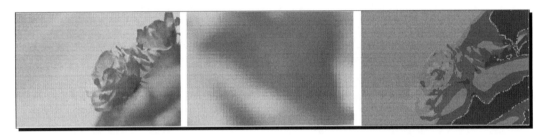

The previous image shows the comparison between a photo on the left-hand side, and the same photo traced in vectors on the right-hand side. In the middle, see how the details of the photo are made up of square pixels that are sometimes difficult to handle to get good printing results.

The first difference is that with photos, you will need to place them in a frame. There are some tips to automatically add the frame, but anyway, a frame will be needed. Vector drawings are imported as shapes and can be manipulated in Scribus like any other Scribus object.

The second difference is that when working with photos, you will have to import them within Scribus. The term "import" is precise here. Most text processors don't import but insert images. In the case of "insert", the images are definitely stored in your document. So you can send this document to anyone via e-mail or can store it on any external storage device without caring about whether these images will still be present later. Scribus does it differently: it adds to the frame a reference to the imported file's own storage position. Scribus will look for the file each time it needs it, and if the file is not where it should be, problems may arise. Basically, the steps you go through while performing a DTP import and while performing a text processor insert are the same, but the global workflows are different because the professional needs to which they refer to are different. All the communication software, layout programs, website building software, as well as video editing software perform the same steps. Once you're used to it, it's really handy: it results in lighter and more adaptable files.

However, while teaching Scribus, I have many times received mails from students who have trouble with the images in their documents, just because they didn't take enough care of this little difference. Remembering it will really help you to work peacefully. We will of course go through the details several times in this chapter.

DTP versus text processors again

Here we are talking about the default behavior of the software. As text processors can now work with frames, they often import the image as a link. Scribus itself should be able to embed pictures in its next release. Will the difference between these two pieces software one day disappear?

The next difference is about the color space of the pictures. Cameras use RAW or JPEG (which are RGB documents). Offset printers, which everyone usually refers to, are based on the CMYK (Cyan, Magenta, Yellow, and Black) model. Traditionally, most proprietary packages ask the users to convert RGB files into CMYK. With Scribus there is no need to do so. You can import your graphics as RGB and Scribus will export them all as desired at the end of the process (which most of the time is exporting to PDF). If you want an on-screen, accurate preview of the colors as they will be printed, refer to the color management section of Chapter 9. So, if you use GIMP, you shouldn't be embarrassed by its default lack of CMYK support.

CMYK in GIMP

If you really want to import CMYK photos into Scribus, you can use the GIMP Separate plugin to convert an RGB document to a CMYK. Batch converting can be easily done using the convert utility of ImageMagick. Consider using the new CMYKTool software too, which gives some nice color test tools and options, including ink coverage.

That said, we now have to see how it really works in Scribus.

Importing photos

To import photos, you simply have to:

1. Create an Image Frame with the **Insert Image Frame** tool (*I*) or with a shape or polygon converted to an Image Frame.

2. Go to **File | Import | Get Image** or use *Ctrl + D*.

This is the most common way to do it. On some systems, you can even drag the picture from your folder into the frame. The thing that you should never do is copy the photo (wherever it is) and paste it into your frame. When doing this, Scribus has no knowledge of the initial picture's storage location (because the copied image is placed in a special buffer shared among the applications), and that's what it needs.

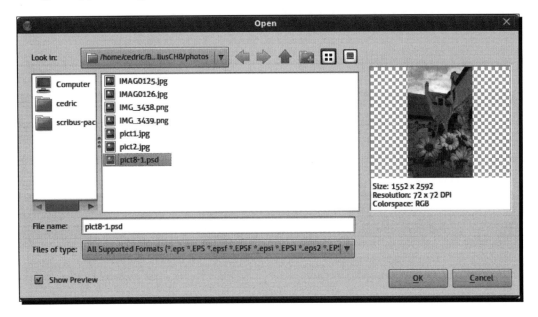

There are other ways to import an image. You can use:

- ◆ The DirectImageImport script
- ◆ The Picture Browser on some very new and experimental Scribus versions (this one might change so we won't talk about it for now)

The **DirectImageImport** script is placed in the **Script | Scribus Scripts** menu. It will display a window waiting for you to specify which image to import. Once you validate, Scribus automatically creates the frame and places the image within. Some people find it useful because it seems that you can save one step this way. But, in fact, the frame size is a default based on the page width, so you will have to customize it. You might have to draw it directly with a good size and it should be as easy. But anyway, you'll choose the one you prefer. Always remember that each image needs a frame.

The image might be smaller or bigger than the frame. In the first case it won't fill it, and in the second case it will appear cropped. You can adapt the frame size as you want; the photo won't change at all. However, one thing you will certainly want to do is move the picture within the frame to select a better area. To do this, double-click on the frame to go into the Content Editing mode; you can now drag the picture inside to place it more precisely.

The contextual menu of the Image Frame will give you two menus that will help to make the size of the image the same as that of the frame:

- **Adjust Image to Frame** will extend or reduce the photo so that it fills the frame but keeps the photo's height to width ratio
- **Adjust Frame to Image** will modify the frame size so that it fits the image

In both cases, once applied, you can change the size of the frame as you need to and the photo will automatically be scaled to fit the frame size. Using such options is really interesting because it is fast and easy, but it is not without some risk. We'll see how to prepare the image for optimal results in the *Image resolution and scaling* section of this chapter.

When a frame shape is changed after the image is imported, the image itself doesn't change. For example, if you use any of the skew buttons in the **Node** window (**Edit** button of the **Shape** tab of PP) you'll see that the frame will be skewed but not the picture itself. Image changes have to be made in an image manipulation program.

Relinking photos

Once your photos have been imported and they fit perfectly in your page content, you may wish to stop for a day or show this to some other people. It's always a good idea to make your decisions later, as you'll see more weaknesses a few days later.

It is generally at this point that problems appear. If you send your Scribus `.sla` document for proofreading, the photos won't be displayed on the proofreader's screen as they are not embedded into the file.

The same issue arises if you decide to move or rename some folders or photos on your own computer. Since Scribus just saves the location of your files and loads them when necessary, it won't be able to find them anymore.

In this case, don't worry at all. Nothing is lost; it is just that Scribus has no idea of what you have done to your file—you will just need to tell it. At this point, you have two possibilities:

- Import the photos that have disappeared, again, so that Scribus can save their new location.

◆ Go to **Extra | Manage Images.** Show where the photos have gone by choosing the missing photo (shown with red diagonals crossing the image display area) and clicking on the **Search** button just below it.

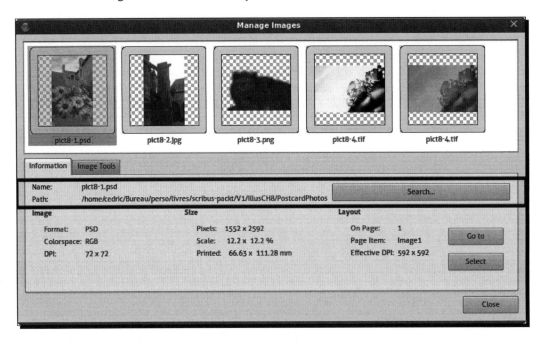

When relinking, you can link to another image if you wish; these images just need to have the same name to make Scribus guess it's the good one. So it will be very important that you give unique names to your photos. You can define some naming rules, or keep the camera automatic numbering.

If you need to send your document to someone, you can either send a PDF that can't be modified, just annotated, or the whole Scribus document along with the photos. The best thing for this is not to compress the photo folder. It won't make the link into Scribus for they are absolute and the folder path name will differ on your reader's computer. They would need to relink every picture and that might take long for some documents. The best technique is to use the built-in **File | Collect for Output** window. It will ask you to create a new directory in which all the files needed for that document will be copied with relative paths, so that it will work everywhere. Compress this folder and send it.

Time for action – creating a postcard

As an example, let's create a postcard. It's an easy document that won't need many features and, therefore, we can concentrate on our image issues. We'll go through the dos and don'ts to let you experiment with the problems that you might have with a bad workflow. We will use this example throughout the chapter and get back to it later to explain some parts.

1. Let's create a two page, A6 landscape document with a small margin guide of 6mm.

2. After creating the page, use **Page | Manage Guides** and add one vertical guide with a gap of 5mm and one horizontal guide with a gap of 20mm.

3. In the first frame, import (**File | Import | Get Image**) the pict8-1.psd file. Notice that it is in a folder called Photos, with some other files that we will use in this document. When you're in the file selector, Scribus shows some file information: you can see the size in pixels (1552x2592), the resolution (72x72), and the colorspace (RGB). This information will help us later.

4. This image will look very big in the frame. Right-click and choose **Adjust Image to Frame**. It fits the height but not the width. Also we'd want the bottom of the flower image to be at the bottom of the frame. Open the Properties Palette and in the **Image** tab, select the **Free Scaling** option and change the X-scale and Y-scale up to 12 or a value close to it. Now it might be better.

5. In the top right-hand side frame, import pict8-2.jpg and set it in the best way you can using the same procedure. Double-click on the frame and drag the picture to find the best placement.

6. Then in the last frame of the first page, import the pict8-3.png file.

7. You can add frame text and type something inside it, such as "Utopia through centuries", and set it nicely.

8. On the second page we'll use one horizontal column without gap and one vertical column with a 5mm gap.

9. On the right-hand part of the horizontal guide (use **Page | Snap to Guides** if you want to be sure) draw an horizontal line from one vertical to another bordering that one.

10. Keep this line selected and go to **Item | Multiple Duplicate**. In the window, choose 4 copies, leave the next option selected, and define a 0.4 inch vertical gap. Here it is necessary to write the address.

11. At the bottom left-hand corner of the same page, draw a new Image Frame in which you can import the pict8-4.tif file.

12. In the **Image** properties, scale the image to the frame size and deselect **Proportional** so that the image fills the frame perfectly, even if it is distorted.

13. Then in the **XYZ** tab of the PP, click on the **Flip Horizontally** button (the blue double arrow icon). We'll deal with the sky of this picture later.

14. We have now set our pages and the photos are placed correctly. Let's create some errors voluntarily. First, let's say we rename the Photos folder to PostcardPhotos. This must be done in your file browser; you cannot do it from Scribus.

15. Go back to Scribus. Things might not have changed for now, but if you right-click on an image and choose **Update Image** you will see that it won't be displayed anymore.

16. If you want everything to go well again, you can rename your folder again or go to **Extras | Manage Images**. You see there that each Image Frame of the document is listed and that they contain nothing because the photos are not found anymore. For each image selected in this window, you'll have to click on the **Search** button and specify which directory it has been moved into in the next window. Scribus will display the image found (image with a similar name only). Select one of the listed images and click on **Select**. Everything should go well now.

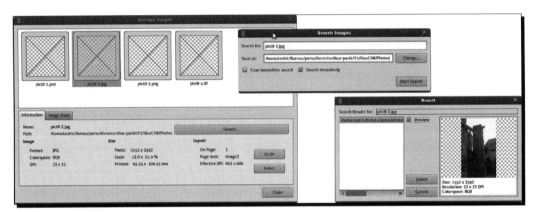

What just happened?

After having created our page, we placed our photos inside the frames. By renaming the folder we broke the link between Scribus and the image files. The **Manage Images** window lets us see what happened. The full paths to the pictures are displayed here. In our example, all the pictures are in the same folder, but you could have imported pictures from several directories. In this case, only those being included in the renamed folder would have disappeared from the Scribus frames.

By clicking on **Search**, we told Scribus what happened to those pictures and that those pictures still exist but somewhere else. Notice that if you deleted the photos they will be lost forever. The best advice would be to keep a copy of everything: the original as well as the modified photos. Notice that if your images are stored on an external device, it should be plugged and mounted.

In fact, renaming the folder is not the only reason why an image might disappear. It happens when:

- ◆ We rename the image folder
- ◆ We rename any parent folder of the image folder
- ◆ We rename the picture
- ◆ We delete the picture
- ◆ We delete the whole folder containing the picture

Giving the documents and the pictures to someone else by an e-mail or an USB-key will certainly be similar to the second case. In the first three cases, using the **Manage Images** window will help you find the images (it's better to know where they are). In the last two cases, you should be ready to look for new pictures and import them into the frames.

The Scribus paste special

What happens if you paste an image into a frame? Normally, nothing should happen and the frame should remain empty. If in any case it gets filled, you should not trust what you see. It's a good idea to go to **Manage Images** and check the path for each image. If a pasted image exists, there should be no name under the picture and the path should be wrong or empty.

On the other hand, if you imported a picture using the right method, you can copy-paste the frame without trouble.

We have already used another paste option while pasting the content onto more frames. This happens when you use **Edit | Contents | Copy** and **Edit | Contents | Paste (Absolute)** instead of the standard **Edit | Copy** and **Edit | Paste**. In this case, the same picture will be put inside the frames but each copy will have the same coordinates so that it would look as if the same image was going from one frame to another. We have used it before in a Chapter 7 tutorial.

You could, alternatively, have chosen **Edit | Contents | Paste**. In this case, the copied image would have been put in this new frame but with local coordinates. Therefore, the left-hand corner of the picture would have been at the left-hand corner of the frame. It is interesting when you want to put the same image in some existing frames: generally some information icons or so.

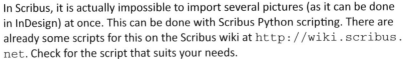

Importing several pictures

In Scribus, it is actually impossible to import several pictures (as it can be done in InDesign) at once. This can be done with Scribus Python scripting. There are already some scripts for this on the Scribus wiki at `http://wiki.scribus.net`. Check for the script that suits your needs.

It's important to check if the frames aren't linked to each other. If you change the picture for one of these frames, the others won't be modified. If you want to change the picture of a frame that has been copied or duplicated and in which some settings, such as scaling or adjustment to frame, have been modified, the new picture of that frame will have these settings applied by default. Copying or duplicating an Image Frame can be a good way to save time when some properties have to be put on several frames.

Placing vector drawings

Vector drawings differ from photos in a way that instead of being a grid of pixels (colored points) they are geometrical formulas defining shapes and are constantly interpreted by the software to calculate their on-screen render on a page. Vector drawings are perfect for graphics that need to be used at several sizes, like logos. They are perfect for documents that need precise rendering such as maps. The trouble with photos is when they need to be resized, they lose their quality, especially when scaled up. So when it's possible (that is, when the graphic result is made up of shapes or lines with flat colors or simple gradients) we try to avoid them. Vector graphics cannot replace the photos because their rendering differs too much. The rule would be: use vector graphics where a photo is not needed.

There is no way to replace a photo by a vector drawing because their graphical qualities are different. Vector drawings are mostly done with simple shapes, flat colors, or gradients. In some killer use case they can have a realistic aspect, but it's not easy to create such drawings with vectors. Vectors are for precise drawings, but they can never be as detailed as a photo can be.

In the tutorial at the beginning of Chapter 2, we already imported a logo, and in the import Openoffice.org Calc tutorial we used a vector file too. What are the specific things to remember about Scribus vector file handling?

- Importing a vector file does not need any Image Frame. It can be imported directly.
- If necessary, vector EPS or PDF files can be placed in an Image Frame. In this case, they will be rasterized at the time of export. The quality of the rasterization can be defined in the **General** tab of the PDF export window (**File | Export | Save as PDF**) as **Resolution for EPS graphics**, where 300 is the default value.
- Scribus won't remember the original vector drawing file path. So, there will be no trouble with the linking, but there is no means to automatically update the file into Scribus when it is changed in another software. Imported vector drawings are not listed in the **Manage Images** window.
- The imported drawing can be freely resized inside Scribus by using the handles around its select box, like a frame or frame group can be.
- Vector files are made of geometrical shapes and Scribus imports those frames as a group. You can affect some of these by ungrouping.
- The colors applied to the shapes of the imported drawings are automatically added to the file swatch and they appear in the color lists in the **Color** tab as well as in the **Text** tab of the PP.

- If the colors are changed in the Scribus color window (see next chapter), the colors will be modified in the drawings that contain it. The color of the logo can be changed on each shape of the ungrouped drawing. It's very practical, for example, when you want to use the same color on text or inside the drawing.

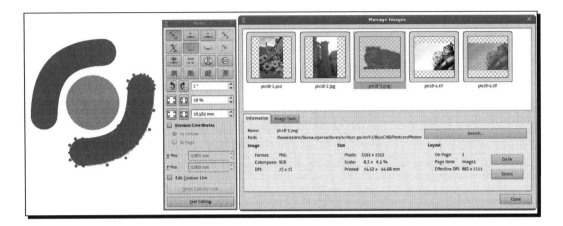

These are the good things about Scribus vector support. But there are some issues too:

- Actually, you can't import any SVG file into a frame, which makes a little difference in format processing and is always difficult to remember.

- Some of the advanced vector functionalities like blurs are not interpreted by Scribus. So when a vector drawing is imported, a message box is displayed. Just validate and continue the import process by clicking on the page. See that the result in the page is good. If not, you can try another vector format or convert your vector to a raster image that will be imported in an Image Frame. Most of the vector drawing programs can do this. In Inkscape use **File | Export as bitmap**.

About graphic file formats

Choosing the right format for the right use case is one of the most important decisions that a designer has to take. The file format is not about which software to use, but about what will be saved by this software inside the picture so that you can use it later in Scribus or any other document. Many users don't care enough about this step and miss very nice possibilities and need to tweak around when it should be so easy.

Mainly, we will have file formats for photos and other raster images, and formats for vector drawings. JPEG, PNG, PSD, or TIF are formats for photos and raster images, and EPS or SVG are formats for vector drawings. PDF is separate.

JPEG

JPEG (Joint Photographic Expert Group) is a well-known image format—maybe the best known. It doesn't steal its place. It has a lot of qualities: it can drastically decrease the size of a file by compressing with a very high-level algorithm that interprets the content of an image and compresses it using some kind of optical compliance. The bad side of JPEG is that whatever you can do, once you choose to save a file in JPEG, you lose some details. Generally, when printing a document, you want to get the best result at the end.

I can remember a time when the print office was saying: "please, everything but JPEG". Of course, things have changed now and they can handle it easily, but I still feel unconfident with this format, at least for high quality prints.

In fact, JPEG can sometimes be interesting: because the files are lightweight, and some processes of the printing workflow will go faster with it. The best thing is to ask your provider if it's a good idea to use it.

In any case, JPEGs will be simple to handle if you use your own camera. Most cameras save your photos in this format. Some others save them as RAW, which is the very best but has a weight increased at least by ten. RAW formats, which are camera specific, cannot be imported into Scribus. Their purpose is to match exactly what the camera grabbed. They need some preprocessing in some dedicated software before being exported into a standard file type and being used in other software.

RAW with UFRaw or digiKam

There are many free software than can open and convert RAW files. UFRaw can be used as a standalone or with a GIMP plugin. digiKam is a very complete photo management program that includes tagging, editing, and other interesting functionality. Some other software, such as Rawstudio or darktable are simpler and very specialized. Do some tests and keep the one that is best for you.

If you decide to use JPEGs in your layouts, you have to take care of the quality. JPEG is very good for photos, but can completely destroy a drawing or any line art document. When saving in JPEG, activate the preview if your photo-editing software can do it. Then you can decrease the quality until the result is nice, the file size will decrease too. Our way is to keep 100 percent of the quality each time, to keep as much as possible. It's a good idea to keep the original file or save your JPEG with a new name so that it doesn't replace the previous file. This way, you can go back to the original if the result is not as good as expected.

PNG

PNG stands for **Portable Network Graphics** and is a World Wide Web Consortium (http://www.w3c.org) recommendation. It is not as famous as JPEG but it is becoming popular in print offices since Mac OS has good support of it. PNG support has been very good in free software for many years.

Scribus can use PNGs without trouble and any free or open-source photo editing program should support it.

PNG files are generally bigger in size than JPEG files, but not always. However, they provide three benefits:

◆ PNG save files with a lossless compression. It means that whatever the compression ratio you use, your image will remain exactly the same, as perfect as the first time you opened and saved it. If the file is a photo, don't use 8-bit PNG, as it can save only 256 colors (which is not enough to keep all the colors).

◆ PNG doesn't modify the pixels and, therefore, the colors are not modified with the saving process. It is important if you want to import graphs or logos saved in that format, especially logos with blurs that could have been done in Inkscape or Adobe Illustrator, or any other vector drawing program.

◆ PNG can have an alpha channel: it means that the background of the PNG file can be transparent, thus allowing some custom borders for the pictures.

In the previous document we have imported a PNG file. Look at the blur around the lion. Move your frame above another and see how they mix perfectly thanks to the alpha information.

TIFF

TIFF (or **TIF Tagged Image File Format**) is a very old format created by Aldus, the company that created the first real layout program called PageMaker. This company was acquired by Adobe in the 90s. TIFF was explicitly made for high-quality image printing thanks to lossless compression. TIFF files are very heady but they can handle CMYK.

In Scribus, we don't really need CMYK pictures because the software can be color managed (see the next chapter). TIFF compression will not be better than PNG, and so we usually prefer the W3C standard when there is no special demand for using TIFF.

You should notice that proprietary TIFFs, especially from Photoshop, can differ from the free format:

◆ They can handle some alpha channels

◆ They can handle layers

Both are unsupported by Scribus. On the other hand, Scribus can perfectly use paths included in TIFF files. These paths are made within the image editing program, such as Photoshop or GIMP, and are saved within the file. The *Working with clipping paths* section will provide us with more information about the use case of such properties. In fact, this use case is the last that makes us choose TIF over PNG when needed.

PSD

PSD stands for **Photoshop Document**, and is the native format of Adobe Photoshop. Since it is the most commonly-used software in the print industry, it's file format became the de facto standard. The trouble with it is that it is not an open format. This legal issue results in the fact that free software can only implement PSD functionalities up to the seventh version of Adobe's software, which is now quite old. But even in this case, PSD does everything TIFF can do plus some other nice goodies.

Mostly, there is no need to provide full access to Photoshop's functionalities, and even InDesign (Adobe's layout software) can import PSD, but with very weak handling capacities. So, the only thing you save in using a PSD file is just not using another one.

But if you need to work in a workflow that uses PSD files, you'll have to do it carefully. Remember that Scribus can open standard layers and can handle them quite well (including layer blending modes even if the rendering can differ a little). If you want to know more about using PSD in Scribus, refer to the *Image layers* section of this chapter.

	EmptyA4-300.jpg	50,2 Kio	JPEG Image
	EmptyA4-300.png	32,5 Kio	image PNG
TIFF	EmptyA4-300-CMYK.tif	33,3 Mio	image TIFF
	FlowerA4-300.jpg	1,5 Mio	JPEG Image
	FlowerA4-300.png	3,3 Mio	image PNG
TIFF	FlowerA4-300-CMYK.tif	33,4 Mio	image TIFF

EPS

EPS is an evolution of the PostScript language. PostScript is THE language, created by Adobe, that made all the actual printing standard workflows happen. Without PostScript, the printing environment would have been very different. PostScript was born in 1981 and has been modified nearly every ten years to take into account new needs and possibilities. PostScript made vector happen in the printing process and typography.

Print offices have got used to considering PostScript as the best format for everything because PostScript is the language that describes the way a page will be printed. Encapsulated PostScript then became one of the natural, default file formats.

Unfortunately, or happily, things are changing:

- Bases of PostScript are old and changes would be too important: it seems that PostScript is not going to be updated anymore.

- PostScript has some weaknesses.

- PostScript files require some special understanding of the print workflow that don't match actual print on demand or WYSIWYG user needs. If, in printing, what you get is never what you see on screen, users will have some bad results and it will take time in the workflow to avoid them.

The EPS file you'll find now will certainly consist of logos or such drawings—nothing more. We used it to import tables from OpenOffice.org Calc passed through OpenOffice.org Draw, which was the EPS exporter. We already saw that the colors of the EPS were added to the document color list. Their name begins with FromEPS followed by hexadecimal values of the color. The colors are kept as RGB, CMYK, or spot.

Inkscape has some nice options to define how text and effects will be exported. If the SVG drawing is not well imported into Scribus, try PDF or EPS and export text as outlines. Rasterize filter effects at a resolution around 300. But even the Inkscape team is not working hard on EPS support because it is not considered as the future and is more of a waste of time.

PDF

Inkscape now prefers PDF to EPS. Remember that PDF has been created by Adobe to replace EPS and tries to avoid the weakness of the Encapsulated file format. But even now, after more than 15 years of existence, PDF is becoming difficult. Everyone knows it because there are many free-of-charge readers including Adobe Acrobat Reader, which is still the best, and some free software like Evince.

Chapter 8

However, very few people know the differences between the PDF versions because PDF is a container that has evolved a lot too. PDF can now contain video or 3D animations, which are really unnecessary in the printing world, and are kind of opposite in the color models. So yes, PDF is the final absolute file format that we use a lot, even in Scribus, but more as an export format. PDFs can be imported within Image Frames and in this case everything will be rasterized, which will result in a loss of quality, even if it's difficult to perceive for a standard reader. The Scribus team is actually working hard on better support, but very few pieces of software can actually do it, because PDF has always been considered by Adobe as everything but the overall saving format. PDF is made for final saving and keeps the result only. You should not consider your PDF file to be modified even if you or other people would sometimes like too.

Adobe Illustrator AI format

`.ai` files are actually a subset of PDF. So, Scribus can handle them as well as PDF. However, AI is a proprietary and closed format; so there might be an unknown amount of unsupported features. There may be difficulties with PDFs coming from many kinds of software, which have very specific features that can't be interpreted by others. Adobe Illustrator users may notice that their software can save in SVG too. So it can sometimes help to try with both formats and just keep the best.

SVG

If you need to use vector drawings in your workflow using free software, you will certainly use **SVG**, the **Scalable Vector Graphics** recommendation of the W3C. It is an Inkscape default format, GIMP can handle it, and it is one of the formats of choice in Scribus too. SVG files are pure vector, even if they can contain pictures. Their source is an XML subset so that they can easily be edited and dynamically modified, while perfectly matching the open source and free software needs.

If you run Inkscape to create your file, you should be advised that Inkscape has its own SVG tags. It is safer to save your document as plain SVG before importing it into Scribus.

Apart from that, SVG is a very broad recommendation and no graphic editor can edit all the specifications at present. Inkscape is certainly the best but Adobe Illustrator can save and open SVG too. If we compare layout programs to them, they are a bit less packed with features, so there might be some loss of some functionality when importing. Scribus warns on that subject: it displays a message that invites you to control the imported result.

The colors of the SVG are added to the document color list. Their name begins with FromSVG, followed by hexadecimal values of the color. SVG color can only be RGB. Scribus can interpret them as CMYK if there is a color profile defined and the color is described in the SVG with a five digit number. Unfortunately, Inkscape cannot do it by itself and we still have to add it manually, which makes this import functionality inefficient. The next SVG recommendation will certainly be compliant with more color models, including spot color, so we'll have to wait a bit.

Scribus in particular can hardly support SVG transparencies, blurs, and primitive filters. When needing them in your layout, you should prefer a raster format like PNG, or may be PDF. Another trick is that SVG uses the system fonts. If the file you use has not been made on your own computer, text might be changed. Tell your graphic artist to convert text to outline before sending you the SVG or ask for a vectorized EPS (it can be done in the Inkscape EPS option dialog). SVG will clearly be more and more supported by free software, and even if you're not used to this format it's a good thing to keep an eye on it.

File information

Now you might have a better idea of what a layout is: a mix of shapes, frames, images, and text; a mix of made and imported documents of several types. It's important to keep an eye on the original documents and be sure we are not faked by some properties.

You will have two ways of getting information about an image:

◆ The Image Frame contextual menu **Info**

◆ The **Manage Images** window

Both display quite similar information. The Info box will display the name of the imported image, its resolution, color space, and whether printing of this frame is enabled. To save memory, printing can be enabled or disabled by clicking on the printer icon in the **XYZ** tab of the PP.

Manage Images will be more precise as this window gives the full path, the scale factor, and the name of the frame in which it is imported, plus some extra functionalities that we'll see in the next pages.

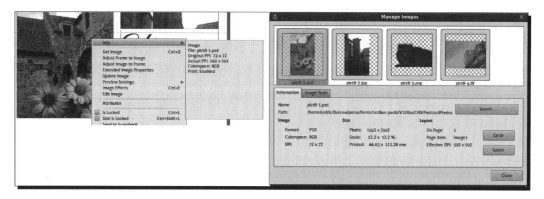

Generally, if you just need to be sure about some properties of a single image, you'll use the **Info** menu. If you really need to control images, it's better to use the **Manage Images** window because it lists all the pictures so that you won't have to browse through your document pages.

Image resolution and scaling

When you import your photos into a frame, you can adapt the photos to the size of the frame by using:

- The Image Frame contextual menu (**Adjust Image to Frame**). With this option the image cannot be dragged inside the frame. Free scaling has to be enabled in the **Image** tab of the PP.

- The **Scale To Frame Size** option of the **Image** tab of the PP. It does the same as **Adjust Image to Frame** and automatically keeps proportions.

- The **X-Scale** and **Y-Scale** values of the same tab when free scaling is enabled. Notice that when using **Free Scaling**, the image doesn't move within the frame. The top left corner remains at its position.

What you should absolutely remember is that any image resizing into the frame will change the image resolution. The best method is to always prepare the photo at the right size in a photo editing program. This is particularly true if your picture needs to be enlarged. If your resolution is too small, the printed image will be ugly and if it's too large Scribus will have to change it with a default setting on which you'll have no control.

GIMP has the **Image | Print Size** option that helps you set the **resolution** and the **Image | Image Size** option to set the size in pixels or any other units. My advice would be to first set the resolution to 300 (which is considered as a standard) and then the best option is to give the picture the exact size of your frame so that you won't have to do any final adjustment in Scribus.

Always choose pictures large in width. Having an image set to 300 PPI gives better printed results, but it will be much smaller on your page. It's very easy to calculate: if you need 300 pixels for an inch and want to have full A4 size, that is, around 12 inches, you'll need a 300x12 = 3600 pixels high picture, which is about a 9 megapixels image (width will be 300x8.2 = 2460, which gives 3600*2460 an average of 8,856,000). Check your camera properties to know if you can safely do so.

Cameras have no resolution and they give as many pixels as they can. The way pixels will be organized is relative to the display device. Screens are between 72 and 100 pixels per inch. So the same image will look about three or four times smaller when it will be converted to 300dpi. A full screen image you download from a website will be about 1000 pixels wide, which means a good print results in around 3 inches only. Always try to get the biggest image you can. The more pixels you have the more free you'll be and the better the results can be. It is easier to down size an image than enlarge it because in this case the software has to create pixels that don't exist, which is a very difficult task. The illustration shows the quality of the original image at 1000 pixels high and on the right the same image set to 250 pixels and back to 1000. We can see that the object edges have been affected and are more or less blurry, especially around the window.

Once the image is properly set in your photo editing software, just import it into your frame. It should have the right width or height or, even better, match the exact size. You can then do a quick adjustment to frame size. Have a quick glance at the image information and verify that the original PPI match what you've done in GIMP (that is, 300 PPI) and that the actual PPI is about the same. The actual PPI should never be under 144 for a document to be printed. If the resolution is too low, Scribus will warn you when exporting to PDF.

Graphic display properties

Up to now, have you already been watching the image quality? I hope so. It might look a bit rough, and you may wonder why because you set it perfectly in your photo editing program as we said previously.

In fact, 300 PPI pictures can be very large in size. An A4 **CMYK** 300 PPI TIF is at least 30MB. If you need to create a hundred pages document, you'll need 3GB of RAM only to display the pictures. To save memory, Scribus doesn't display a picture at its best quality. On some photos you won't see the difference but some others will really become ugly. If you're sure that your image is better than how Scribus shows it, try to change the display setting by right-clicking on the frame and choosing **Preview Settings | Full Resolution**. On the contrary, if you're not so sure of yourself that you do need to see the result, you can choose **Low Resolution** or even disable images by deselecting **Image Visible**. When it is deselected, the content of the frame is not displayed at all; just its filename and some other important information (which we will soon see) are displayed. This way, Scribus will run faster. You can set the default behavior in the Image Frame preferences, in the **Tools** section. Whatever you decide to use, it doesn't affect the printed result. Those options only change the way your image is shown on screen.

Image layers

If you decide to use PSD in your document you'll be able to handle its layers. Image layers have nothing to do with your document layers. They are just relative to the image placed inside the frame.

To set image layers you can open the extended image properties in several ways:

◆ From the Image Frame contextual menu select **Extended Image Properties**

◆ From the **Image** tab of the PP, click on the **Extended Image Properties** button

◆ **Extras | Manage Images** has an **Image Tools** tab that includes an **Extended Image Properties** button too

If those buttons or menus are not there, it is because your image file doesn't have any of these properties that you could be using.

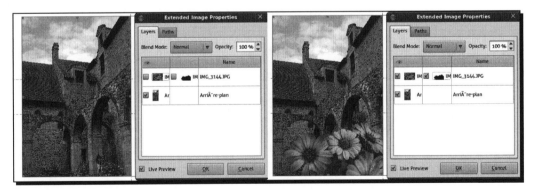

Once you have displayed the **Extended Image Properties** window, you'll see the image structure with several images combined, at the bottom and with the others above each other. The left-hand column shows a preview of the content of the layer, the middle column shows applied masks that are used to hide some parts of the layers, and on the right-hand column you have the layer name. The checkbox on the right-hand side of the preview enables you to completely hide or show a layer. On top of it all, you can set the blending mode or the opacity for each selected layer individually.

Changing those settings doesn't change the image itself, only its instance in the actual frame. So if you use the same image several times in your document, you can use various layer settings. Layers are interesting when you don't exactly know in advance how your picture should look within the page or when you need variations. In other cases, if you don't need layers, just using PNG will be enough.

If you want to do some tests, use the first picture of our preceding tutorial; it is in PSD format with layers and **mask** included.

Working with clipping paths

Clipping paths is another advanced setting that can be used to hide some parts of the picture and isolate some other parts. Unlike layers or masks, clipping will completely hide that part. It can be used to customize the text flow settings. Only one **clipping** can be applied to a single Image Frame.

Clipping is available only with the TIFF file format. In GIMP, we generally use a selection and convert it to a path. GIMP will save all the paths included in your document.

In Scribus they will be available in a tab of the **Extended Image Properties** window that you can simply open in the **Image** tab of the PP.

Time for action – using clipping path twice

The flower picture of our last *Time for action* exercise is a TIFF file and includes a clipping path. Let's go back to this document if you still have it or import this picture in an empty new document to see how to apply the path.

1. Open the **Extended Image Properties** window and you'll see that only the **Path** tab is available. There is no layer in this TIFF because it has been saved in GIMP, which doesn't handle multi-layer support for this format.

2. Only one path is saved in this picture, and it will be easy to choose which you want to apply.

3. Just click on the path and you'll see some parts of the image disappear. These parts are those defined in the path, not necessarily matching any content. If you performed some flipping on the image, you should see that the path doesn't take it into account. If you really need four flippings you'll have to prepare it in the photo editing software. Notice that if you have some color in the frame background, it will show up.

4. If you have some Text Frame under the picture, you can use this clipping path to make the text flow around it. Select the Image Frame and go to the **Shape** tab of the PP.

5. Activate the **Use Image Clip Path** option that is available only if there is a path within the picture.

6. At this point it might not be perfect. We'd like to have some margin between the text and the visible parts of the picture. Click on the **Edit** button of the **Shape** tab to display the **Nodes** window.

7. Click on the **Set Shape to Image Clip Path** button or **Set Contour to Image Clip** if you selected the **Edit Contour Line** option.

8. Put some value in the first field above those buttons and click on the **Enlarge the Size** button at its left-hand side.

9. If you used the contour line in the **Nodes** window, change the flowing values in the **Shape** tab to take that into account.

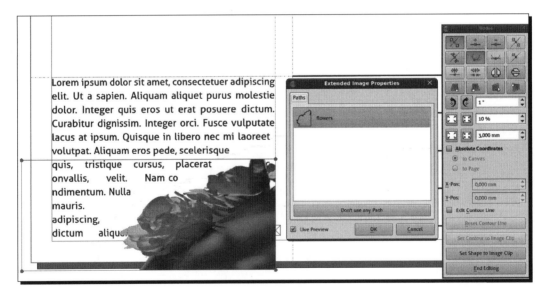

What just happened?

In this example we used the path twice: first to hide some image areas and then to make the text flow around it. You might notice that in some cases the flow is not perfect. It happens generally when a path is made of many points and Scribus seems to have difficulties to actually do its calculation with that. We hope that the new text engine will avoid those issues in the future.

Clipping paths cannot themselves be modified within Scribus, only the usage we have of it. But you can have several paths stored in the file and apply them one by one as you prefer. If you want to have no path applied, just click on the **Don't use any Path** button at the bottom of the **Extended Image Properties** window

Image effects

Scribus has some nice features in editing photos. Generally, you will prefer do that in a photo editing software where you'll have more choice in the functionality and algorithms. However, being able to do some fast, last minute changes is really handy. Plus it will help you to get better results even if you don't want to learn another software.

Image effects can be applied on Image Frames from:

- ◆ The Image Frame contextual menu **Image Effects**
- ◆ The **Image** tab of the PP; click on the **Image Effects** button
- ◆ **Extras | Manage Images** has an **Image Tools** tab that includes an **Image Effects** button too

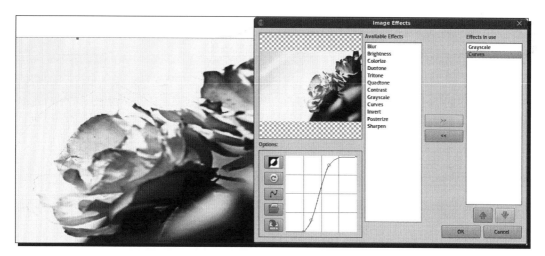

There is a little list of effects and they are very basic operations. You apply an effect by selecting it in the left-hand column and then clicking on the **>>** button. Applied effects are listed in the right-hand column. You can apply as many effects as you need, but generally two or three will be enough. If the effect you chose has some parameters, they appear under the image preview, on the left-hand part of the window.

Some effects, like the curves, can be saved for future use, so that if your picture is taken in the same context it will be very easy to apply similar changes to them. But generally they are so simple they don't need any. If you want to apply the same effect several times, you can just duplicate the frame on which you have the effects applied and replace the image with a new one. This frame can be stored in the **Scrapbook** if you wish.

Applying effects can slow down Scribus because instead of just loading a prepared image it has to do the calculations itself. If you find you applied too many effects, selecting it the right-hand list and clicking the **<<** button will remove it.

Time for action – applying color to an imported graphic

Even if you would preferably apply effects in your photo editing software, it's interesting to have such effects in Scribus when you need duotone documents or you want to use some custom and precise colors on your image.

1. Let's go back to the `pict8-4.tif` file that has some clearly identified colors.

2. Display the **Image Effects** window using the way you like most.

3. First select the **Contrast** and apply it by clicking on **>>**. It should appear in the right-hand column.

4. A slider is now visible under the preview: drag it to the right to increase the contrast as you wish.

5. Then choose the **Grayscale** effect and apply it. It should appear under the previous in the right-hand column. **Grayscale** has no parameter.

6. Then select the **Duotone** effect and apply it. For this **duotone** effect, you'll be able to set the color you want to use and the amount.

7. In the **Color 1** list, choose **Black**, and just under it where 100% is written select 70% instead so that there is less black ink used and we can see more of the next color.

8. In **Color 2**, choose **Cyan**. As we just did, you can change the amount of tint applied to your color or use the right button to display a curve to do the same but with more flexibility.

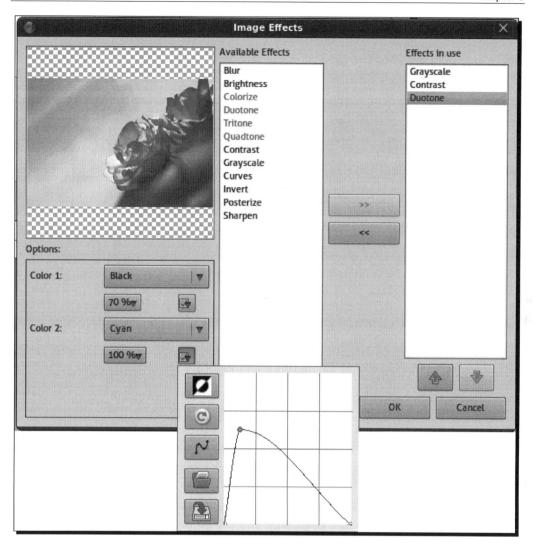

What just happened?

We just used a simple image and applied some effect to it. Some of these effects can be set more precisely thanks to some settings. You should take care of the order: if grayscale is applied after duotone, it is the duotone resampled version that will be converted to grayscale. You can change the order of the effects applied by clicking on the arrows at the bottom of the applied effects lists.

The colors you have in those effects are the colors defined for your document. It is exactly the same color you have available for the frame color and text color. It's very handy. This way you have a very limited choice, which helps you to make a faster choice. You are sure to use the right color and you can easily have the exact same color on any element of your layout. We'll see how to customize this list in the next chapter.

Pop quiz

1. What are the format of choice for your logos?

   a. PSD

   b. EPS

   c. SVG

2. How would you keep transparencies stored in your photos?

   a. Using PSD

   b. Using TIF

   c. Using PNG

3. What resolution would you use for a high-quality document?

   a. 72dpi

   b. 144dpi

   c. 300dpi

   d. 600dpi

4. PNG advantages are:

   a. Lightweight images for fast rendering

   b. An alpha channel that lets the user use transparencies

   c. It enables the use of Spot colors

5. You should use PSD when:

   a. You need clipping path

   b. You need layers

   c. You need effects

6. When scaling an image into a frame:

   a. The original image is scaled at the same time as all instances in your document

   b. Only the current instance is scaled and the resolution doesn't change

   c. Only the current instance is scaled and the resolution changes

   d. The original image is scaled at the same time and applies only to that frame

7. Imported color photos must be:

   a. CMYK images

   b. Grayscale images that we colorize in Scribus

   c. RGB images

Summary

In this chapter we've seen how to use images and drawings. We have dived deeper into some detail to help make your choice between the huge amount of possibilities and software that exist to prepare those photos and help you import the picture with the right settings.

Specifically, we covered:

- How to use bitmap or vector images
- What format can be best used in Scribus
- What advantage you get by using some of these formats in some particular use cases
- How to apply some effects to your image
- And most important, how to prepare the resolution of your image to get a good printed result and how Scribus handles it

In the next chapter, we will see in detail how to customize your colors and what color model you can use in your Scribus documents.

9
Applying and Managing Color

Even though you can see lots of black-only documents (such as books and the daily press) everyday, it's true that there are more and more full-color advertising brochures being printed. So color is becoming an important printing method. An in-between approach of printing with black and only one another color is less interesting, but is still used for many documents and can be considered as a creative approach. In any case, we need to be sure that the color we have on screen matches the printed results. From this, it becomes evident that using color in Scribus is not just a click here or there but is the result of both aesthetic choices and the capacity of the printing process.

In this chapter, we will spend some time on using some color options, and will be able to get a custom render when needed. Especially, we shall:

- ◆ Create and apply CMYK colors
- ◆ Create spot colors
- ◆ Use gradients and patterns
- ◆ Use some transparency options
- ◆ Set the color management render engine

Applying colors in detail

We have already applied colors several times since the beginning of this book. Applying color is as basic as creating a frame or writing text. In our tutorial in Chapter 2, we have used it a lot, and you might find the others if you randomly browse through this book. It is certainly interesting to see more logically what can be done when applying it from where and how.

In this chapter we will often give color values. Each time we need to, we will use the first letter of the color followed by its value. For example, C75 will mean 75 percent of cyan. K will be used for black and B for blue.

There are five main things you could apply colors to:

- Frame or Shape fill
- Frame or Shape border
- Line
- Text
- Text border

You'd like to colorize pictures too. It's a very different method as we have seen in Chapter 8 using duotone or any equivalent image effect.

Applying a color to a frame means that you will use the **Colors** tab of the PP, whereas applying color to text will require you to go to the **Color & Effects** expander in the **Text** tab. In both cases you'll find what's needed to apply color to the fill and the border, but the user interfaces are a bit different.

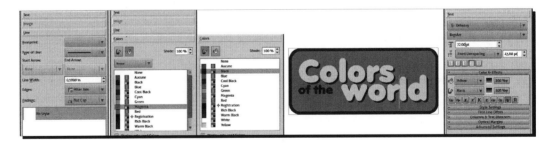

Time for action – applying colors to a Text Frame's text

Colors on frames will use the same color list. Let's follow some steps to see how this is done.

1. Draw a Text Frame where you want it on a page.

2. Type some text inside like "colors of the world" or use **Insert | Sample Text**.

3. Go to the **Colors** tab of the **PP** (*F2*). Click on the second button placed above the color list to specify that you want to apply the changes to the fill.

4. Then click on the color you want in the list below, for example, **Magenta**.

5. Click on the paintbrush button, and apply a black color that will be applied to the border (we could call it stroke too).

6. Don't forget that applying a stroke color will need some border refinements in the **Line** tab to set the width and style of the border. If you need more information about these options, refer to the *Using lines* section of Chapter 7.

7. Now, you can select the text or some part of it and go to the **Colors & Effects** expander of the **Text** tab.

8. Here you will again see the same icon we used previously. Each has its own color list. Let's choose **Yellow** for the text color.

The stroke color cannot be changed. To change this, click on the **Shadow** button placed below, and now choose black as the stroke color. The text shadow should be black.

What just happened?

Color on text is quicker than frame colors in some ways because each has its own list. So, there is no need to click on any button, and you can see both at a glance. Just remember that text has no stroke color activated when setting it first. You need to add the stroke or shadow to a selection to activate the border color for that selection.

Quick apply in story editor

If, like me, you like the **Story Editor** (**Edit | Edit Text**), notice that colors can be applied from there. They are not displayed in the editor but will be displayed when the changes will be applied to the layout. This is much faster, but you need to know exactly what you're doing and need to be precise in your selection.

If you need to apply the same color setting to a word in the overall document, you can alternatively use the **Edit | Search/Replace** window. You can set there the word you're looking for in the first field, and in the right-hand side, replace with the same word, and choose the **Fill** and **Stroke** color that you want to apply. Of course, it would be nice if this window could let us apply character styles to make future changes easier.

The Scribus new document receives a default color list, which is the same all over your document. In this chapter, we will deal with many ways of adapting existing colors or creating new ones.

Applying shade or transparency

Shade and transparency are two ways of setting more precisely how a specific color will be applied on your items. Shades and transparencies are fake effects that will be interpreted by some later elements of the printing workflow, such as Raster Image Processors, to know how the set color can be rendered with pure colors. This is the key point of reproducing colors: if you want a gray, you'll generally have a black color for that. In offset printing which is the reference, the size of the point will vary relatively to the darkness of the black you chose. This will be optically interpreted by the reader.

Using shades

Each color property has a **Shade** value. The default is set to 100 percent, meaning that the color will be printed fully saturated. Reducing the shade value will produce a lighter color. When at 0 percent, the color, whatever it may be, will be interpreted as white.

On a pure color item like any primary or spot, changing the shade won't affect the color composition. However, on processed colors that are made by mixing several primary colors, modifying the shade will proportionally change the amount of each ink used in the process. Our C75 M49 Y7 K12 at a 50 percent shade value will become a C37 M25 Y4 K6 color in the final PDF. Less color means less ink on the paper and more white (or paper color), which results in a lighter color.

You should remember that **Shade** is a frame property and not a color property. So, if you apply a new color to the frame, the shade value will be kept and applied immediately.

To change the shade of the color applied to some characters, it will be a bit different: we don't have a field to fill but a drop-down list with predefined values of 10 percent increments. If you need another value, just choose **Other** to display a window in which you'll add the amount that you exactly need. You can do the same in the **Text Editor**.

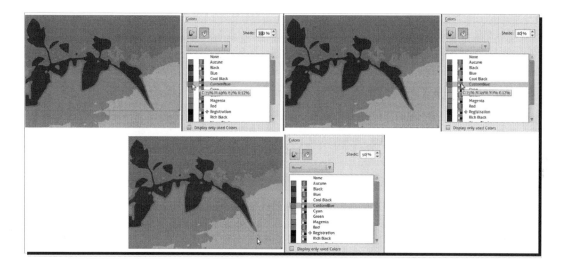

Using transparency

While shade is used to lighten a color, the **Opacity** value will tell you how the color will be less solid. Once again, the range goes from **0%**, meaning the object is completely **transparent** and invisible, to **100%** to make it opaque.

The latter value is the default. When two objects overlap, the top object hides the bottom object. But when **Opacity** is decreased, the object at the bottom will become more and more visible.

One difference to notice is that **Opacity** won't affect only the color rendering but the content too (if there is some).

As for **Shade**, **Opacity** too is applied separately to the fill and to the stroke. So you'll need to set both if needed. One important aspect is that **Shade** and **Opacity** can both be applied on the frame and a value **50%** of each will give a lighter color than if only one was used. Several opacity values applied to objects show how they can act and add to each other:

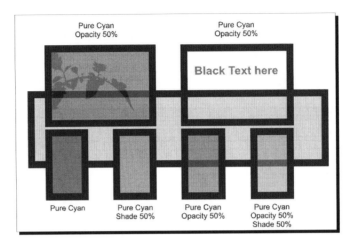

The background for the text in the title, in the following screenshot, is done in the same color as the background at the top of the page. Using transparency or shade can help create this background and decrease the number of used colors.

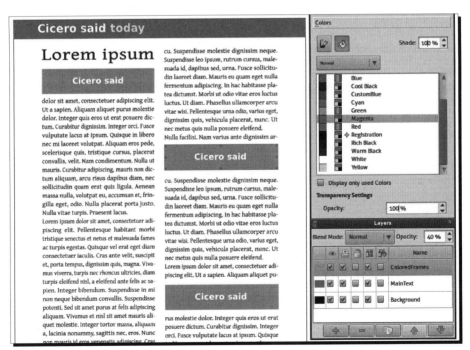

Time for action – transparency and layers

Let's now use transparency and layers to create some custom effects over a picture, as can often be done for covers.

1. Create a new document and display the **Layers** window from the **Windows** menu.

2. This window will already contain a line called **Background**. You can add a layer by clicking on the **+** button at the bottom left-hand side of the window: it will be called **New Layer 1**. You can rename it by double-clicking on its name.

3. On the first page of it, add an Image Frame that covers the entire page.

4. Then draw a rectangular shape that covers almost half of the page height.

5. Duplicate this layer by clicking on the middle button placed at the bottom of the **Layers** window.

6. Select the visibility checkbox (it is the first column headed with an eye icon) of this layer to hide it.

7. We'll modify the transparency of each object. Click on **New Layer 1** to specify that you want to work on this layer; otherwise you won't be able to select its frames.

8. The frames or shapes you'll create from now on will be added to this layer called **New Layer 1**.

9. Select the black shape and decrease the **Opacity** value of the **Colors** tab of the PP to **50%**. Do the same for the Image Frame.

10. Now, hide this layer by clicking on its visibility icon and show the top layer.

11. In the **Layers** window, verify if this layer is selected and decrease its opacity.

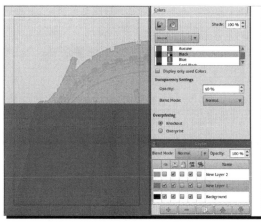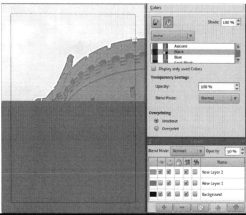

What just happened?

If there is a need to make several objects transparent at once, an idea would be to put them on a layer and set the layer **Opacity**. This way, the same amount of transparency will be applied to the whole. You can open the **Layer** window from the **Window** menu.

When working with layers, it's important to have the right layer selected to work on it. Basically, any new layer will be added at the top of the stack and will be activated once created.

When a layer is selected, you can change the **Opacity** of this layer by using the field on the top right-hand side of the **Layer** window. Since it is applied to the layer itself, all the objects placed on it will be affected, but their own opacity values won't be changed. If you look at the differences between the two layers we have made, you'll see that the area in the first black rectangle explicitly becomes transparent by itself because you can see the photo through it. This is not seen in the second.

So using layer, as we have seen, can help us work faster when we need to apply the same opacity setting to several objects, but we have to take care, because the result is slightly different.

Using layers to blend colors

More rarely, layers can be used to mix colors. **Blend Mode** is originally set to **Normal**, which does no blending. But if you use any other mode on a layer, its colors will be mixed with colors of the item placed on a lower layer, relatively to the chosen mode. This can be very creative. If you need a more precise action, **Blend Mode** can be set to **Single Object** from the **Colors** tab of the PP. Just give it a try.

Layers are still most commonly used to organize a document: a layer for text, a layer for images, a layer for each language for a multi-lingual document, and so on. They are a smart way to work, but are not necessary in your documents and really we can work without them in a layout program.

Gradients and pattern fill

Even if most of the layout objects are filled with flat and well chosen colors, it happens that we need more complex visual effects. Gradients that can be of two- or n-color and pattern fills that can be made of very complex shapes are some of the options that Scribus provides.

Applying gradients

Of course, flat colors are not the only fill that you can add. We generally use flat colors, but **gradients** are used in some cases too. The problem with gradients is that they are not easy to print and readability can be worse. Beginners often use gradients to fill areas and backgrounds. Of course, it is possible, but where another solution could be used, it should be used.

In Scribus, gradients will be made of swatch colors from the document color list. Unfortunately, gradients cannot be added to this list. So, if you need to use the same gradients several times you should consider:

- ◆ Seeing if the gradient cannot be part of a master page
- ◆ Adding the frame with the gradient applied in the Scrapbook
- ◆ Copying and pasting a frame containing the gradient

Of course, you can keep the composition of your gradient somewhere to be able to use it later without duplicating old frames. It will be easy for a simple two-color gradient but difficult with a more complex gradient.

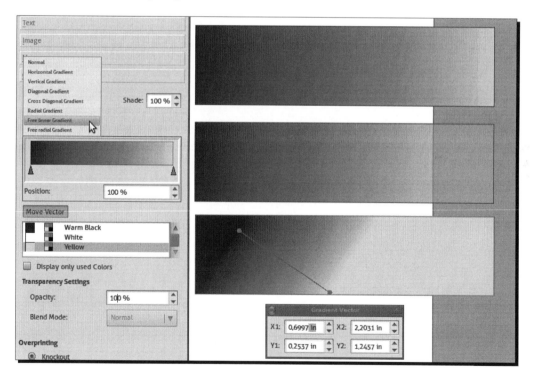

There is no special tool to apply a gradient manually. Everything is done from the **Colors** tab of the PP. This means gradients cannot be applied to text unless they are converted to polygons or frames. In the drop-down list above the color swatch, you'll specify which gradient type you need. From now on, something new will be displayed in the window that gives you everything needed to customize the gradient. The little triangles below the gradients are color handles. They can be dragged and new colors can be applied to them when they are selected. If a color uses transparency or shade, it will be used for that stop color too. So it's quite easy to get a gradient going from a solid color to a completely transparent one. You can use gradients of identical, partially-transparent colors to have a custom-color fill, instead of using the standard opacity setting to prevent content from being affected.

The **Free linear Gradient** or **Free radial Gradient** types will add a **Move Vector** button. Clicking on it will make some new pink handles appear. It will be possible to drag them inside or outside the frame using the right mouse button (to specify in which direction the gradient needs exactly to go) or, instead of dragging, using the **Gradient Vector** window to place them precisely. Other types are predefined.

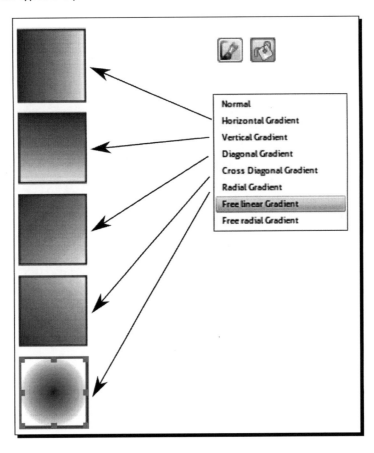

Using patterns

Not only gradient and solid colors but patterns too can be applied to the frames. If solid colors are the most commonly used, patterns are certainly the least. Patterns make background fills very complex and can drastically decrease the readability of a document. Using patterns will mean taking a lot of care and doing tests, not only on screen but in print too, to be sure that contrasts and colors are correct on paper.

If you want to use patterns to fill a frame or shape, you'll need to use the drop-down list at the top of the **Colors** tab, as for gradients, and choose **Pattern** from here. It will be available if there is an existing pattern. Scribus has no built-in patterns to begin with so you'll have to create your own pattern.

It will be very easy to create your own patterns. Just select the frame or frame group you want to use as pattern. Right-click on it and choose **Send to Pattern**. Now **Pattern** will be available in the fill type of the **Colors** tab in the PP. Select it to display the list of available patterns. Click on the pattern to apply it. You can then set the scaling of the applied pattern as well as its rotation and beginning point.

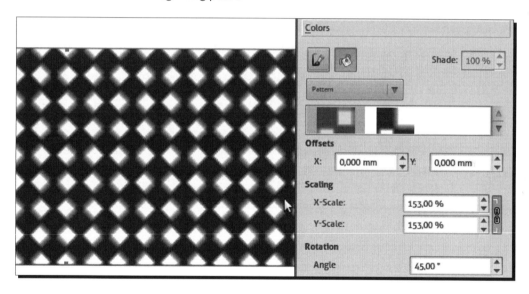

Time for action – using patterns and gradients in a layout

It's time to make something out of these nice features. We will try to layout a page that will be graphically based on a checkerboard pattern, and we will add gradients here and there. We won't care too much about texts and images; we will just focus on what is most important for us right now. So let's first have a look at the result and then go on to the steps involved.

1. On an A5 page, begin by creating a 1 inch square: activate the **Insert Shape** tool and click to display a window in which you can specify the width and the height.

2. Go to **Item | Multiple Duplicate**. Specify that you need only one copy, and set **Shift Created Item By** at **1** both horizontally and vertically. Validate and you'll have a new square at the bottom-right corner of the first.

3. Select them both and group them with *Ctrl + G*.

4. Right-click on the group and choose **Send to Patterns**. You'll be prompted to give a name to your pattern: just type a name (for example, checkerboard) and go on.

5. Now that the pattern is done, let's build the page. First, delete the shapes or drag them outside the page.

6. At the top of the page draw a rectangle that fills it from left to right. The height of this rectangle will be around 1.5 inches and can be set afterwards in the **XYZ** tab of the PP.

7. Give it a yellow color and then copy and paste (*Ctrl + C* then *Ctrl + V*). This yellow will fill the spaces between the black squares of our checkerboard.

8. The top rectangle is created last. Keep it selected and in the **Colors** tab of the PP, change the **Normal** fill to a **Pattern** fill. Click on the pattern preview that you want to use below (there should be only one at this point).

9. Decrease the **X-scaling** and **Y-scaling** by about **25%**. The amount can be different if the size of your pattern is not 2 inches—set the size you prefer.

10. Now add a rectangle shape and text on top of it and set it nicely. We kept the color as simple as possible: black, white, and yellow.

11. Let's go on with the morning schedule. First, draw a Text Frame and write **Morning** inside it. Choose a nice font, set the size, and add some effects. Here we used a white Armalite Rifle (`http://www.dafont.com/armalite-rifle.font`) uppercase font (at 92 pt, with default black outline and shadow) and the Appendix3 font, which is free (`http://www.dafont.com/appendix3.font`).

12. Now draw a rectangle to its left-hand side and one at its right-hand side. Try to make the height of your rectangles fit the height of the text.

13. Apply the pattern to them and set the scaling to **5%** or **6%**. You can then duplicate this set of frames, twice, and move the copies downward.

14. It's OK with the pattern now. Let's go on with the gradients. Draw a 0.23in by 1.12in rectangle under the Morning first letter.

15. In the **Colors** tab of the PP, choose **Vertical Gradient**. You'll get a completely black gradient from the beginning to the end.

16. In the gradient editing part of the tab, click on the left-hand triangle handle. If your cursor is a black arrow, it means that you will create a color stop if you click. If you added a stop by error, just drag it outside the editing area to delete it. A double white arrow is what the cursor should look like when it is on select mode.

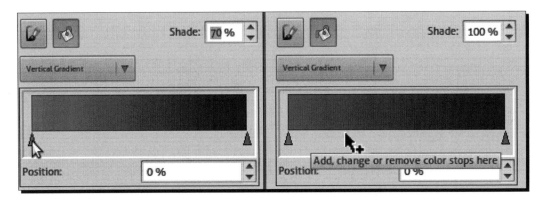

17. Change the **Shade** of this stop color to **70%**. You can immediately see the result on the page. We've added a SVG graphic at the bottom of the gradient to make things nicer and simulate a gauge.

18. Let's now add the text for some events: draw a Text Frame at the right-hand side of this and write some event title and description. You may use paragraph styles for this purpose.

19. We will now add bullets to each event. Draw a little circle and in the **Colors** tab of the PP, choose **Free radial Gradient**.

20. Select the left-hand handle and give it a white color to create a specular highlight.

21. Place the mouse between the two gradient handles to add a stop there. Give it a black **50%** shaded color and drag it the left-hand side until its position is around **20%**.

22. Now, click on the **Move Vector** button and drag the left-hand side pink handle with the right mouse button to position the highlight a bit inside of the sphere.

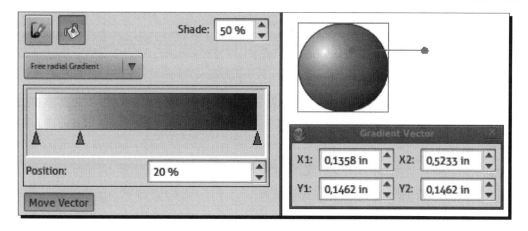

23. Resize the circle to the size of your event title, copy it, select the Text Frame, and place the text cursor before an event and paste. Do the same everywhere you need a bullet.

24. The first part of our flyer is done; you just need to go on and do the same with the rest.

What just happened?

Patterns and gradients are more complex fill options that can be used instead of a flat color. Gradients are the easiest to handle. They can be added to any shape by turning the **Normal** option list to a gradient type and then choosing the color for each stop triangle that represents the gradient stops.

Patterns will need more to get prepared. You'll first have to draw the shapes that will be the basis of your patterns—the shapes you exactly want to repeat. Then after selecting them all you can send them to patterns with the right-click option. To apply your new pattern on a frame, you'll just have to select that frame, choose **Pattern** as fill type in the same **Normal** options list that we changed for gradients, then choose your pattern in the pattern list that appears, and set it for the current object.

When repeated on several objects, gradients, and patterns can really modify the visual aspect of a page.

Have a go hero – gradients, transparencies, and patterns for creativity

Layouts are usually a simple combination of simple objects. But with all the advanced features Scribus is giving you, you could have a try and use it as a very creative software to generate visual effects. Try to reproduce the following geometrical picture by using:

- One pattern
- One gradient
- One transparency effect (Opacity or Blend mode)

We have made non-overlapping areas to give you clues on how it is made. Good luck!

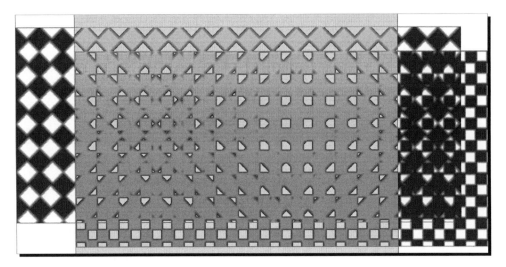

Create and import colors

Until now, we have used only default, primary colors. It's incredible how many things you can do with one single color or a small set of them. Even though black is still the most important color, you will certainly need custom colors very soon.

Time for action – managing new colors

To define your own color set, you'll need to go to **Edit | Colors**. Here you will have several options. The most import will be the **New** button, which displays a window that will give you all that you need to define your color perfectly.

1. Give a unique and meaningful name to your color; it will help you recognize it in the color lists later.

2. For the color model, you'll need to choose between CMYK, RGB, or Web safe RGB. If you intend to print the document, choose CMYK. If you need to put it on a website, you can choose the RGB model. Web safe, will be more restricted but you'll be sure that the chosen colors will have a similar render on every kind of monitor.

3. **Old** and **New** show an overview of the previous state of a color when editing an existing color and the state of the actual, chosen color. It's very practical to compare.

4. To choose your color, everything is placed on the right-hand side. You can click in the color spectrum area, drag the primary sliders, or enter the value of each primary in the field if you already know exactly which color you want.

5. The **HSV Color Map** on top is the setting that gives you the spectrum. If you choose another, you'll see predefined swatches. Most of them are RGB and should not be used directly for printed documents.

6. Click on **OK** to validate it in the **Edit Color** window and in the **Colors** window too.

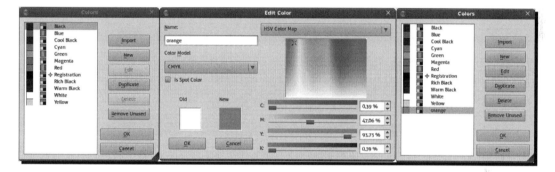

7. If no document is opened, the **Colors** window will have some more buttons that will be very helpful.

8. The **Current Color Set** should be set to **Scribus Basic**, which is the simplest color set. You can choose any other set but they contain RGB colors only.

9. Then you can add your own colors, if you haven't already done so.

10. Click on **Save Color Set** and give it a name.

11. Your set will now be listed in the list and will be available for every new document.

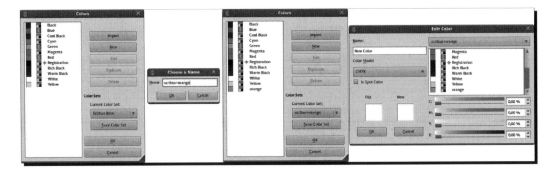

What just happened?

Creating colors is very simple and can be done in few steps. In fact, creating some colors is much faster than having to choose the same color from a long, default color list. My advice would be: don't lose your time looking for a color in a predefined swatch unless you really need this color (like a Pantone or any other spot). Consider the following points:

- ◆ You should know the average color you need before looking for it
- ◆ It will take some time to take a look at all the available colors
- ◆ The color might not be in a predefined swatch
- ◆ Don't use the set everybody uses, it will help you make your document recognizable

If no document is opened, the color will be added to the default swatch unless you create your own color name. If a Scribus document is open, even empty, the color will be saved in the document. Let's see how to reuse it if needed.

Reusing colors from other files

If you already have the colors somewhere, there might be a way to pick it without having to create it again.

If the color is defined in an imported vector (mainly EPS or SVG) file, the colors will automatically be added in the color list with a name beginning with **FromEPS** or **FromSVG** followed by **hexadecimal** values of the color. In an EPS, colors can be CMYK or spot, but in SVG they will be RGB.

CMYK between Inkscape and Scribus

Inkscape colors are RGB but this software is color managed, so you can have an accurate on screen-rendering and you can add a 5-digit color-profile value to the color style property. Actually, no software adds this automatically. Doing it manually in Inkscape through the XML editor will require some knowledge of SVG and **CSS**. It will be easier to simply get your RGB colors and then go, after import, to the **Edit | Colors** window and refine the colors by clicking on the **Edit** button.

If your color is in an imported picture or is placed somewhere else, you can use the **Eye Dropper** tool (the last icon of the toolbar). When you click on a color, you will be asked for a name and the color will be added as RGB in the color list. If you want to use it in CMYK, just edit the color and change the color model.

The last important use case is an internal Scribus case. The color list swatch defined in a document is available only in that document and saved within it. The bad point of this is that they won't automatically be available for future documents. But the good point is that you can send your file to anyone and your colors will still be there. You have several ways of doing this.

Time for action – importing from a Scribus document

We have already seen how to import style and master pages from other existing Scribus documents; importing colors will be very similar.

1. The simplest method to reuse existing already defined colors is to go to **Edit | Colors**.

2. Click on the **Import** button.

3. Browse your directories to find the Scribus file that contains the colors you want and select it.

4. All the colors of this document will be added to your new document swatch.

5. If you don't need some colors, just select them in the **Edit | Colors** list and click on the **Delete** button.

Scribus will ask you which color will replace this deleted color. If this color is unused in your new document, it doesn't matter.

What just happened?

The **Edit Colors** window provides a simple way to import the colors from another Scribus document: if the colors are already set in it, you just have to choose it. But there are many other ways to do it, especially because colors are considered as frame options and can be imported with them.

In fact, if you really need the same colors, you certainly won't like importing them each time you create a new document. The best you can do is create a file with your master pages, styles, and colors defined and save it as a model. Each new document will be created from this model, so you'll get them easily each time. The same will happen if you use a scrapbook. Performing those steps can help you get in few seconds everything you have already defined in another similar document.

Finally, you may need to reuse those colors but not in the same kind of document. You can create a swatch in GIMP `.gpl` format or use any EPS or AI file. GIMP `.gpl` format is very simple but can be only RGB. Give the value of each RGB color. Press the *Tab* key and write the name of the color (for example, medium grey would be: 127 127 127 grey50). Each color has to be alone on its line. GPL, EPS, and AI files have to be placed in the Scribus swatch install directory (on Linux `/usr/lib/scribus/swatches`, on Macs `Applications/Scribus/Contents/lib/scribus/swatches`, and on Microsoft Windows `Programs/scribus/lib/scribus/swatches`).

When using an EPS file you might get too many colors. Create as many sample shapes as needed on a page and apply a color that you want to keep on each. Then go to **Edit | Colors** and click on **Remove Unused**. Then close this window and delete the shapes.

The best way will be the one you'll prefer. Test them all and maybe find your own.

Spot colors

Another kind of color that we haven't already dealt with much is spot color. In Scribus, creating and using a spot color is really easy. To create a spot color, just do as you would do for any other color and select the **Is Spot Color** checkbox. If you use a color from a reference catalog like Pantone or other, the name of the color you define in Scribus should be the same as the name in the catalog.

In the color list, spot colors will be identified by a red circle and you can apply it as you would do for any other color.

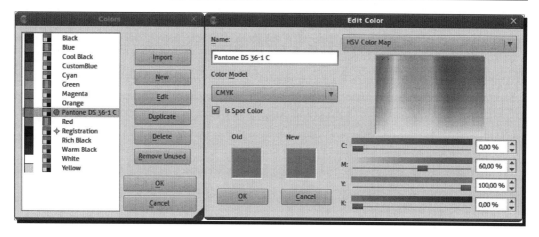

So then what's the difference with other colors? When printing colors in CMYK, all the colors will be a composite of those primaries (we call that process colors). So printing a color document will necessarily need those four colors and the plates (in Offset) that go with it. There are few issues with this process:

◆ You can't be sure you'll get the exact color you want at the end. Primaries will give a different result depending on the shapes, angle, or frequency of the dots as well as the temperature within the building, the paper type, and other parameters that are really difficult to handle and foresee.

◆ If you need to print only in two colors, let's say black and orange, you'll need four plates or inks where you could use only two if you could directly deal with orange ink.

◆ If you need to have metallic, fluorescent, varnish, or other kinds of weird colors, they can't be done with primaries.

◆ Finally, the gamut you can reproduce with primaries is not large and some important documents (an art book for example) need more accurate printing. Having more inks can help extend the gamut.

If you have to manage one of these use cases, spot colors will be your friend. The colors defined as spot will be printed in pure inks. Orange will not be processed anymore but prepared in advanced and put as is on the paper. This is perfect or quite right. The trouble is that the more colors you'll need to use as primaries (let's say that spot is like a primary for easiness), the more expensive it will become. So, generally, using spot colors for a two-color document will reduce the price but a five-color document (CMYK+1 spot) will be more expensive.

The best is to know in advance:

- How the document will be printed and choose the print office to talk about the possibilities
- What spot colors you'll need to use

If you don't know the answers to these questions, and you are used to spot colors, make your document with them and if it happens that you can't print them as spot because of a technical or financial issue, you'll be able to transform all of your spot colors in CMYK when exporting your document in PDF before sending it.

If you are used to some specific spot color provider like Pantone, you should be advised that Scribus can't integrate them because of legal issues. If you have got them through Adobe software licensing, it will be OK. Know that Pantone (and some others too) provides standalone applications that store spot colors into EPS files. In Scribus, you can use them by simply importing them as explained in the previous section.

Converting swatches with Swatchbooker

Swatchbooker is a nice and easy-to-use application that can convert many swatch file formats to others. I often use it and you could have a try. Get it at: `http://www.selapa.net/swatchbooker`.

If you need more information on Scribus and Pantone, have a look at this webpage too: `http://wiki.scribus.net/index.php/How_to_legally_obtain_spot_colour_palettes_for_use_in_Scribus_1.3.3.x_and_later_versions`.

If you use spot colors, you'll have to take care of few things when exporting:

- Before exporting, verify that you don't have too many spot colors or that the number of the inks you'll use will match the requested colors. If you're unsure, **File | Print Preview** will display a window that will show the inks. Read the next chapter if you want to know more on this functionality.
- You'll need to export the PDF as **Printer** PDF, not **Screen / Web** PDF, in which all the colors will be converted to RGB, and neither **Grayscale** PDF where everything will become shades of black.
- Verify if you need to select (or not) the **Convert Spot Colors to Process Color** checkbox.

Colors from an EPS file

EPS files are often used to save and share logos. Encapsulated PostScript format can handle CMYK and Spot Colors. When you import such a file, its colors are automatically added to your document swatch and are kept as CMYK or spot, as they are. It's a good idea to have a look at the swatch after import. It's not a good idea to have too many swatch colors in a document for they will be very expensive to print.

Time for action – replacing colors

Replacing colors is a very simple task because we often need to use it. You have three ways to replace colors in the document swatch:

1. In **Edit | Colors**, click on the **Delete** button. You'll need to choose which color will be applied to the object having the deleted color.

2. But you can also use the **Replace Colors** window as shown in the next screenshot.

3. Create a document and import a vector file or logo, which can be the sample ColorShade.svg file or the logo used in Chapter 2.

4. Go to **Edit | Replace Colors** where you will be able to define several replacements at once that Scribus will make just after you validate.

5. Click on the **Add** button to display a new window that will let you choose the color you want to replace (Scribus shows only used colors): here we have chosen the **CustomBlue** color.

6. Don't forget to mention which color will replace it, and which color you want to be applied to the objects; here we changed it to red.

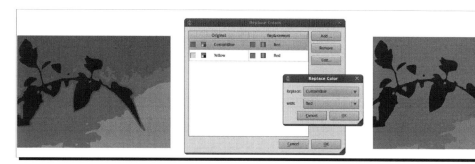

What just happened?

The **Replace Colors** window is a very nice feature when you reach the end of your layout and some bad people inform you that the colors of the document will need to be changed for whatever the reason.

Notice that replacing the color in the swatch is the only way to automatically modify the color of several objects. There is no frame style that could allow it. But you still can use the Magic Wand tool to copy the properties of a frame to another.

Choosing colors that suit

If you need to define the color of the document yourself, and you don't feel comfortable doing so, Scribus has an old built-in plugin that can help you. This plugin is called **Color Wheel** and can be launched from the **Extras** menu.

The top part of the window lets you choose a base color.

- ◆ It can be a color you will choose by dragging the red circle around the wheel. The chosen base color is displayed at the center of the wheel.

- ◆ If you already know how the base color is processed, just go to a **CMYK**, **RGB**, or **HSV** tab and enter the values of each primary or setting.

- ◆ If you have already added the base color to the document swatch, go to the last tab named **Document** and select it in the list. The red handle will be automatically placed at the right place on the wheel.

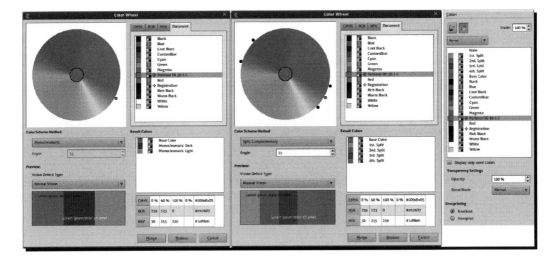

Then, choose one **Color Scheme Method**. Each scheme will give you different results from two to six colors. The colors are displayed on the right-hand side, in the **Result Colors** part, and below in the **Preview** part.

In the **Result Colors** list, you can click on each proposal and see the ink values at the bottom for **CMYK**, **RGB**, and **HSV** models. It will help you compare each one with some ink values that you already have or see if you can avoid the usage of some ink.

In the **Preview**, you can select a Preview mode that tries to simulate some usual color blindness on screen. This can help you choose your color by considering if they will give enough contrast and will be readable enough for everyone.

If some of the colors please you, click on the **Merge** button and they will be added to the document swatch. You can edit those colors from the **Edit | Colors** window to adapt them a bit and get better results if needed.

Color management

The color management system is a very advanced feature and is certainly why Scribus is getting popular. Of all the free software we use such as GIMP, Inkscape, Scribus, and some others, they all share the same color management process based on the famous Little CMS libraries.

For the user this is very handy:

- ♦ All the software will have the same options. So if you know them in one, you know them for all and if you have set a certain color management in one application, it's easy to set the others.
- ♦ The color result in the different software will be very similar.

But what is that made for. Isn't it enough to define colors and take care that they are CMYK? In some ways, yes. It depends on your needs and of the quality that you want.

We have already discussed about some printing issues: paper type and color, quality of the inks, and so on. There are so many possibilities and we generally use very little; so some standard presets have been defined. We call them profiles. Profiles will remember how a color is printed on some context. So you can tell your software which profile will be used by the print office. If you don't know, just ask them or use a standard like Fogra27 or Fogra29, which are Adobe's defaults.

But if you want to have the right colors displayed on your monitor, it gets more difficult because all monitors display colors differently. You'll need a profile for the rendering on screen, and that will be your own job. Scribus cannot create the profile for you. Some manufacturers give them on a CD or on their website. Just check for yours. But if you really need a perfect preview of the printed result, you'll need a custom profile of your screen because the way these colors are rendered vary in the peripherals life and even within a day. If you need such a custom profile, you can use Argyll with many colorimeters or spectrometers.

Profiling with Argyll

Argyll is a color management system that can create profiles of your monitors, scanners, and printers. To use Argyll you'll need a peripheral that can analyze the colors rendered on your screen or printer and compare it to a reference to know the difference that will be stored in the profile. Those measuring instruments can cost from 100 £ to several thousands, but you won't have as much choice as for your printers. Most of the cheapest color management systems can only profile the monitor and not the printers. It just depends on whether you need it.

Argyll is a command-line tool, but DispcalGui provides an easy and graphical way to create your profile. You can download them from `http://www.argyllcms.com/` and `http://hoech.net/dispcalGUI`.

Time for action – managing colors in Scribus

That said, how do you manage colors in Scribus?

1. First of all, Scribus needs to know where the profiles are stored on your system. This will usually be:

    ❑ `/usr/share/color/icc` on Linux.

    ❑ `spool/drivers/colors` of your Microsoft Windows system folder.

    ❑ `Libray/ColorSync/Profiles` on Mac.

    ❑ But you can store them where you want and tell Scribus where they are when you go to the **General** tab of the **Preferences** window and change the directory for the ICC profile. This can be done only if no document is opened.

2. Then you need to configure the color management tools. You can do it from:

- ❑ The monitor icon that is placed at the right-hand side of the status bar. Keeping the mouse button pressed on it will display the **Configure CMS** menu.

- ❑ The **File | Document Setup | Color Management** pane to set it only for the current document.

- ❑ The **File | Preferences | Color Management** pane to set it for all the following documents.

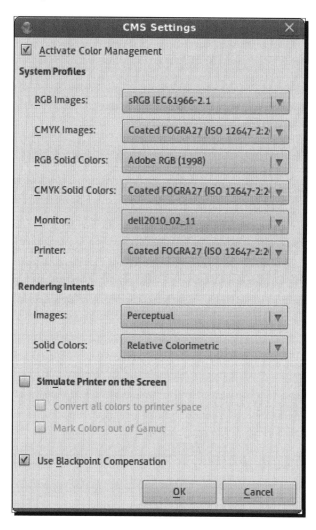

3. In those windows you will need to give the best profile for each type of document input or output. The settings used in the screenshot are for CMYK printing on coated paper, and displayed on a DELL monitor, for which I have a custom profile named by the date **dell2010_02_11**. It is supposed that the inputs will be:

   ❑ Photos interpreted with the sRGB profile, which is not the best but is still the most-commonly used. If you use your own photos from a known camera, check if you have a profile for it.

   ❑ Photos in CMYK that have been modified in a photo editing software and are saved as CMYK. It can be Adobe Photoshop, GIMP, or any other software. Some vector applications, such as Adobe Illustrator or free SK1, can save as CMYK raster images. Personally, by using the CMYK profile to convert an image to CMYK, it makes it simple for me to specify which profile I have used in GIMP.

4. Do the same for the solid colors that you will define in your Scribus swatch and use it in your document.

5. Once you've done that, you have to set the rendering intent. The rendering intent will tell the color management system how it should adjust colors, especially what it should do with the gamut of colors. As industry standards are different in North America, Europe, and in Japan, it will be hard to specify what you need to use.

What just happened?

The hard part of the color management is that it is not made to be used with default values. It should be set exactly for your monitors, sources, and printing methods. Your print provider may have that last bit of information, and you can ask him.

Rendering intents are also important in modifying the result.

   ◆ **Perceptual**: It preserves the smoothness between colors and tries to avoid color bands.

   ◆ **Saturation**: It preserves the saturation and can be a good choice for drawings like logos or maps with solid colors.

   ◆ **Relative Colorimetric**: In this, the gamut colors are shifted to the closest reproducible of the output color space and all the colors are shifted accordingly to preserve color relationship.

   ◆ **Absolute Colorimetric**: It is similar to relative colorimetric except that the colors that fall inside the output gamut are not shifted.

Then, if you decide to activate color management, you will be likely to simulate the printer's result on screen. You will, for example, have non-reproducible colors displayed in pure green if the **Mark Color out of Gamut** checkbox is selected, so that you can easily see what part of the pictures will be modified by the color management adjustments. But don't worry, this green color is only an on-screen rendering and won't be present in the printed document.

Color management can't prevent errors, even human errors. Using color management is not a safe process in itself. You should not expect miracles from it. But if you have time to do it well, you will really get more accurate results. You will generally use the same settings. So you could define your needs in the preferences, and then activate and deactivate color management when needed by pressing the CMS icon of the status bar. Let Scribus do the calculation, and the rendering that you will get will match the printed result.

Pop quiz

1. Colors for print document can be:

    a. RGB

    b. CMYK

    c. Spot

2. Import colors from SVG Inkscape files will generally be:

    a. RGB

    b. CMYK

    c. Spot

3. To convert RGB colors to CMYK we need to:

    a. Use the Color Picker tool

    b. Use the **Edit Color** window

    c. Nothing

4. What are CMYK colors in Scribus made for?

    a. To match the common print primary colors

    b. To match the monitor primary color and get nice results on screen

    c. To display the colors of the photos correctly

5. Spot colors can be created in:

    a. The Color Wheel

    b. The **Edit Color** window

    c. The **Colors** tab of the PP

6. Shade is:

    a. Similar to transparency

    b. A way to define color opacity

    c. A way to define color saturation

7. Color management is based on:

    a. ICC profiles only

    b. ICC profiles and rendering intents

    c. A colorimeter input

Summary

In this chapter, we've seen how to use simple and advanced color features to improve the workflow and the printed results.

Specifically, we covered:

- How to create custom CMYK colors and spot colors
- How to apply patterns or gradients
- How to use some transparency effects like Opacity or Blending mode
- How to find colors that match
- How to set the color management to get better printed colors

In the next chapter, we will now see how to export the document and what's need to be checked before and saved after, to have a complete and safe workflow.

10
Print Your Layout

When the layout is done, it's time to print it. Knowing whether the document will be printed or not, and eventually how, is an important point that should be defined at the beginning of the layout process and that we refer to while creating the document. This helps us with choosing colors, fonts, and so on.

Printing on a desktop printer will help to get an overview of the result. Even if the result given by a print office using offset can be different, it is a good proof of what is working and what's not. Generally, the print provider will ask for a PDF of some kind, with some elements like printing marks. In Scribus, we'll have to check if the document matches the request—thanks to the print preview or the Preflight Verifier.

When everything is done, we just have to save it the right way, for future use if needed.

This chapter is one of the most theoretic of all the chapters in the book. No actions are particularly to be performed. Everything here is related to the print office's needs and the only result you can trust is the one your print shop will provide you with. Most of the options we'll see won't affect the on-screen display of your Scribus document, but they are made to help you get the most accurate printed results.

In this chapter, we will see in detail how Scribus can help us check the quality of our layout with:

- ◆ Proof printing
- ◆ Preflight Verifier and PDF export
- ◆ Preview color separation
- ◆ Collect for output

Printing from Scribus

Printing on your local printer is something that you will sometimes like to do while doing the layout. The quality of what you'll get printed is highly dependent on your printer. Is it inkjet, laser, black only, or CMYK or using spot colors, PostScript, or not? Anyway, you should not trust the colors that you'll get here. You certainly won't have the right paper and you won't have perfect profiles for your printer. Therefore, the proof print is only an average of what you'll finally get.

Install Ghostscript absolutely

Ghostscript is a standalone software specializing in the printing processes and printing file formats. Many software use it as a background library. Scribus uses it to load EPS vector drawings or some printing options like print preview. You should absolutely install Ghostscript on your system if you want to use the advanced printing feature implemented in Scribus. Get it from `http://sourceforge.net/projects/ghostscript/files/`, and install or uncompress. If Scribus can't find it, go to the **Preferences | External Tools** section, and modify the **PostScript Interpreter** section to specify where you installed it.

But this average is very important to have a good overview of your page and is much better than what the print preview can give you. In fact, it's not a technical problem but more of an optical one. You don't have the same proportion feeling when reading on screen and on paper because of zoom factors or screen resolutions, which differ highly from print. So having a physical proof is something that your print provider can ask for as a basis of what you want at the end.

The Scribus print dialog can be called from **File | Print**. It will display a verifier window that you can ignore for now. Read the next section if you want to know more about it. The print dialog will then appear and it lets you print in two ways:

- On a printer that is installed on your computer
- In a file

In the latter case, you'll get a PostScript file unless you have **PDF** listed in the **Print Destination** available. **PDF** will be present only if you install a virtual PDF printer. On Linux, CUPS can provide it and it might be in your repository. On Windows, PDFCreator can do it too. By choosing **File**, you'll need to define where the file will be saved, whereas **PDF** will automatically store it in the print service default directory. If you have used advanced features, such as transparencies (opacity, blend modes, and gradients) or pattern in your file, you will lose them all, as PostScript cannot handle such features.

If you decide to use a printer, you'll need to choose it in the available printer list. The **Options** button will then be available to define some printer specific settings.

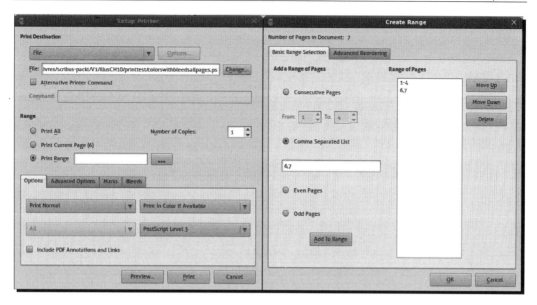

In both cases you can of course define how many copies of each will be created and the page/pages you want to print. The current page is displayed between parenthesis so that you can be sure that the right page is selected. If not, just close the window, click on the page, and verify the selection red rectangle is around it and come back to that window. If you choose to print several pages, you'll need to define these in the field (use "–" for range and "," to list single pages) or in the separate window available from the **…** button. Once in there, choose an option between each, write the page number, and add them to the range with the button placed at the bottom. They will be added to the right-hand part that lists all the pages to print. Click on **OK** when you're done and everything will be added to the field.

All the settings placed in the tabs below are Scribus specific.

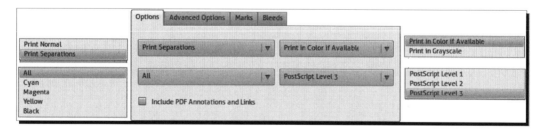

You can deal with the most important settings in the **Options** tab.

Print Normal will print all your colors processed on a sheet whereas **Print Separations** will print each primary CMYK color on a separate sheet, in black. When the second is chosen, the field **All** is made available and you can choose only one plate if you wish. This is important because the separation is one of the most important actions an offset print office will have to do: separation is the action that tries to understand how much Cyan, Magenta, Yellow, or Black are contained in any color you used for your layout and the photos. You have here the means to evaluate everything in advance. It can help you evaluate the amount of each color used and see if some can be avoided.

You can then choose to print in color or grayscale and eventually the PostScript level, but shouldn't change it unless your print shop asks for an .eps file of some ancient fashion.

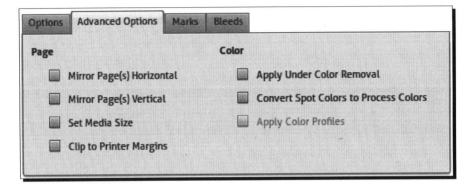

In the next tab, the settings of choice are those of the color group.

Apply Under Color Removal will try to replace some color amount of your file and replace it with black. By doing this, Scribus tries, of course, to keep the colors as similar as possible. The result will be a file with little ink coverage that can fit more easily for some very exigent providers. Actually, since you're printing at home, you'll use more of the black color and less of CMY, and black is cheaper. So do a test on an important and regularly printed document, and keep the option selected if you like the result.

Convert Spot Colors to Process Colors, will use the CMYK value used in the **Edit Color** window instead of the spot itself. It is useful if you used some spot catalogs to choose your colors but don't want to print with them in the end. If you print on your own printer, it is certainly impossible for you to get spot color on it for you to check it in anyway.

Apply Color Profiles will simply print the result as set in the color management window.

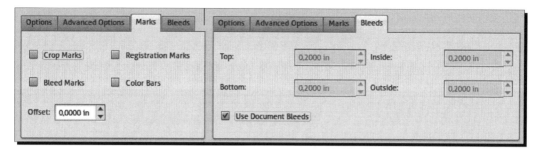

In the **Marks** tab you'll find everything you need to help you see if your document is well printed. **Crop Marks** are lines placed around each corner of the page to show you where the limit of your sheet is and where you can cut. **Bleed Marks** are lines parallel to the previous lines that will show the limit of the bleeds if you defined some in the **New Document** window or the **Document Properties,** or at least in the **Bleeds** tab of the current window. Bleeds is an external margin that helps you play with the colored frames or shapes that should be placed next to the page border. As it can be difficult or long to be so precise, they can go a bit outside of the page, in the bleeds. Bleeds are generally around 0.2 inches. There's no need to add more.

Registration Marks are a kind of target that can be used to precisely place the plates in the presses. You won't need them if you print on a desktop printer. And finally, **Color Bars** will show some colors (primaries and shaded black) to help you check if the primary applied by your printer is good.

You can use **Offset** to move the marks away from the pages. But you should remember that those options will help you only if the size of your page is smaller than the maximum printing size of your printer. If you try to print a letter or A4 document on a letter or A4 paper, this can't be done properly for the marks are printed outside the document page. However, this will work perfectly for an A5 document, for example. If you need to print A4 with marks you'll need A4+ and A3+ for an A3 document or 2 facing A4 pages. If you need to print a booklet or several pages at once, we'll talk about it later but our advise is to leave Scribus at this point, and let the print shop use a really specialized software for this.

Preflight Verifier

Would you be sure your layout is perfectly done? Are you sure that you did not forget something that could transform the printing process or its result into a nightmare ? We are never sure and we really like this little **Preflight Verifier** Scribus window. It has been here for a while now, but people don't use it as often as they should, and it sometimes would really help them.

The **Preflight Verifier** window can be launched:

◆ From the **Windows** menu if you want to keep it permanently

◆ From the **Preflight Verifier** button of the main action bar, near the **Save as PDF** button

◆ Automatically when you use the **Print** or the **Save as PDF** command unless you deselect the **Automatic check before printing and exporting** checkbox of the Preflight Verifier preferences

We find a lot of other interesting information in these preferences. In fact, every error category that the verifier can inform you about is listed. Some are already deselected. Actually, the deselected values are part of a default profile. You can choose the verifier profile in the first drop-down list. The default profile is **PostScript;** we will change it to **PDF 1.4,** which is the PDF type we mostly use. In fact, each export format has some capacities and weaknesses. The verifier will try to find if you used some unsupported feature regarding the format you have chosen.

Time for action – detecting errors before exporting

The Preflight Verifier will help you get the most accurate PDF you need. To apply modification to any of these objects:

1. Try to reproduce the page in the following illustration or open `preflight.sla`.

2. Open the **Preflight Verifier** from the **Windows** menu.

3. Choose the **PostScript** profile and look at the errors displayed.

4. Then choose the **PDF 1.4** profile and look at the errors.

5. We have an empty Image Frame error: the right rectangle to the right-hand side of "Preflight", a frame named **Image5**. In this case, the frame should really get the photo of the author, so we should import a picture or delete the frame.

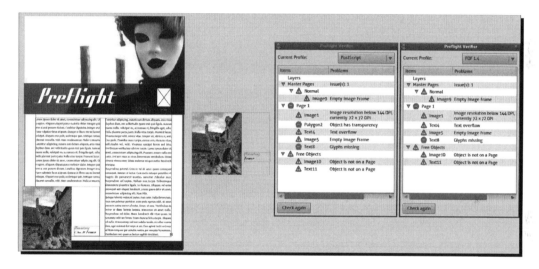

6. Click on its entry in the preflight verifier and the object is automatically selected on the layout and displayed.

7. Do the changes to make it match the needs.

What just happened?

When the Preflight Verifier appears, it displays the errors corresponding to the default selected profile. If you're asked for a different format or version, you can select it in the verifier window and it will automatically be updated. On the illustration we can see that the transparency error is not displayed with **PDF 1.4**. But if you need to give a PostScript file to your print provider, you'll be in trouble.

Errors are listed in the order they appear: the master page and then the pages from the first to the last. The **Free Objects** class shows objects that are outside the page. You could delete them.

Other errors we see here are simple.

- On the Normal Master Page, the frame named Image9 (see **XYZ** tab of the PP) is empty. In the layout, this is the black rectangle at the bottom. If it has to be empty on every page, it could be converted to a shape.

- Image1 in Page 1 contains the main top image, which is under 144dpi. In fact it is 72dpi. We forgot to change the resolution in GIMP. Do the change and update it in Scribus and everything will be OK for that point. As we can see, the picture at the bottom displays no error.

- Text overflow simply tells us that the Text4 frame contains too much text, and that some text is not displayed. We could modify the font properties (font size, kerning, glyph extension, and so on) to save space throughout the page, if it is enough, or link this frame to another.

- Lastly, the text near the photo contains some special and exotic French accentuated character that the font doesn't have. The only solution here is to update the font with FontForge if it is a free font or use a more simple method: choose another font.

In the end, the verifier should display no errors and you can go ahead. It is your choice to have a permanent look at the errors with the verifier window or just check for errors at the end.

Previewing before printing

We have already seen that we could print separation from the Print window. But in fact, the most important thing is not that you print it but that you make sure that the color settings are as they should be at the end.

The **Print Preview** window available in the **File** menu, uses Ghostscript if it is installed to check some of the printing prerequisites. If you are a Microsoft Windows user, the display of this window can be a bit different for the printing process and is driven by a Microsoft GDI engine and not PostScript.

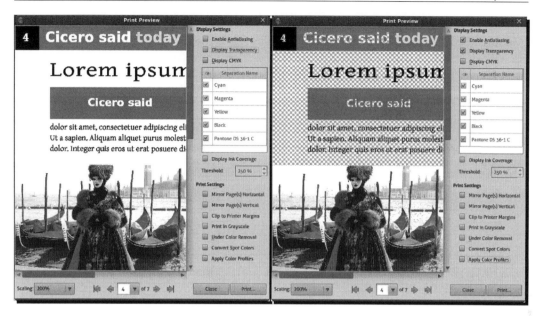

The first basic options are:

◆ Play with the zoom factor at the left-hand bottom to have better approach on details. The green buttons on the right-hand side let's you navigate through document pages, and the number (**4** in the illustration) is the current page.

◆ **Enable Antialiasing** will improve the rendering of the text in the preview window. Changes will take longer to be applied but text will be smoother.

◆ **Display Transparency** shows the part of the page were no ink will be put, meaning that the paper will be completely free. It doesn't mean that a transparency effect is applied, but, for example, that white color is used. Be careful, this option cannot read in pictures and don't bother about overprint, which might result is some changes.

◆ **Mirror Page** will flip the page horizontally or vertically and **Clip to Printer Margins** will display only what is placed inside the document margins.

◆ **Print in Grayscale** will show what the document will look like if everything is converted to black only, which can result in grey tone visual appearance. This is a nice functionality if you created a color document and didn't know it would be printed in black, or because you didn't have time to create a color document to put on a website and a black only for print purpose. We have the same option in the PDF export window.

Time for action – previewing color separation

Certainly the most important functionality of this window is to check whether the primaries and spot colors used in the file match those defined for the print process. This way you can see each plate or ink usage without printing separation in the print dialog, which will help you save ink and paper as well as time. If you select the **Display CMYK** checkbox, the lines placed in the list just below are made available.

1. Open the colors.sla file and display Page 4.

2. There are several color objects on that page and a picture.

3. You can have a look at the color list in the PP to see what colors are used.

4. Now go to **File | Print Preview.**

5. Deselect all colors except **Cyan** to see where cyan is used.

6. Deselect all colors except our pantone orange to see where it is used and if it could eventually be replaced by a process color at exporting time.

7. When you've done all the tests, close the window.

What just happened?

When all the separations are selected, you see the page with all the processed colors. But if you deactivate some, these colors won't be displayed anymore. It can help you check, for example, if you can do your layout and avoid the use of some color and print cheaper. In this example, deactivating yellow doesn't change much except for the word "today" on top on the reds in the photos where no reader could know that there was red inside. If price is an issue and you need color, check it sometimes.

On the other hand, you can see that a spot color is added: it is a pantone orange color that is used only on top as shown in the last preview. The question here is that is it so important to keep that spot color and not better to have a processed orange, which might need yellow but will allow richer results. If you select **Convert Spot Colors**, and wait a bit for the preview to be rerendered, you'll see that you can deactivate the orange pantone line and that you'll still have every color you need at a good quality.

It's important to notice that if a spot color is used with black to create a single, cheap colored (or two if you consider black as color) document called duotone, having spot color with standard CMYK will increase the price of the printing as well as other fifth plate like varnish, which should be defined as spot too. Unless you know exactly what you're doing, spot colors will not be the most common setting so that you can convert spot.

It's important to remember that all the changes made in this dialog won't affect the printed or exported result.

Ink coverage

As all the teachers would say: you shouldn't draw on the table. In offset printing it's not good to have too many colors on the paper too. **Under Color Removal** can be used to reduce the amount of ink by replacing them with black when possible. Even if it helps avoiding some inking issues, it results in some dull colors and is generally used for basic and cheap printing.

Generally, you should consider that having an amount of ink above 250 percent can put you in trouble in some printing contexts, especially with some cheap paper and inks. Some providers can print up to 320 percent, but unless they tell you something, use the minimum as possible for your needs.

This amount is calculated by adding the percentage of each colors used somewhere on a page. A pure color like black, will be 100 percent. If we convert the **Pantone DS 36-1 C** to CMYK we will have 60 of **Magenta** and 100 of **Yellow** so that we are still under 250. Even if you use colors like warm, rich, or cool blacks, which are black mixed with other color to give it more depth, you'll be at 240 for rich black.

If you go to print preview and check for colors one by one, you'll see that the color of the top-left square will be composed of each primary, spots included. When doing the layout, we filled it with the registration color, which looks like black but is 100 percent of each ink printed color. We should never use registration color in the layout and only use it to give information to the provider. For example, crop marks will be automatically be generated in registration color and they are not part of the layout, just manufacturing indicators. If you use some dark spot color, take care of it too. For example, PANTONE 276 EC is C100 M100 Y10 K79, a dark blue, which gives 289 if the spot is converted. However, there are many other colors like that and it's up to you to check whether the color you're using can be printed.

To test the ink coverage of your document, just activate the **Display Ink Coverage** option of the print preview window and change the **Threshold** value to the one given by the print shop. The colors of the page will turn to grey if they are under the value and will be red if they are above it. If it's the case, you'll have to modify the color you define to make it match the request. Do it in **Edit | Colors** as you would for any color and come back to this window to check. If you need to use spot colors and know that you'll print them in process CMYK, don't forget to select the **Convert Spot Colors** checkbox, otherwise the print preview won't display the right ink coverage for them. But if you do it well, you should know when creating the color that it might be tricky at the end.

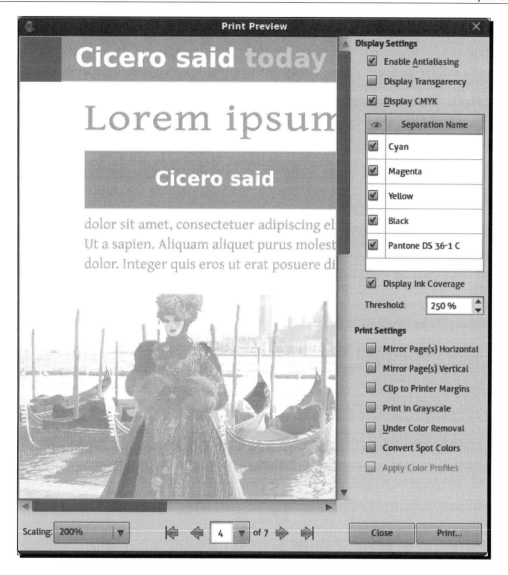

Printing booklets

Scribus is not a printing software and our advice to print your documents with other software applies here again. If you want to do a print test like we did previously, Scribus is quite good, but if you want a complete document ready to be read, like a booklet, Scribus won't help you much. If you send your file to a print office you shouldn't prepare the booklet; the office will do this by itself and will use its own production presets. This action is called Imposition and some specialized pieces of software can do it, taking care of many parameters to have the best result.

But for your own proof reading you might need it sometimes. Booklets are defined by some characteristics:

- Double-sided print
- Facing pages print, that is, two page per sheet side, which will certainly need a fold
- First page faces the last and so on

Printing on each side of a piece of paper is a printer option, so if your printer can do it, you should be able to have it set in Scribus.

Facing pages will be different. Scribus creates a document page per page; this is what it is made for and joining two pages in one is not possible in Scribus and no print option gives it from Scribus.

At last, modifying the page order can be done from the PDF export, or print to a file. In this case just choose the order of the page you need. It means not 1,2,3,4,5,6,7,8 but 8,1,2,7,6,3,4,5 or so. You can then open the file in any PDF viewer and print it with two pages per sheet.

If you have Adobe Acrobat Reader, which is still the best PDF viewer even today, you could use the Booklet printing option to print a normal PDF with pages in the standard crescent order.

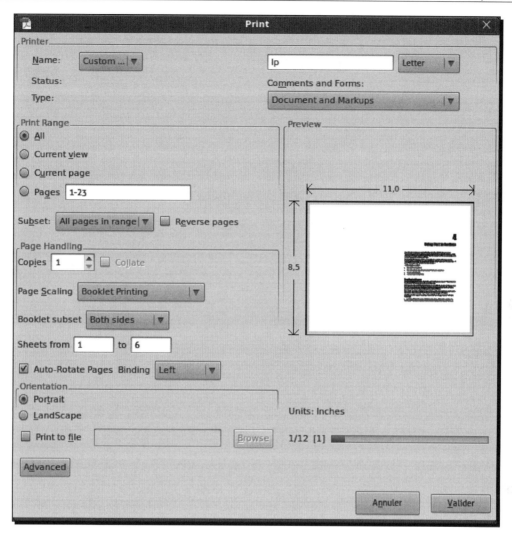

Exporting to PDF

Once the layout is done and you've checked with a print output if it is OK, you can send your document to a professional print provider. They used to ask for an EPS file in the past but PDF is now really becoming the default. You shouldn't have to send the Scribus document unless there is a real problem with your layout. Of course, the best thing is that the print office gets a print-ready file: it will be cheaper and faster. Sending a PDF is smarter than sending a Scribus file for many reasons:

◆ You're sure that the document you'll get will be the exact print copy of the file you sent because a PDF file is not made to be modified.

- You'll avoid some trouble, with fonts for example if the print doesn't have some font that you used, and as we'll see they will all embed into the PDF.

- You can add some extra information in your PDF, like printing marks.

- PDF is a very commonly used file format and you can easily send you file for proof reading or other reasons and be really confident. Sending a Scribus file would be more difficult, you need to send the font, pictures, as well as be sure that you have compliant Scribus version.

There might be many more reasons to use PDF. The best thing is to give the provider what he asks for. He may have some workflow that he manages better than others. Just ask if you're not sure. Talking to people is never a bad thing and it's better to know in advance than watch a bad result when printed. So you should really care about the PDF export to make it as suitable as needed.

To export to PDF just press the **Save as PDF** button in the toolbar or choose **File | Export | Save as PDF**. The Preflight Verifier might appear to check for some last minute errors. Do what's needed at this point as seen in the *Preflight Verifier* section of this chapter. When everything is perfect, you'll reach the export window. The top part of it displays a default file name abstracted from your Scribus filename. You can change it, that's the easy part.

Export to other formats

Sometimes you can experience that the Scribus PDF export won't match the needs. In this case you can have a look at other entries of the **File | Export** menu. Particularly, the safest will certainly be to **Save as EPS** or as a bitmap where you can choose the TIFF file format. Designers and print professionals use them a lot too.

There is one option just below telling that you can **Output one file for each page**. Using this, you'll have as many PDF files as the number of pages you have. This is very useful if you made notes using master page. Doing one Scribus file for each note would be less productive. You can then have each note as a separate document and send them to clients or anyone who could need it. Each exported page is named by the name you gave in the previous field, followed by the page number like this: `Document-1-Page001.pdf`, `Document-1-Page002.pdf`.

PDF versions and general options

Exporting to PDF is quite easy but some options are available and it's important to know them to control the quality of the file. It's a good thing to have an idea of the several PDF versions to know which one to use to keep your exported layout as consistent as possible.

PDF 1.3

This is the older PDF version that Scribus supports. In fact there is no need to be compliant with previous versions for they are not press-ready. Defined in 1999, it is quite old and is a good base if you're not sure of the version you'll use. It can support gradients, color management, and all kinds of font we really need. It also adds interactivity with JavaScript to have a more complex Web PDF. Scribus can support those functionalities too even though they are not intended for print.

PDF 1.4

The next PDF version is the default in Scribus. You could wonder why if PDF 1.3 is the safest. In fact PDF 1.4 didn't add much functionality for our purpose, except transparency support that is very often used. Compared to PostScript, transparency was just a simple addition to it as some printers might not render transparency correctly. If you use transparencies in your documents, you need to use this one otherwise you'll get colored changes. But ask your office if they can easily print real transparencies.

PDF 1.5

If you used layers and want to keep them in your PDF file, you should use the PDF 1.5 version. You will keep their opacity and blend modes as well. But be careful, the newer the PDF version you use, the less compliant providers you will find.

PDF/X-3

PDF/X-3 is an abstract of PDF 1.3. The main difference is that it requests some information. It needs color management enabled and well configured. You won't be able to export in PDF/X-3 if your document doesn't match the criteria. PDF/X files should be sent to a print office only if they ask for. Other PDF/X-3 requests are automatically handled by Scribus.

The PDF window is divided in tabs. Each of these tabs are dedicated to a special task. In a print workflow some will be more important than others. Let's begin with the **General** tab, which is already open.

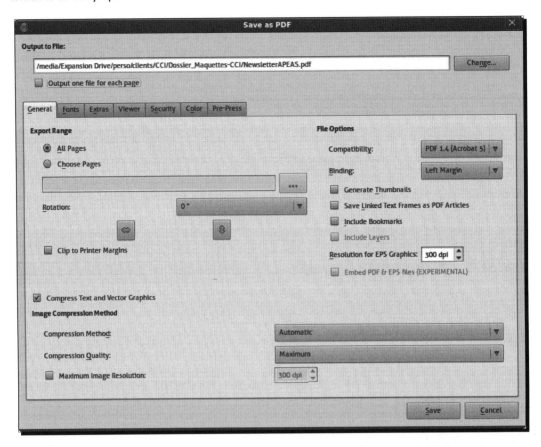

Time for action – quick export method

There are many export options in Scribus and the export option that you choose once are saved within the file so that you don't have to redo everything each time. Here is a fast method that shows the most important fields to control:

1. Go to **File | Export | Save as PDF**.

2. In the **Save as PDF** window, give a name and verify that the PDF **Compatibility** is on **PDF 1.4** at least.

3. Then go to **Fonts** tab and verify if all the fonts listed in the left-hand part of the window are listed in the right-hand part. If not, select it on the left-hand part and click the arrow button activated to pass it or click on the **Outline All** button.

4. In the **Color** tab, you will choose the way the document will be exported. Generally, you will choose **Printer**.

5. If needed, go to **Pre-Press** tab, and check for crop and bleed marks.

6. You now just have to click on the **Save** button.

What just happened?

Creating a PDF should be related to the printing process. However, using PDF under 1.4 will make you lose all the transparency effects. Mostly, the print office can print PDF 1.4 without trouble. Verifying the font will be important if you want to keep the aspect of your text. Remember that there are rights on fonts and to use fonts that can be embedded into documents. Choosing **Printer** will help you get colors in the document. You could get colors with the **Web** option too, but they wouldn't be prepared for the printing process.

Choosing how to export pages

In the **Export Range** part of the **General** tab, you'll see some of the options we have already talked about in the print dialog. You can:

♦ Specify if you want to export all the pages or only some. In this case, you'll have to say which. If this is a range write the first and last of the range separated by a hyphen (1-10). If you need only some of the pages, write the numbers separated by a comma (1,10). Both methods can be mixed if needed. The difference with the **Output one file for each page** option is that you can here set which page you want whereas the previous would export all.

♦ You can rotate the page by some of predefined values: 90, 180, or 270 degrees.

♦ Flip the page horizontally or vertically.

♦ **Clip to Printer Margins** will export only what is placed inside the page margins of the document. It changes only what is visible but the size of the page is not modified. The size of the exported page is exactly the size of the page of the document.

Fonts and outline documents

The next tab is made to define the way text and fonts will be handled in the PDF. It is one of the advantages PDF has over EPS: incorporating the font inside the PDF. Before that, there were only two ways:

◆ Vectorize the text; it is still possible in the PDF.

◆ Give the font apart from the PDF so that the provider could install it on its own machines. There were two main issues with this method:

   ❑ Many people often forgot to send font files, so there was a loss of time; same when they sent the bad font

   ❑ Legally, this was complex for nobody should install something he doesn't have the license for

Actually, we make it simpler with PDF. But some people like to make things difficult. It would not be exciting if there were no issues. Now that we can embed font files into the PDF, it is possible to extract those files from the PDF. To protect their work, some type foundries decided that their fonts could not be embedded into PDF. So to do things well, you should read the license of every font you use or use it is as a criteria when you choose your fonts. As it is very important to keep it legal, we'll see the only quote of this book right now. Here's what the PDF 1.7 specification says:

> *Font programs are subject to copyright, and the copyright owner may impose conditions under which a font program may be used. These permissions are recorded either in the font program or as part of a separate license. One of the conditions may be that the font program cannot be embedded, in which case it should not be incorporated into a PDF file. A font program may allow embedding for the sole purpose of viewing and printing the document but not for creating new or modified text that uses the font (in either the same document or other documents). The latter operation would require the user performing the operation to have a licensed copy of the font program, not a copy extracted from the PDF file. In the absence of explicit information to the contrary, embedded font programs shall be used only to view and print the document and not for any other purposes.*

The specification doesn't say more about what it means by "print": is it only local desktop print or not? Some Microsoft advice seems to indicate that. So, as always, be careful if you use proprietary fonts or try to use open source fonts as much as possible to avoid all kinds of trouble.

Actually, a weakness of the Scribus text engine makes it more difficult than we would like too. In this context, Scribus tries to avoid the bad surprises and is very demanding. It's another reason why you should give attention to this current tab. There are three important parts:

- ◆ On the left—the list of the fonts used in the document
- ◆ On the right, top list—the list of the fonts that Scribus wants to embed
- ◆ On the right, bottom list—the fonts that Scribus wants to vectorize or outline

If Scribus thinks the fonts can be handled easily, all the fonts used will be added automatically to the embed list. In some cases, it will be added in the outline list, for example, when the font is a really complete and Unicode openType font format. It's not so important where they are. But the real thing is that you should have as many fonts in the two right-hand side lists as in the first. If not, look for the fonts that are not added in the PDF, select it in the list and click on the green arrow that should now be available. If there are several, you can try the **Embed all** button.

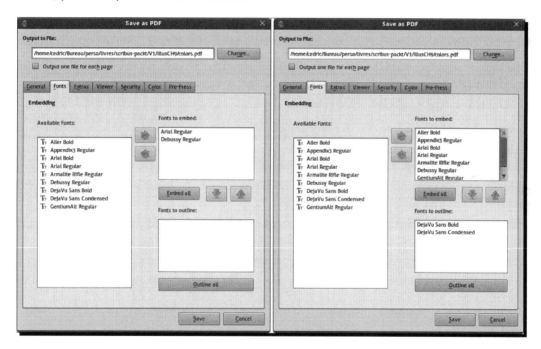

Finally, if your office wants to get outlined text, click the **Outline all** button. This is the safest option for everything—even for legal issues. But your PDF file will certainly be much heavier, especially if you have a lot of text inside. Consider it because it is possible to experience some crashes in huge files.

Colors handling

Once we're done with fonts we go directly to the **Colors** tab as **Extra**, **Viewer**, and the **Security** tabs are intended more for Web PDFs. They deal with page effects, the way the file will be displayed in a reader, or with passwords to avoid printing or other actions. It would be bad to add a password that the employees of your print shop wouldn't have. And if you give it to everyone, there is no need to have a password.

In the **Colors** tab, you can choose how the color of your file will be handled by the Scribus export system. It is very easy to change because you have only one list available in this tab. It shows **Screen/Web**, meaning that at this point Scribus wants to export your document with common RGB colors. As the name says, it will be perfect for a PDF file you put on a website or send by e-mail if it is intended to be viewed on a screen.

If you need to print the file or make it printed, you can choose between one of the last two options:

- ◆ **Grayscale** will export every item and content as black shades so that it can be printed only with black. You could have created your document in black but it wouldn't be the same and you have to prepare all your images as grayscale in GIMP or any other photo editing program. This method is much easier, even if you don't keep control of everything. The best method is to view the grayscale PDF after export to see if contrast is enough on text (especially Text Frames that have background colors) and pictures. Colors of the frame can easily be changed using the **Edit | Color** window; any shade changes and pictures can be adjusted with a Curve Effect if needed, and exported again.

- ◆ **Printer** will export the document as CMYK + spot, if there are any, unless you select the **Convert Spot Colors to Process Colors** checkbox. With **Use Custom Rendering Settings** you can change the way dots and halftones will be output. The **Frequency** is the number of halftone cells per inch and the **Angle** is the amount of rotation for each primary line. For best results none of the primary should have the same angle. In **Spot Function**, you can set the shape of the printed dots. In fact, unless you're really accustomed with those settings, it's better to leave that part to the printer himself or explain if you want some special result.

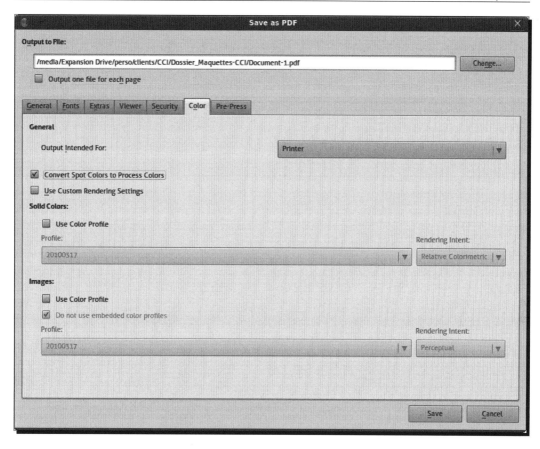

If you enable color management in your document, you'll have some other settings available with which you can define the way the colors of the layout will be exported. You can set separately the solid colors (like frame fills) and pictures. You'll have to activate the one you want to use and inform of the right profile and rendering intent. If you want to remind yourself about them, read the end of Chapter 9. When activating the **Use Color Profile** for images, Scribus will use profiles embedded in your photos (in GIMP this can be done with **Image | Mode | Apply a color profile** or maybe your camera has embedded one into your photos). If your pictures actually have no profiles, or if you're not sure of the profiles embedded, do not use an embedded color profile and add your own.

Marks and bleed

In the **Pre-Press** tab you'll have the ability to define some options that your office could ask for:

- **Crops Marks**
- **Bleed Marks**—use the bleeding settings to define the bleeds unless you defined them previously while creating the document or in document properties. You can then simply use the document bleeds.
- **Registration Marks**
- **Color Bars**
- **Page Information**
- **Offset**

These options are the same you get in the print dialog. So there is nothing new here.

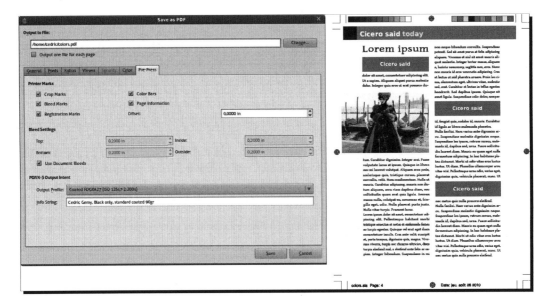

The **PDF/X-3 Output Intent** contains information that is required to have a fully PDF/X-3 compliant file. You need to save your file in this format only if you're asked to. This is a very special PDF specification applied to professional printing but some offices might not support it as they should. To have those options available, you have to choose the PDF/X-3 version in the **General** tab instead of 1.4. If it's not available, enable **Color Management** and configure it if it's not done. You can then specify which output profile you will use (your print shop might have told you which or you may have to ask). Enter the **Info String** with what you need; this is required. You could add your name, phone, and print information. It can be a good idea to fill the **Document Information** of the **Document Setup**, too. This is defined in the PDF/X specifications.

Once the PDF is made, it's a good thing to watch it precisely and look for errors. Actually there are many free PDF viewers, but the best is still Acrobat Reader.

Collect for output

This last action you should absolutely do in two cases:

◆ When you're done with your document, and there's is nothing left to do

◆ When you need to work on several computers or send your Scribus file to someone else

Remember what we said about the fact that doing a layout was using resources from several parts of the computer. Especially, fonts and pictures are considered as links and are never embedded in the Scribus file itself. So if you move the file anywhere:

◆ Fonts won't be found on the next computer, so that all the text won't be rendered right.

◆ Pictures won't be found either, because they might not be on the new computer either and even if they are, they surely won't be stored at the right path. Using the **Manage Images** window could help but it would take very long to redefine all the paths if you have many photos.

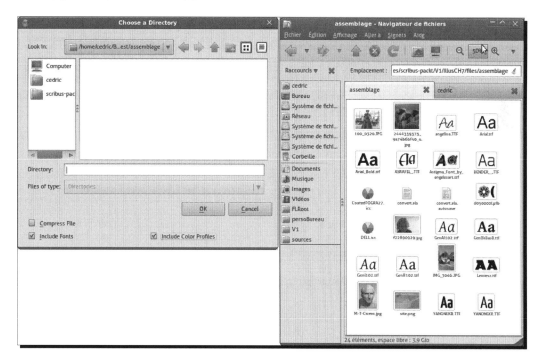

If you want to archive, send, or move your files you should collect them. In the **File** menu, you can use **Collect for Output**. In the window choose the directory you want to collect the file in. If the directory doesn't exist use the **Create New Folder** button to add it in the current selected directory.

There is no real need to compress the file but **Include Fonts** is a need if you wish to use the file on another computer and **Include Color Profiles** at the same time.

You can then simply compress the folder and send or store it where you want it for future needs.

Pop quiz

1. What kind of PDFs allow transparencies?
    a. 1.3
    b. 1.4
    c. 1.5
    d. PDF/X-3

2. Preflight Verifier checks:
    a. For errors in the layout according to an output format
    b. For errors in the graphical aspect of the layout
    c. For errors in the PDF that you will export

3. Ink coverage value tells us:
    a. If there is ink somewhere
    b. If a color is used in the layout
    c. The total amount of ink used at one place

4. Bleeds are:
    a. Margins
    b. External crop safety areas
    c. Comments for the printer

Summary

In this chapter we've seen how to print and export the Scribus file to another famous format called PDF.

Specifically, we covered:

- How to create custom CMYK colors and spot colors
- How to apply patterns or gradients
- How to use some transparency effects like opacity or blending mode
- How to find colors that match
- How to set the color management to get better printed colors

In the next chapter, we will see how to export the document and what needs to be checked before and saved after, to have a complete and safe workflow.

11
Customizing the Creation or Viewing Process

Even if it is not the main goal, Scribus has many features to help enhance user experience. We can analyze it from two points of view.

For the reader, the document author can add some basic interactivity with buttons, links, or transitions.

For the author themselves, they will be able to use the power of open source by customizing Scribus source code, adding Python scripts to automate some tasks, or defining how the interactivity will work within the PDF document using JavaScript.

Most of the options we will deal with in this chapter won't have much impact on the printing result. But they can be a handy approach for the people who have to play with the document in some ways, generally with repetitive actions.

In this chapter, we see in detail how to:

- ◆ Add links or bookmarks
- ◆ Add buttons and fields
- ◆ Have auto-generated content in the PDF with JavaScript
- ◆ Perform repetitive actions with Python scripts, especially importing content from an external source

Among all the PDF capabilities, Scribus absolutely ignores those related to movie or sound embedding. This is not really what it is made for but may be incorporated one day if someone needs it and contributes it.

PDF option toolbar overview

Most of the Scribus PDF tools interactivity are available from the PDF toolbar, which is, by default, displayed at the extreme right-hand side of the standard toolbar. If you don't see it, just go to **Windows | PDF Tools**.

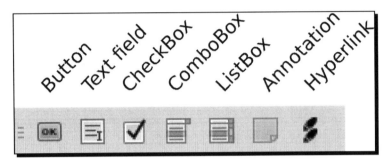

Some of the options can be found in the **Item | PDF Options** menu as well in any item contextual menu.

Finally, some options will be defined when exporting the file. Some of these options will require some basic programming knowledge and viewing all the capabilities is out of the scope of this book.

Time for action – adding hyperlinks

Just follow a few steps:

1. Select the **Insert Link Annotation** (Hyperlink) tool.

2. Draw a rectangle above the source text.

3. Double-click on that rectangle to display the link properties.

4. Enter the details and click on OK.

What just happened?

Actually, the link is placed above and is separate from the text of the frame it tries to link. So if you do some changes in the text, or in the layout, it will be important to have a look at what could be placed badly after the changes.

You can define your link among several types:

◆ **Link** will just go to another part of the document. You can say in this case which page the link must go to and eventually which place of the page. You'll have to write the X and Y coordinates or click in the page preview you have in the window. As page preview is quite small, if you need a more precise position, you'll need to get the page coordinates before being in the link properties. Just put the mouse pointer over the element that you want to link to and look at the cursor position in the Scribus status bar—make a note of it. There's no need to be very precise to the decimal, an approximation is generally enough. Unlike the next two kinds of links where the shape will be active, here the text itself will become linked and the reader will have to click on it even if he or she doesn't see any hand cursor. It can be a good idea to apply some specific styles to the linked text so that they can easily be recognized.

◆ **External Link** will provide an easy way to link to any kind of document apart from the current one. When displaying the properties, you'll be prompted to choose the file: just browse your directory and choose it. Then if you want to immediately reach some page and position on the page, just fill the fields below as for normal links. This way, it can be more tricky to get the position: opening the file in an Image Editor Program can help a lot.

◆ Finally, **External Web-Link** will contain the URL of a website where the reader will immediately be redirected to, if he clicks on it, as if he was reading a webpage.

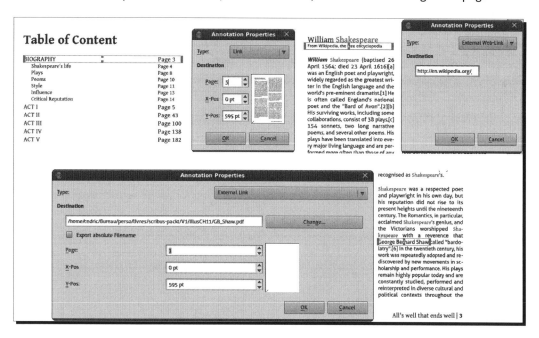

Of course, a link frame can only be one of that type. If you decide to set the colors or line of the hyperlink shape, notice that those properties will be ignored by the Scribus PDF exporter.

Bookmarks

A bookmark is another kind of link that you can add to your PDF files. Unlike hyperlinks, a bookmark will be used only to enhance the navigation within the current document. In fact, you can add bookmarks to many parts of your content, but generally it's a good idea to add bookmarks to the table of content destination because PDF viewer generally displays bookmarks in a sidebar. This makes it very handy to navigate through the document. It is much more usable than regular Table of Contents.

Of course, bookmarks can be added to any other content of the document. In Scribus, you can do this by:

- Right-clicking on the frame you want to bookmark and choosing **PDF Options | Is PDF Bookmark**

- Going to Item **| PDF Options | Is PDF Bookmark** to bookmark the currently selected frame

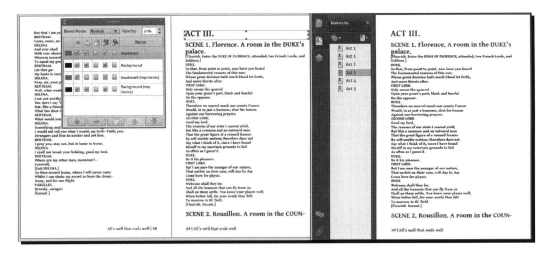

Time for action – adding bookmarks to your PDF documents

The way Scribus creates bookmarks is unfortunately not the most practical: the bookmark window or sidebar will display the text content of the bookmarked frame. So if you bookmark a frame with a long text, it becomes unusable. What we usually do is:

1. Display the **Layers** window from **Windows | Layers**.

2. Create a layer in the **Layers** window by clicking on the **+** at the bottom left.

3. Browse to a page or frame that needs to be bookmarked and draw a new Text Frame over it.

4. Inside that frame, write the text you want to display in the bookmark sidebar, generally a small text like a title.

5. You can set the **Opacity** of this layer to **0%**.

6. Then, when exporting to PDF, enable the **Include Bookmarks** option of the **General** tab and choose at least the 1.4 version of PDF to keep transparencies.

7. If you want the tab to be displayed when the reader opens your PDF, just enable **Display Bookmarks Tab** in the **Viewer** tab of the PDF export window.

What just happened?

Bookmarks will not be like Table of Contents. They can show the same information but not necessarily. Bookmarks should give another way to read the document, based on keywords for example. The only way to get this custom browsing system done is to create each bookmark one by one. Some people think that it would be nice if Scribus could itself add the text of the bookmarks because it would be much faster. I personally like to be able to customize it easily when I need to. Imagine our text about William Shakespeare, who can be called author, poet, and a dramatist. Being able to customize it allows us to use the same bookmark text for each to make it clearer for the reader.

Annotations

Annotations are another type of interactive tool. Scribus enables text annotations by converting any selected text frame and using:

- **Edit | PDF Options | Is PDF Annotation** menu
- Right-click on the frame to convert and choose **PDF Options | Is PDF Annotation**

Annotations are a convenient way to:

◆ Replace footnotes for documents if they don't need to be printed, especially when they are considered as comment

◆ Add layout information when you're working with other people who will use Scribus too

It's a good idea to draw your annotations frame on a separate layer, the same way we did for bookmarks in the previous section. But the reason is different. We used a bookmark layer to be able to hide the bookmark text of the page in the PDF viewer, but we will use an annotation layer to hide the annotation frames that would overlap and hide other frames.

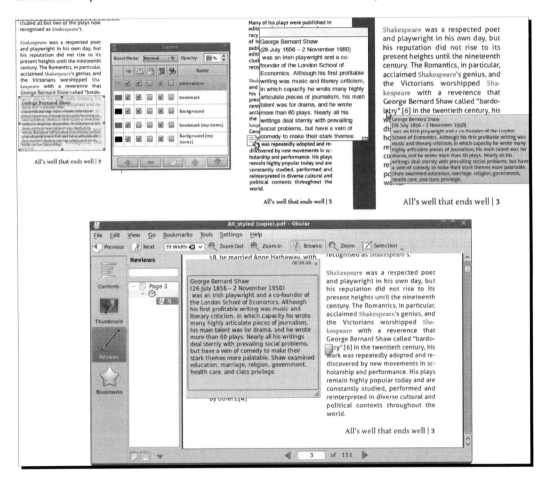

It's good to remember that an annotation is not printed. The way it is rendered on screen is up to the viewer too. In the illustration, you can see that the colors and font settings used are not displayed in both the viewers used. But the first, which is Adobe Acrobat Reader, and the third, Okular, have an advantage by inserting an icon at the annotation position, so that they are easier to find. They can display the annotations list in the Comment window (Acrobat Reader) or the Review sidebar (Okular), which is very practical to browse annotations and improve a professional layout workflow.

Buttons and form tools

With Scribus you can add objects that you can use to communicate with a user. As on a website, these options are often used to build forms that can be filled, printed, or sent by e-mail.

The PDF toolbar shows all the form control elements you can add in your layout:

- The button is the standard way to launch an action. The user clicks on it and all the magic happens.

- Text field will give a place for the user to add some information. A text field is the kind of field you use on a website when you write your e-mail address to subscribe or log in.

- Checkboxes are commonly used for questions that have only two possible answers: true or false. These are often used at the end of a form like: "if check, I agree the terms of conditions written on the xxx document", or "check here to receive our daily newsletter".

- List Box and Combo Box will both list the possible answers from which the user will have to choose. Typically, it is used to know if you are a male or female, or to know your age (you could have ranges listed such as 0-18, 18-40, 40-60, and 60 and up). List Box and Combo Box values just have to be typed in the form frame and they will be displayed in a list in the PDF viewer.

You can look at the field's properties by double-clicking on a field or from **Item | PDF Options | Field Properties**. The aspect of all these form object types can be set with standard form properties. The **Appearance** tab gives some possibilities that will replace any kind of properties set by the well-known Properties Palette (*F2*). They all share the **Action** tab too, which contains a default list that will help you enable JavaScript for your document.

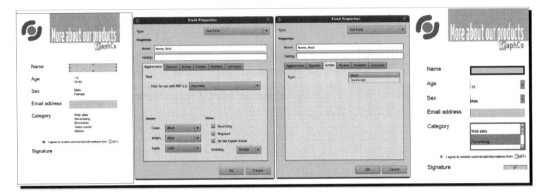

In the **Others** part of the **Appearance** setting you can specify how the user will be able to act with this field:

- **Read Only** specifies that the field value can't be modified. This can be used, for example, for the prices in a catalog.

- **Required** will constrain the reader to fill that field, it's very common on websites where you need to write a password to login or in a terms of exchange agreement.

- **Visibility** is usually used to hide some values that will be used in some calculations but that the reader does not need to know.

Text Field options will have some interesting settings:

- **Multi-Line** if you want the user to be able to write several lines of text. This will usually be for comments. This is really similar to HTML textareas.

- **Password** will hide what the user is writing and replace letters with bullets.

- If **Limit of Characters** is set, the reader won't be able to enter more characters than defined here. Just think of how you could use the Scribus form to send messages to your Twitter account.

Lists fields only have an option that can make them editable, especially if you are expecting unlisted answers.

Checkbox can be defined as checked when the document is opened. And the style of the checkbox when enabled can be set with some predefined shapes, such as cross, diamonds, and others. Just have a try a keep the one you prefer.

The button object type is more complete. You can freely set its aspect including the addition of icons or text for each step of the mouse action on it: mouse over, mouse pressed. Just click on the button named as those states in the **Options** tab and Scribus will give you the window to browse your directories and choose your images. We will use it more as well as some special text field properties in the *PDF interaction* section of this chapter.

Time for action – sell your shoes and help clients choose!

Let's do a simple layout that will list some products that you'd like to sell online. We will need fields for photos, product name, price, and quantity. These fields will be of numeric types to prevent errors. The client will have to write his address so that we can send him the products, which can be done with a text field. Finally, he will have to agree that he will receive the products when his payment will be verified and validated.

1. Create a A4 Portrait document on top of which you can add our GraphCo logo and a name over a pinkish rectangle filled with R255 G128 B128 color with a 50% shade.

2. Add some white text on top with our now common Yanone font.

3. Now create the form header with a rectangle of 0.73in length and 0.27in height. Fill it with R170 G0 B0.

4. Duplicate it (or copy-paste) five times and change the size of each rectangle so that it fits the content need (Product name, Price, Quantity, and Subtotal) and available space on the right. Distribute them on the line and avoid overlapping. Above each, add the name of the 'column'. It could be a good idea to create a style for it.

5. Under this header, prepare the first product row by drawing a rectangle filled with the pinkish color. Then, select all the text frames of the header, copy-paste them, and drag them to this first row.

6. For the second 'column', draw a white image frame.

7. Over each Text Frame of this row except Name and description, draw a text field frame and change is properties by double-clicking on it: specify that it has no border and exit.

8. Type some text inside each frame and fields and apply some style to it.

9. Duplicate all the objects of this row and drag them below. You can do it several times. Using the **Multiple Duplicate** dialog can be a good idea.

10. Make the changes you need on the copies such as changing background colors alternatively or changing values of the Text Frames and fields.

11. At the bottom, add a new, darker rectangle and draw a Text Frame on it. Type "Total" inside it.

12. Below this one draw two Text Frames and draw one checkbox at the left-hand side of each. The checkbox can be without a border too and its fill color can be as pink as the rows.

13. Add some text or pictures around them to make things nicer and save your file; we will use it later.

What just happened?

As we can see, creating a catalog and form in Scribus can be very easy. It stands in some frames duplicated several times with text or pictures within. This is generally simple and common in layout usage. Using PDF fields can really ease the experience the customer will have of your catalog if they read it on screen. Adding fields is as easy as drawing frames. The difference is in the fact that some of the properties will be defined in the PP and some, like the border, in the **Field Properties** window. PDF fields enable you to add several kind of interface and help the user choose products, quantities, or any other quality.

As we'll see in the *PDF interaction* section, having a well-done PDF form will be the basis of the interaction between the reader and the catalog (for example, to perform a calculation) and eventually between the form and you (for example, if you want to receive the command in a mail or store it in the database).

Display and viewing options

As a Scribus user and document creator, you can define how your document will be displayed in the reader's viewer, if it supports it. Those options can be found in the **Viewer** or **Extras** tabs of the PDF export window.

Time for action – communicating with the reader application

Let's briefly look at the most commonly-used viewing options.

1. Display the **Viewer** tab of the PDF export dialog. In this tab you can choose between a predefined action or, at the bottom of the window, define your own custom actions if you've added some with your own JavaScript functions.

2. Let's begin with the default options, which are quite easy to understand. Click on the **Double Page Right** in the **Document Layout** category.

3. In **Visual Appearance**, choose the **Display Bookmarks** tab to help the user navigate in your document.

4. Finally, if you want to define some advanced display option, you will have to do so with your own JavaScript actions. If you want to choose your script from the drop-down list of the **Viewer** tab, you'll need to inform Scribus first about the JavaScript functions that you want to create. By going to **Edit | JavaScripts**, you will get a new window in which you can **Add** some scripts. Click on the button and give it a name; here we named it "hello". When validating, an editor window will appear in which you'll see the following lines:

```
function hello()
{
}
```

5. If you can just add some lines between the opening and closing braces. As an example we have added a simple message:

```
app.alert('Hello. Fill the fields, print and send.')
```

6. You can then choose **Save and Exit** in the Script editor **File** menu and quit those windows. The hello function will now be available in the JavaScript field of the **Viewer** tab in the PDF export options.

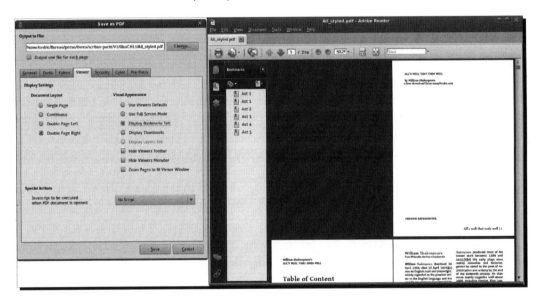

What just happened?

On the right-hand side, the **Document Layout** group will help you define how the pages will be displayed. The default is **Single Page** because it's the more comfortable for the reader, unless your document is done in a small paper size or with a huge font-size. But using **Double Page Right** will simulate a real book: two pages side by side with the first page alone on the right. This display mode can be important if your layout contains text or pictures that are placed above the fold.

Visual Appearance should be left to the user's preferences too. However, using full screen mode can be useful if your PDF is a presentation. Displaying bookmarks will just help if you defined **bookmarks** in your document. **Thumbnails** will help if you have no Table of Contents. Browsing thumbnails will help the reader understand the structure of your document, because chapters or parts of it will certainly have different layouts, especially the first pages of each. If all the pages are really similar, just filled with plain text, this won't help much and, therefore, it's best not to overload the user interface with such details.

Notice that if you choose **Use Full Screen Mode**, you can display tabs.

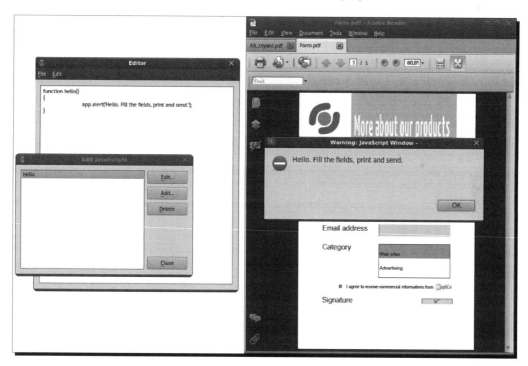

Generally, Scribus won't help you in writing your scripts. There are many books and websites on the subject of JavaScript, as it is one of the most important programming languages for web applications. If you want to know more about how PDF can deal with it, read `http://www.adobe.com/devnet/acrobat/pdfs/js_api_reference.pdf` and you'll get the detailed information. Learning JavaScript is outside the scope of this book.

If you are a JavaScript beginner, there are many websites explaining the basis of the programming language. I could recommend `http://www.w3schools.com`; but you could find your own.

You will often appreciate the benefits of keeping your JavaScripts apart from your Scribus file. This is more convenient if you want to reuse them. Form the Scribus script editor, you can choose **File | Save As** to save the current script. Or if you already wrote your scripts, may be with another external text editor, you can use **File | Open** to import their content into the Scribus file.

Page transitions

The **Extras** tab of the PDF export window will help you set the page **transitions** and effects as you could create them in Microsoft PowerPoint or OpenOffice.org Impress. It doesn't mean that Scribus can efficiently replace these pieces of software. But if you're used to Scribus productivity tools, such as master pages and styles, it will be nearly as easy to create it with Scribus than with specialized software.

The main difference is that it will work only if the file is exported to PDF, because transitions can only be rendered in a PDF viewer. The pages that you have created in Scribus will become slides and you can use buttons or links to modify the browsing of the file as you would do with any other software.

Page transitions cannot be printed; so you can't see the effect on these pages. Having a try is the best way to discover them. The only advice we could give you is to keep it simple: use the same effect or transition for the whole document if possible, it will help the listener or reader to concentrate on the content, which is more important. Plus, if your document needs to be rendered on screen or publicly during a conference, for example, it can be a good idea to do it in a landscape document and set it to fullscreen from the PDF Viewer's options.

To use transitions, in the **Extras** tab, **Enable Presentation Effects** should be selected and then simply use the settings Scribus gives you: durations for the page (**Display Duration**) and for the transition (**Effect Duration**), **Effect Type,** and other available settings to modify the behavior for the type you've chosen. Then click on **Apply Effect to all Pages**. If you want to apply the transition only to a single page, it should be selected in the left-hand part of the window before applying the effect to it.

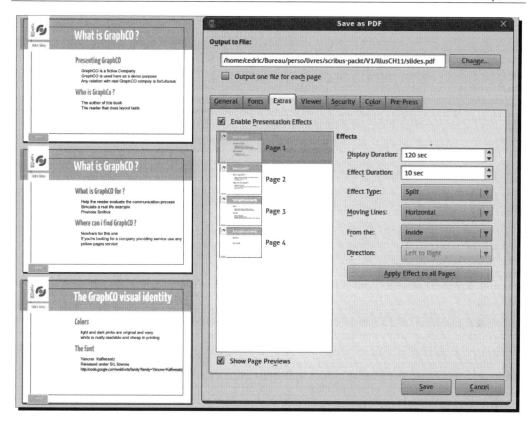

Light-weight PDFs

Scribus PDFs are quite heavy. And if you produce a web PDF with a standard Scribus export to Web options, you'll see that your file can take long to download because Scribus is mainly made to create print documents, for which the quality criteria will be very different. If you want the PDF files to be easily available on your website, it's particularly important to make them as light as possible to decrease download duration.

Reducing the size of your Scribus PDF will require the modification of some options here and there, especially in the PDF Export dialog. In fact, there is no absolute way to do it. It depends on the result that you want and the content of the file.

First of all, reduce the number of primary colors. If you need to print or display only in black, just use **Grayscale** PDF in the **Color** tab of the PDF Export dialog. If you want a web PDF, **Screen/Web** will be enough and avoid the use of the fourth primary and spot colors. Our postcard export to the Web instead of print is 6MB instead of 20MB.

The second most important setting is to reduce the picture resolution if you used several or a lot of them. Shrink all the pictures with the **Image Compression Method** part of the **General** tab of PDF Export, using **Lossy-JPEG** in M**edium** quality at a 72dpi **Maximum Image Resolution** will decrease our PDF size to 233KB. This is particularly true if you used TIFF or PSD containing paths and layers.

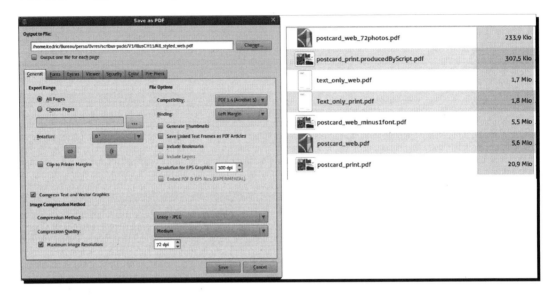

You can then reduce the amount of fonts you're using. Font files can be heavy, going from 20Kb up to several MBs. Using many fonts is not the best idea for readability and doesn't help with the file size. The best would be to use only standard PDF fonts, such as Courier or Helvetica. Avoid outlining the text too. However, if you want to keep your fonts, look for unused styles and delete them, and avoid local font replacement, which won't give you full control.

You can then remove all unwanted objects, such as invisible or non-printable objects or layers, as well as unused frames, be they below some other or outside the page. You can delete unused pages too, don't use bookmarks, thumbnails, and links if not necessary.

Time for action – using a predefined script to reduce file size

If you run a Linux machine, you should try a simple script:

1. Go to http://wiki.scribus.net/index.php/Reduce_the_size_of_ Scribus_generated_PDFs.

2. Copy all the code you find on that page and paste it into a text editor and save it with the extension `.py` as `reduce_PDF_size.py`. If you don't have an Internet connection, use the code provided in the code bundle.

3. Go to **Script | Execute Script**, pick your script and follow the instructions.

What just happened?

The script is a list of several tasks that can be redone each time the script is launched. Scripts are handy ways to handle repetitive series of actions in Scribus. They are written in Python. You won't actually need to know how exactly that script works—just focus on the result.

Our sample document is exported to a 307KB PDF with a better average quality than we got with other methods. It was the case that some other files got heavier. We think it's worth a try because its much simpler and it doesn't need to modify the export options, which can be kept for the best quality (remember that Scribus remembers the last setting you used for a document).

ePUB

Scribus cannot actually export in ePUB format. ePUB is an adaptable layout format when Scribus is aimed for fixed layout mainly for print, not screens. If you need more information about ePUB go to the International Digital Publishing Forum at `http://www.idpf.org/`. If you want to use free, open source software to do this, have a look at Calibre `http://calibre-ebook.com`.

PDF interaction

We've seen previously how we can add some forms into a PDF file. We have already shown how it was possible to add some JavaScript to display some information when the file is opened in the viewer. JavaScript can be used to add interaction in the PDF too. Many things could be done using JavaScript, such as video controls or 3D modeling and viewing. But as Scribus is a layout software it won't be useful to add all this.

In Scribus, it will be more interesting to define simple actions, such as form field calculations and data transfer by e-mail, or with any kind of server-side language connection like PHP that could add data to a MySQL database.

Teaching these languages is out of the scope of this book. In the following example, we will just show you some tips on how to implement them in Scribus. But the learning will be long if you don't know them yet. Just do some research on the Internet with keywords, such as PHP and JavaScript, and you'll find many websites or books to help you succeed with any task. Having a look at the PDF JavaScript API reference is not a bad idea too. You can find it at http://www.adobe.com/devnet/acrobat/pdfs/js_api_reference.pdf.

Time for action – calculate the sum of the fields

Let's take the form we created before, in its present state, and modify some details to enable calculations and see how we can receive the command in a mail.

1. The first thing we will need for our calculation is the unique name for each field. Names can be set in the **Field Properties** window of the PP. For easy remembering let's name them by their column name and row number. The first field of the first column will be **Ref1**, the price of the same row will be **Price 1**, and then **Qty1** and **Subtotal1**. The next row will be **Ref2**, **Price 2**, and so on.

2. The first calculation must be done at the end of each row. Select the first Subtotal field and display its properties by double-clicking on it.

3. Specify that it is **Read Only** in the first tab and then go to the **Calculate** tab.

4. Activate **Custom calculation script**, and click on the **Edit** button. In the editing window, enter the following:

```
this.getField('Subtotal1').value=this.getField('Price1').
value*this.getField('Qty1').value
```

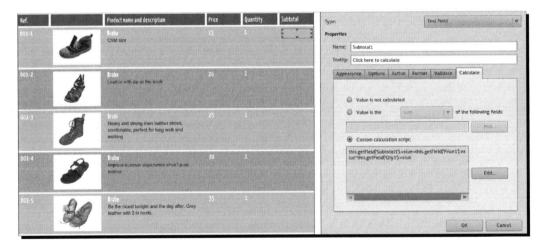

5. In the **Editor** window, choose **File | Save and Exit** and repeat the same process for each subtotal, replacing the names of the fields for each row calculation.

6. If you don't already have a "Total" field below the subtotals, it's time to add one. Of course, it must be read only too.

7. Go back to the **Calculate** tab. This time we'll try another method by using the second option. The value should be the **sum**.

8. Then, click on the **Pick** button and in the new widow select each subtotal one by one and pass them to the second list by pressing the **>>** button.

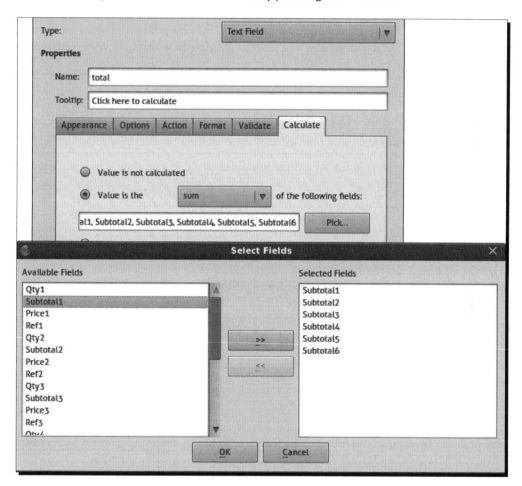

9. You might be wondering how you will get this information from the client. The client could print and send it, or save the file content and send by mail. But you can help him in doing it. Add a button field and enter `mail this!` or something similar.

10. In the **Action** tab of the **Field Properties** window, choose the **Submit Form** type.

11. Then, in **Submit to URL**, enter `mailto:` followed by the e-mail address that needs to receive those important submissions.

12. Finally, choose a submit format. **HTML** or **XFDF** will be the easiest to manage later.

13. Everything is perfect, or nearly so. Add some fields for the postal address, the agreement boxes, and export to PDF.

What just happened?

If we want to perform calculations of A+B, we need to know exactly what A and B are. Giving unique and well-known names to each field makes it easier for us to remember and use them. When giving such names, avoid the use of special characters, including spaces. Be as simple and rational as possible. Once we have done this, we can use this field name to get their values. Those values can be defined when the form is created and even if set to read only, this is the case for the product reference number. For all the numbers that have to be used, it is important to store them in a form field as JavaScript can easily get the value than with standard Text Frames.

Then it's easy to say that the value of Subtotal fields must be the product of the Price fields and Quantity fields.

In the end, when submitting, we choose to submit by e-mail and the form content will be send as an attached file. The mail client will be launched but everything will be ready and the reader will just need to press the "Send" button. But it could be a good choice to submit to a URL. It could be some PHP file that would store the values into a database and eventually send an e-mail both to you and your client to confirm that everything is OK.

Scripting basics to extend Scribus

It's well-known that the most important advantage of Free Software stands in the fact that the source code is available and that the user can adapt this source to his needs. Scribus is developed in C++ and QT and anyone who knows these programming languages can go deeper into Scribus functions and add their own. However, C++ is a very complex language that is not really easy to learn. Most of the free software, such as GIMP, Inkscape, and Blender choose to define a Python API to let the user interact with the program itself. Python is a powerful interpreted language, and it:

◆ Is easy to learn
◆ Is easy to read
◆ Makes it easy to share the scripts

- Doesn't need to be compiled and, therefore, makes tests easier and faster
- Has many modules that can do specific tasks
- Has a very large and active community

For a Scribus user, what does that mean? It's very simple. With Python you will be able to add your own functionality to Scribus. Maybe you have experienced a lack of tools, or maybe you need to perform a repetitive task for which a script would be perfect. Some Python scripts are already distributed with Scribus. You use them from the **Script | Scribus Scripts** menu. They are made to help you in the following tasks:

- **CalendarWizard**—creating calendars.
- **color2csv**—exporting the color list into a CSV file format.
- **ColorChart**—creating a reference with the color list of a file showing a sample frame and color value in CMYK, RGB, and hexadecimal.
- **DirectImageImport**—importing an image by automatically adding the frame.
- **FontSample**—creating a Scribus document containing a sample of each font available on your system. It can take a while so it might be a good idea to choose only some of them in the script window.
- **importcsv2table**—importing CSV data from a spreadsheet into a Scribus document and automatically creating the table to put them in. This is an alternative method of the EPS import we've seen previously, useful when text needs to be modified in the layout.
- **InfoBox**—displaying some information about the selected object and writing them in a frame. It is a good complement to ColorChart to remember the settings of important items of the layout.

There are many other scripts available. Most of them can be found in the Scribus wiki at `http://wiki.scribus.net/index.php/Category:Scripts_%26_Plugins`.

The other important place to go to is the Scribus Python API reference available at `http://docs.scribus.net/index.php?lang=fr&page=scripterapi`. The API documentation is split into several sections listed in the left-hand column.

Time for action – adding a script

Scribus will usually be interesting when you want to add some new functionality to Scribus or do some repetitive task. If you want to use a Scribus script, you have to save your script content into a `.py` file. For example, if we want to use the text vertical alignment script, stored at this URL `http://wiki.scribus.net/index.php/Adjust_a_text_frame_ to_fit_its_content` you'll have to:

1. Select the Python code from the website (it is shown with a blue background).

2. Open your favorite text editor. Be careful, use a real text editor, not a text processor, on Windows, Notepad or Notepad++ will be OK, on Mac, use Smultron or Textwrangler, and on Linux, use gedit, vim, or Kate.

3. Paste the content inside a new document.

4. Save this file where you want with a `.py` extension.

5. On the website, read the recommendations or explanations if there are any.

6. Back in Scribus, do what is needed by the script (here it is having a filled text frame selected) and go to **Script | Execute Script** and choose it from the window.

What just happened?

The script we have used has been written by one or several authors who add their names in the first part of the script. This, generally, is the place where the script licence and the modifications are listed. By saving it on your computer it will be available for use any time you want. You can call it with a simple menu that can help you find it in your directories and the script does the rest. If you need to use this script again on other frames, just go to **Script | Recent Scripts** and the last script used will be listed there. Some scripts will need things to be prepared, such as having a frame or two selected, and so on. Generally, they will display messages that will help you understand what happens; read them carefully.

Time for action – importing from databases with a script

Now that we have installed a simple script we can proceed further and see how we can use a more complex one. Our use case here is simple and very common in a company: using data stored in a database to fill your document.

For example, at the beginning of this book we have created a business card. However, we would like all of the employees of our fictive GraphCo company to have their own business card. If the company has very few people involved, creating the cards manually might be fast enough. But if your company has more than 50 or 100 people, it could take very long to do them one by one. You certainly have the employees list somewhere. In our case, we have created the Scribus template, without the employee frame. We have created a MySQL table for the employees, but, Python might be able to read other kinds of database systems too.

When writing Python script for Scribus the important place to go to is the Scribus Python API reference available at `http://docs.scribus.net/index.php?lang=fr&page=scripterapi`. The API documentation is split in several sections listed in the left-hand column. It will help you find the name of Scribus methods to add or manipulate the content of your document.

We have customized the default Scribus script to make it easier.

1. Copy the following lines in your text editor, and keep the indentation:

```python
#!/usr/bin/env python
# -*- coding: utf-8 -*-

import sys

# environment checking
try:
    import scribus
except ImportError:
    print "This script only runs from within Scribus."
    sys.exit(1)

try:
    import MySQLdb
except ImportError:
    print "You must have 'MySQLdb' installed."
    sys.exit(1)

# connection parameters
hostname = 'localhost'
dbname = 'company'
username = 'company'
password = 'companypassword'

# connection to the network wide server would be time consuming.
So get the hint to the user.
scribus.statusMessage('Connecting to the ' + hostname + ' server.
Be patient, please...')
```

```
# Database related issues
try:
    conn = MySQLdb.connect(passwd=password, db=dbname,
host=hostname, user=username)
except:
  scribus.messageBox('DB connection example', 'Connection error.
You should specify your login in the script')
  sys.exit(1)

cursor=conn.cursor()
cursor.execute("""SELECT * FROM people""")
results=cursor.fetchall()

# Scribus presentation part
for row in results:
  txtName = scribus.createText(44, 32, 35, 22)
  scribus.setText(row[1], txtName)

scribus.statusMessage('Script done.')
```

2. Save your file as a Python file, for example, `biz-card.py`.

3. To make this script work, we will need to verify if we have the dependencies with some Python modules:

   ❑ **Python** installed on our computer. If you run a Unix-like OS it's probably already there. You can type `which python` in a terminal window to check if it's there. If you can't find it or if you run Microsoft Windows, check the download page on the Python official website `http://python.org/download/`.

   ❑ **MySQLdb** python module available at `http://sourceforge.net/projects/mysql-python/`.

   ❑ Data stored in a MySQL database—in our example, it is installed locally. The name of our database is `company`, and the name of the table is `people`. The database access user login is `company` and the password is `companypassword`.

   ❑ A Scribus template—in this case, this is our business card.

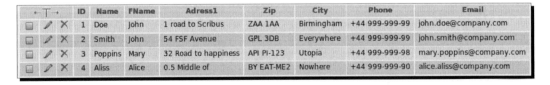

			ID	Name	FName	Adress1	Zip	City	Phone	Email
☐	✎	✗	1	Doe	John	1 road to Scribus	ZAA 1AA	Birmingham	+44 999-999-99	john.doe@company.com
☐	✎	✗	2	Smith	John	54 FSF Avenue	GPL 3DB	Everywhere	+44 999-999-99	john.smith@company.com
☐	✎	✗	3	Poppins	Mary	32 Road to happiness	API PI-123	Utopia	+44 999-999-98	mary.poppins@company.com
☐	✎	✗	4	Aliss	Alice	0.5 Middle of	BY EAT-ME2	Nowhere	+44 999-999-90	alice.aliss@company.com

4. Modify the connection parameters to make them match your own database system.

5. Then in Scribus, go to **Script | Execute Script** and choose your script from the window.

What just happened?

In any case, you'll need to import Scribus module for your Python script to access the Scribus-specific functions using `import scribus`. The connection parameters will need the database name and user login and password. Change them to what matches the ones for your database. Ask your system administrator if needed.

```
cursor.execute("""SELECT * FROM people""")
```

This above line is important. It tells the script to get all the data from the `people` table. Then we take each result and store it in a temporary row list (`for row in results:`), create a Text Frame with its positions and size (`scribus.createText(44, 32, 35, 22)`), and finally add text to it (`scribus.setText(row[1], txtName)`). `row[1]` refers to Name, `row[2]` to Fname, and so on.

If you use this, you'll see that all the frames will overlap, because they all have the same position. We'll need to customize it a bit to make it match what we need. The simplest way will be to add a page for each card and define styles for the name, address, and phone number. First be sure that everything on the business card is put in the Normal master page and create those three styles.

To add a new page for each row, type the following line before the `createText` one:

```
scribus.newPage(-1)
```

`-1` means that the page is added at the end. If your master page is not named Normal, add a comma followed by the master page name after `-1`. Keep the indentation because Python is both indentation and case sensitive.

Now should get as many pages as there are people in your database, a frame inside, and the name written in it. Then to add the first name and apply styles on them, add the following:

```
scribus.setText(row[2]+' '+row[1], txtName)
scribus.selectText(0, len(row[1])+len(row[2])+1, txtName)
scribus.setStyle("name", txtName)
```

The first line adds a frame and the content into that frame. We added the first name before the last name and a space in between. `txtName` still refers to the variable representing the frame created. The second line selects the text from the 0 position, that is, the first letter of the frame for a length equal to the length of each piece of information plus the space: `len(row[1])+len(row[2])+1`. Finally, `setStyle` applies the style `name`.

To add some text within your frame, the equivalent of **Append Text** is in the **File | Import** menu; you can use `scribus.insertText()`. Knowing that, just simply repeat that for each piece of information and add a break line before each record by concatenating the row value with '\n'.

```
scribus.insertText ('\n'+row[3], -1, txtName)
scribus.setStyle("adress", txtName)
scribus.insertText ('\n'+row[4], -1, txtName)
scribus.setStyle("adress", txtName)
scribus.insertText ('\n'+row[5], -1, txtName)
scribus.setStyle("adress", txtName)
scribus.insertText ('\n'+row[6], -1, txtName)
scribus.setStyle("phone", txtName)
```

At this point everything should be good. You'll just have to verify, especially if the text fits in the frame. We could automatically export to PDF with the script but it seems a good idea to do it manually after a control.

Of course, customizing this script takes a while. But think of the time it would take to request adding add all this information one piece at a time. If we'd like to make things easier to use later, we could add a nice dialog window to this script. This window could help giving database information and fields that we would like to use as well as the styles. This can been actually done with Tk. Of course, the Tk Python module will have to be installed before being able to use it. To begin with Tk in Scribus, you can have a look at these nice scripts and websites:

- `http://wiki.scribus.net/index.php/Drawing_a_grid`
- `http://wiki.scribus.net/index.php/Automatic_import_of_images_from_a_directory_using_a_script`
- `http://www.tkdocs.com/tutorial/`
- And of course `http://wiki.python.org/moin/TkInter`

Have a go hero – frame styles

Another thing you can often need is the ability to automatically update frame or fields settings and properties. For example, you might change your mind once the document is already in a well advanced state. Using Python script, you can have a try at doing this and write for frames something that could be quite similar to text styles. Frame selection could be done with some naming coding style and you should find all the necessary information to change the frame at `http://docs.scribus.net/index.php?lang=fr&page=scripterapi-setobjprop`. Good luck!

Pop quiz

1. A PDF hyperlink made in Scribus can:

   a. Help the user go to a page within the document only

   b. Help the user reach a website from the PDF file

   c. Do both

2. Displaying thumbnails in the views:

   a. Can be defined in **General** tab of the PDF Export dialog

   b. Can be defined in **Viewer** tab of the PDF Export dialog

   c. Is the default

   d. Cannot be set

3. In PDF forms you can add:

   a. JavaScript scripts

   b. Python scripts

   c. C++ scripts

4. Scribus can be extended with:

   a. JavaScript scripts

   b. Python scripts

   c. C++ scripts

   d. Tk scripts

Summary

In this chapter, we've seen how to use some tools to create more complex PDFs, especially when they are made for Web use. We saw how to add interactivity to these PDFs and how to extend Scribus if you need custom action.

Specifically, we covered how to add PDF fields and use these fields to store data or receive data as an attached file in a mail. We have seen how to perform some calculation using JavaScript scripting or standard Scribus options. Finally, we searched for user scripts on the Web, especially the Scribus script repository, and we also used Python scripts that were eventually customized using common methods.

Pop Quiz Answers

Chapter 2

1	a
2	b
3	b

Chapter 3

1	b, c
2	b
3	a

Chapter 4

1	b
2	c
3	b
4	b

Chapter 5

1	b
2	c
3	a
4	c

Chapter 6

1	b
2	b
3	a
4	c
5	a
6	c
7	b

Chapter 7

1	b
2	b
3	b
4	d
5	c
6	c
7	a, b, c

Chapter 8

1	b, c
2	a, c
3	c
4	a, b
5	b
6	c
7	a, c

Chapter 9

1	b, c
2	a
3	b
4	a
5	b
6	c
7	b

Chapter 10

1	b, c
2	a
3	c
4	b

Chapter 11

1	c
2	b
3	a
4	b

Index

CMYK model 203
CMYK photos
    importing, in Scribus 203
Collect for Output option
    using 285, 286
color group
    settings 264
color management system
    about 255
    Argyll 256
colors
    applying, to frames 232
    applying, to imported graphics 226-228
    applying, to text frame's text 233
    blending, layers used 238
    creating 246, 248
    importing 246, 248
    importing, from Scribus document 249, 250
    managing 246
    managing, in Scribus 256-259
    replacing 253
    reusing, from other files 248, 249
    selecting, with Color Wheel plugin 255
color separation
    previewing 270, 271
colors handling 282, 283
Color Wheel plugin
    about 254
    colors, selecting 255
column
    modifying, in tables 154
comma separated value. *See* CSV
company name
    scaling 50
content
    bookmark, adding to 292
    linking, via cells 155-157
    modifying, in tables 155
coordinates
    setting 44
CSV 158
custom effects
    creating, layers used 237, 238
    creating, transparency used 237, 238
custom font directory
    setting 136, 137

Cyan, Magenta, Yellow, and Black model. *See* CMYK model

D

default font
    defining 134, 135
default master pages
    about 76
    managing, with Edit Master Pages window 78, 79
    using 76-78
desktop publishing software
    versus text processors 8, 9
digiKam 213
DirectImageImport script 204
DispcalGui 256
display options, Scribus 299, 301
document
    glyph, reusing 114
document setup window, Scribus 21, 22
DTP
    versus text processors 203
dynamic settings
    using 120

E

Edit Colors window 250
Edit Master Pages window
    custom master pages, managing 78, 79
EPS 216
EPS files 253
ePUB 305
Extras tab
    page transitions 302

F

fields
    values, modifying in 24
file size
    reducing, predefined script used 304
file version, Scribus 36, 37
flat colors 239
Fontmatrix
    fonts, managing with 137

fonts
   about 123
   changing 121, 123
   managing 134
   managing, with Fontmatrix 137
   new fonts, adding in Scribus 136
   size, changing 123

font size
   about 124
   changing 123
   example 124

form
   calculations, enabling 306-308
   details, modifying 306-308

format
   setting, for document in Scribus 36

frame conversion 176

frame margins 95

frames
   about 176
   colors, applying to 232
   text, converting to 177

Free linear Gradient types 240

G

game grid
   creating 153, 154

General Public License 7

Ghostscript
   about 28, 262
   URL, for installing 262

GIMP
   about 255
   CMYK photos, importing in Scribus 203

glyph extension 134

glyphs
   adding, on page 114
   reusing, between document 115
   reusing, in document 114

GnuPlot
   about 162
   URL 163

gradients
   about 238, 239
   applying 240
   Free linear Gradient types 240

using, in layout 242-245

graphic file formats
   about 212
   EPS 216
   JPEG 213
   PDF 216
   PNG 214
   PSD 215
   SVG 217, 218
   TIFF 214

graphics
   display properties 221, 222

graphic workflow, Scribus 9-12

Graphviz
   about 162
   URL 163

grids
   about 88
   displaying 88
   major grids 88
   minor grids 88

guides
   about 87
   benefits 87
   creating 55
   issues 87
   pages, structuring 87

guide snapping 151

H

horizontal scaling 126

hyperlinks
   adding 290, 291

hyphenation 105

I

image
   file information 218, 219
   resolution 219, 220
   scaling 219, 220

image effects
   applying 225, 226

image layers
   about 222
   setting 222, 223

Thank you for buying
Scribus 1.3.5 Beginner's Guide

About Packt Publishing

Packt, pronounced 'packed', published its first book "*Mastering phpMyAdmin for Effective MySQL Management*" in April 2004 and subsequently continued to specialize in publishing highly focused books on specific technologies and solutions.

Our books and publications share the experiences of your fellow IT professionals in adapting and customizing today's systems, applications, and frameworks. Our solution based books give you the knowledge and power to customize the software and technologies you're using to get the job done. Packt books are more specific and less general than the IT books you have seen in the past. Our unique business model allows us to bring you more focused information, giving you more of what you need to know, and less of what you don't.

Packt is a modern, yet unique publishing company, which focuses on producing quality, cutting-edge books for communities of developers, administrators, and newbies alike. For more information, please visit our website: www.packtpub.com.

About Packt Open Source

In 2010, Packt launched two new brands, Packt Open Source and Packt Enterprise, in order to continue its focus on specialization. This book is part of the Packt Open Source brand, home to books published on software built around Open Source licences, and offering information to anybody from advanced developers to budding web designers. The Open Source brand also runs Packt's Open Source Royalty Scheme, by which Packt gives a royalty to each Open Source project about whose software a book is sold.

Writing for Packt

We welcome all inquiries from people who are interested in authoring. Book proposals should be sent to author@packtpub.com. If your book idea is still at an early stage and you would like to discuss it first before writing a formal book proposal, contact us; one of our commissioning editors will get in touch with you.

We're not just looking for published authors; if you have strong technical skills but no writing experience, our experienced editors can help you develop a writing career, or simply get some additional reward for your expertise.

Inkscape 0.48 Essentials for Web Designers

ISBN: 978-1-84951-268-8   Paperback: 306 pages

Use the fascinating Inkscape graphics editor to create attractive layout designs, images, and icons for your website

1. The first book on the newly released Inkscape version 0.48, with an exclusive focus on web design

2. Comprehensive coverage of all aspects of Inkscape required for web design

3. Incorporate eye-catching designs, patterns, and other visual elements to spice up your web pages

Processing XML documents with Oracle JDeveloper 11g

ISBN: 978-1-847196-66-8   Paperback: 384 pages

Creating, validating, and transforming XML documents with Oracle's IDE

1. Will get the reader developing applications for processing XML in JDeveloper 11g quickly and easily

2. Self-contained chapters provide thorough, comprehensive instructions on how to use JDeveloper to create, validate, parse, transform, and compare XML documents.

3. The only title to cover XML processing in Oracle JDeveloper 11g, this book includes information on the Oracle XDK 11g APIs.

Please check **www.PacktPub.com** for information on our titles

6764882R00193

Printed in Great Britain
by Amazon.co.uk, Ltd.,
Marston Gate.